Diversity in Family Constellations

Diversity in Family Constellations

IMPLICATIONS FOR PRACTICE

EDITED BY

Krishna L. Guadalupe
California State University, Sacramento

Debra L. Welkley
California State University, Sacramento

LYCEUM
BOOKS, INC.
Chicago, IL

© Lyceum Books, Inc., 2012

Published by

LYCEUM BOOKS, INC.
5758 S. Blackstone Ave.
Chicago, Illinois 60637
773+643-1903 (Fax)
773+643-1902 (Phone)
lyceum@lyceumbooks.com
http://www.lyceumbooks.com

Cover image © Nikolay Mamluke—Dreamstime.com

6 5 4 3 2 1   12 13 14 15

ISBN 978-1-933478-46-3

Printed in the United States of America.

Library of Congress Cataloging-in-Publication Data

Diversity in family constellations : implications for practice / edited by Krishna L.
Guadalupe, Debra L. Welkley.
    p. cm.
Includes bibliographical references and index.
ISBN 978-1-933478-46-3 (pbk. : alk. paper)
 1. Families. 2. Extended families. I. Guadalupe, Krishna L. II. Welkley, Debra L.
HQ728.D58   2012
306.85'7—dc23

2011020101

Dedication

To my children Isaiah, Elijah, and Rhia, for exposing me to an amazing journey filled with love, bliss, magic, and possibilities. To my partner, Judy, for being one of my greatest, most delightful teachers in the school of truth, trust, and remembrance of our true essence beyond conventional reality. To the diverse family constellations that breathe in this planet, encouraging magical probabilities for living, learning, laughing, and loving. KLG

    I dedicate this work to my grandparents (Stanley and Marion Welkley and Vernon and Arlene Frost) who provided a foundation of unconditional love, and who always believed in my capabilities . . . to my parents (Lee and Caroline Welkley) who have always given support and encouragement as I continued my journey . . . and to my many friends who have become a part of my "extended family" and at times "immediate family" constellation for all the laughter, support, and listening ears they have provided over the years. It is through these experiences that I have become aware of the multidimensionality of "family" and what that means for me. DLW

Contents

List of Figures and Tables

Tables

Preface

Current times reveal the importance of recognizing and honoring diverse ways of being, and the notion of family seems to create a space for navigating through a multidimensional exploration of our human existence and complexities. From that space, this text, *Diversity in Family Constellations: Implications for Practice*, attempts to present the reader with an opportunity to examine the family as a living entity in constant movement and evolution. While engaging in this exploration, these authors introduce and explore five premises:

1. The family as a multidimensional contextual nonstatic living entity

2. Individuals as experiencing simultaneous memberships within diverse family constellations

3. The family and its members as being in a constant space of being and becoming

4. Reciprocity of forces—diverse realms of existence (i.e., intrapersonal [micro] domains, interpersonal [mezzo] domains, environmental [macro] domains, as well as nonordinary reality [magna] domains) as being continuously affecting and being affected by the family

5. An eclectic approach, vital when servicing diverse family constellations

We live in a world that reflects a universal law of impermanence. Change is constant and inevitable, and so is the space of possibilities and transformation. There are multiple ways through which experiences are defined and arranged. Historically, though, we observe that the search for absolute truth is a work in progress and in some ways a sacred task for each individual sharing this human existence. The authors of this text believe this notion has been mirrored in the way the word "family" has been defined and experienced through perceptions of time. As language has changed, so have the definitions given to the experiences or lenses of family.

Diversity in Family Constellations: Implications for Practice provides readers with an opportunity to explore the aforementioned premises within diverse family constellations (i.e., the notion of nuclear families, multigenerational family constellations, single-parent family constellations, lesbian and gay families, foster family systems, and blended family groups). This text intends to offer practitioners, students, and others in the field of family practice an opportunity to glimpse and examine some of the complexities of family dynamics within the context of societal socioeconomic–political–environmental domains.

The purpose of *Diversity in Family Constellations: Implications for Practice* is not to conclude how the experience of a family should be perceived, but rather to afford some considerations for a multidimensional vision that encourages inclusiveness when addressing diverse family constellations. *Diversity in Family Constellations: Implications for Practice* supports an emerging body of knowledge that contributes to the education of current and future practitioners. Practice wisdom (a combined forty-plus years of working in various social service nonprofits that range from providing direct practice to administrative roles), scholarship and research, and a combined forty years of teaching in the disciplines of social work and sociology have contributed to the ideas and explanations addressed in the premises provided in this book. The authors do not claim any specific truth through the content addressed, yet simply wish to present a lens that honors, respects, and demonstrates integrity to diverse family constellations.

Organization of the Text

Diversity in Family Constellations: Implications for Practice is organized into three major parts. Part 1 of the text presents the reader with an opportunity to explore emerging and traditional perspectives of family constellations. In part 1, the authors introduce the five premises, previously identified, with the intention to move beyond stereotypical lenses likely to marginalize family experiences. While creating a foundation for this framework, the authors discuss how the five premises intersect and overlap.

Part 2 provides the reader with an opportunity to apply the five premises within the context of six different yet connected family constellations: (1) opposite-sex family ideal, (2) multigenerational families,

(3) single-parenting families, (4) gay and lesbian families (gamilies), (5) foster families, and (6) blended family units. Although there are many additional forms of family arrangements, these six are used by experts in the field as a way of illustrating application of the developing framework to family experiences that have been addressed in other texts, as well as to some that are frequently overlooked when thinking about the family in today's society. The authors intend for this to be a starting place for readers to begin exploring how the emerging framework can be used when understanding and working with individuals and families.

Finally, part 3 begins with a summary of major ideas addressed throughout the text and proposes areas for further consideration and expansion. The authors present a template for determining practical approaches useful for assessing and intervening with diverse family constellations. Readers are encouraged to continue an exploration of family constellations from a space of nonabsoluteness in order to embrace infinite possibilities when attempting to understand the notion of family.

Acknowledgments

The authors wish to thank their families for their support and love throughout the process of this project. In addition to offering us their steadfastness, many people contributed to the development of this book. We thank our many students and colleagues, as well as clients, throughout our years of learning and teaching that have provided impetus for many of the ideas presented in this text. Much gratitude is expressed to the contributing authors and their willingness to explore application of the framework constructed. We also thank the reviewers who provided valuable feedback as we strengthened the development of the content addressed in this text: Karen Jick, Diane A. Kempson, Thomas Meenaghan, and two anonymous reviewers. For assistance with graphically representing our model and premises, we offer appreciation to Valerie Mighetto, California State University, Sacramento. We wish especially to thank David Follmer, publisher; Reese-Anna Baker, editorial coordinator; Catherine Dixon, editorial associate; Alison Hope, copy editor; and Lyceum Books, Inc., for their encouragement and technical support throughout our writing. Finally, a heartfelt thanks to the many families we have worked with whose stories are reflected throughout case studies and other aspects of this work.

PART I

The Family Within the Context of Multidimensionality and Contextualization

This text begins with the introduction of an eclectic lens for raising an understanding of family practice during the process of assessment and intervention. The content is intended to expand the readers' conceptualization of the family beyond stereotypical lenses and marginalization of family experiences. Five major premises are discussed: (1) the family as a multidimensional contextual nonstatic living entity, (2) individuals constantly experience multiple family memberships, (3) the family in a constant space of being and becoming, (4) diverse realms of existence affecting and being affected by the family, and (5) the importance of an eclectic approach to family practice. The reader is exposed to the notion of multiple lenses and ways of understanding social or cultural factors affecting and being affected by diverse family constellations. (Note: the term "family constellation" is used throughout this text to represent the union of a group of people under the umbrella of family experience.) The reader is encouraged to incorporate a multidimensional eclectic lens to his or her study and work with families.

Whereas some of the concepts addressed in part 1 of this text are based on ideas, thoughts, and experiences published by numerous writers or practitioners within the field of family practice, some of the views presented have not yet been shared publicly, since they reflect these authors' current developed orientations and observations. As the authors share perspectives that are not widespread, it is their hope that readers will use these ideas to continue strengthening and exploring family experiences beyond notions of absolute truths. It is stressed throughout this text that the family is a socially and culturally con-structed phenomenon inclusive of experiences that are not always eas-ily operational or explained through reasoning and logic. Enjoy the ride!

CHAPTER ONE

Creation of a Baseline

Krishna L. Guadalupe
Debra L. Welkley

When I think I know, I lose.
When I open myself to uncertainties my
being is extended into worlds never imagined.

KLG

The experience of the family is ancient and can be viewed as an evolutionary progression into new manifestations of human creations. Therefore, a degree of awareness or alertness of historical encounters and current possibilities is imperative to understanding the family and its diversity. Is the human race ready and willing to be mindfully present and active in the ongoing transformation of consciousness as it relates to the experience of the family? While exploring the historic evolution of the experience currently referred to as the "family," one can observe that change is constant and inevitable. Transformation, although generated through the process of change, seems optional, requiring a degree of awareness and intentionality that provides one or more specific directions. That said, it is obvious that changes in the experience of the family will continue to occur. The degree to which we consciously participate and contribute to those changes can influence the direction(s) and purpose(s) that the family may provide throughout our ongoing human evolution. For instance, some may argue that the major purpose of the family is to procreate, to perpetuate the species. Although procreation is essential for preserving any species, anyone can procreate, regardless of whether or not he or she is part of a family. Procreation may not be essential to what constitutes a family. Thus, procreation may or may not be a fundamental role of the family.

This chapter presents various interpretations of the family within the context of dominant orientations (concepts strongly influencing our current understanding of family) as well as what we like to refer to as nonordinary orientations (ideas and experiences not widely recognized or empirically addressed). The content encourages readers to be mindful as to the lens or lenses that they use to understand and address family dynamics. It also proposes that an understanding of families as multidimensional–contextual nonstatic living entities, which are continuously transforming, is imperative for cultivating and sustaining a degree of professional competence within the context of servicing diverse family constellations experiencing a variety of strengths and challenges. From this point of reference, the content introduces five major premises guiding the focus of this text.

This book is not interested in convincing the reader of a "best" or "right" way to approach the family, but rather in presenting areas for consideration. By doing so, the intention is to add to the realm of possibilities. As an experience, the family is a moving target. Therefore, this conversation can be considered boundless and readers are invited to join in as this journey continues.

Dominant and Non-widely Recognized Orientations

When encouraged to contemplate the meaning of family, people will most likely engage in an exploration that reflects their personal experiences or particular societal dominant models of normalcy. By this we mean the formal and informal systemic norms created by conscious and unconscious social–cultural agreements that convey a conceptualization of what "should" or "should not" be considered a family constellation. When reading different books or articles, or during conversations around the concept of family, one may notice that, whereas some views of what constitute a family constellation are comprehensive, that is, inclusive of multiple variables (e.g., familial agreements or commitments, family structures, functions, nature of diverse family constellations, dynamics of interactions and exchanges, etc.), other views are not comprehensive. Furthermore, ideas generated by one person often differ from those generated by another. The image(s) of what constitutes a family constellation has evolved in many ways and for many reasons, mirroring diverse contexts, settings, and times in history. Changes have often reflected human creation or transformation of social phenomena generated by interactions (i.e., contact-connectedness among and between people) and exchanges (i.e., inputs and outputs created by dynamics of interactions-connections) that yield results (figure 1.1).

The aforementioned observations briefly reveal the complexity of the experience currently identified as family. It also momentarily reminds us that, whereas "families are the foundation of most societies" (Hull & Mather, 2006, p. 2), families are not static experiences. Families are not discovered, but rather are individually and socially constructed. Therefore, individual interpretations or meanings given to the experience of family frequently do not carry absolute truth, yet these interpretations are often representations of diverse perspectives.

Within different historical times and contexts, dominant or traditional perspectives (governing views or orientations heavily influencing social conditions and interpretations of experiences) as well as not widely recognized orientations (i.e., existing or emerging views not greatly represented within social norms and standards) have existed. Although dominant perspectives often have promoted exclusive definitions that do not reflect diverse ways through which the family has been experienced, other not widely recognized orientations have persisted, often surviving while facing marginalization due to unpopularity. Dominant definitions of the family, through the course of social times, have been generally understood by the majority of the population. However, they have not been representative of all forms of family constellations. For instance, Coontz (2000) stresses that the term "family" was initially used to refer to a band of slaves. As time has passed, this term has been used within broader contexts and expanded as an attempt to define what constitutes family constellations within new evolutionary times.

The endurance of non-widely recognized orientations related to the experience of the family has been remarkable and undeniable. Such

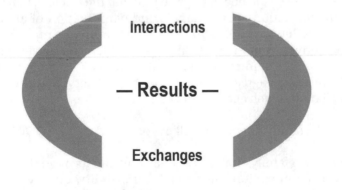

© Guadalupe & Welkley

FIGURE 1.1 *Dynamics of Interactions and Exchanges*

endurance is especially observed when exploring emerging orientations within the context of attributed social power often given to dominant perspectives to disgrace views cherishing experiences that are not socially or culturally widely represented. For instance, in the twentieth and twenty-first centuries, the dominant definition of a family has habitually been referred to as the "nuclear family." Although the notion of the nuclear family has historically demonstrated different characteristics affecting its social establishment and modifications throughout time, several major themes associated with the nuclear ideal have historically been preserved. An example of one theme historically perpetuated within the notion of the nuclear family is the impression that familial nuclear unions are fundamentally based on relationships between individuals of opposite sexes: one man and one woman. A nuclear family has often been defined as a married heterosexual couple, often with children, all of whom live together in the same home independently from extended family members such as grandparents, aunts, uncles, and cousins. The experience of the nuclear family often seems to be viewed as child-centered, where the lives and activities of the children are the main focus of the family as a whole. This idea of family has been powerfully upheld throughout the United States' society and perpetuated through major establishments, including the media, schools, political organizations, and religious institutions, regardless of evidence that reflects the existence of family constellations not represented by the aforementioned experience. However, non-widely recognized orientations related to the experience of the family have not ceased to exist. Diverse forms of family constellations have coexisted or struggled historically, as will be further discussed in chapter 2.

Dominant perspectives have historically attempted to promote the notion that a normal or typical family is nuclear, often further interpreted as heterosexual, neglecting the role that the nucleus plays in promoting the formation, maintenance, and perpetuation of all forms of family constellations, including same-sex family groups. The term "nuclear" derives from the term "nucleus," which can be viewed as the core unifying force or intentionality that assembles, sustains, and is promoted by relational agreements such as those observed by diverse family constellations. Such agreements affect the

- nature of a family: that is, overall purpose;

- structure of a family: that is, sets of arrangements or guiding patterns of family composition (membership flexibility, quality of interactions, duration, and intensity of relationships), and exchanges within and between familial members as well as with those considered to be outsiders;

- family's culture or multicultures: that is, beliefs, values, life orientations, attitudes, rules, codes (language, norms), shared expectations influencing behavior, as well as sense of being, identity, belonging, and direction;

- function(s) of a family: that is, crucial activities that promote healthy or unhealthy family well-being as well as procedures intended to stimulate, encourage, or fulfill the family or members' optimal purpose; and

- familial roles: that is, behaviors related to one's familial position and tasks assumed by individual members within different contexts or settings.

Figure 1.2 is a hierogram to help readers better visualize these observations.

Whereas many families effortlessly fit into the nuclear family experience, a significant number of families fit only partially or not at all, including, but not limited to, multipartner family groups, blended family units, foster family systems, communal family structures, spiritually based family forms, cohabitation, single-parent family units, and same-sex family constellations. Thus, solely viewing the family through the lens of nuclear family, as a union between a man and a woman, is negligent. It minimizes the experience of diverse family constellations as well

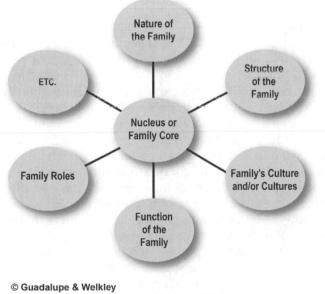

© Guadalupe & Welkley

FIGURE 1.2 *Nucleus Effects*

as the encounters that human beings often have while they are simultaneously part of multiple family groups (i.e., an individual can be a member of a family of origin, a cohabitation group, a blended family unit, and/or a spiritually based family).

In *A New Earth*, Eckhart Tolle (2005) makes an interesting observation: "Humans suffered more at the hands of each other than through natural disasters" (p. 10). He goes on to stress that devastating human conditions (inherited human insanity resulting in dynamics of destructive living patterns encouraged by fear of the unknown, greed, and the desire for power) have been psychological motivating forces reinforcing painful human interactions and exchanges. Tolle's observation is applicable when exploring experiences encountered by diverse family constellations.

It is important to recognize that when groups of family constellations are not recognized by a dominant societal definition(s) they often are not treated equally; as a result, a structure of social stratification is created. Unequal treatment often reflects and promotes marginalization of specific family constellations. Guadalupe and Lum (2005) view marginalization as "the exclusion of attributes and experiences that can help reveal a more comprehensive view of an individual, family, group, or community" (p. 10). The traditional legal definition of the nuclear family in the United States has strongly guided the formation of legislations surrounding marriage, child custody, health or retirement benefits, and adoption, which tend to exclude or create difficulties for nontraditional—or should we say non-widely recognized—family groups. The U.S. Census Bureau has historically defined the family as two or more persons living together and related by blood, marriage, or legal adoption. This definition does not consider same-sex family constellations or cohabitation as family types, but rather as groups of people living together in a household. As a result of current legislations, gay marriages are recognized in only six states in the United States as of this writing, and domestic partnerships are often not eligible to receive the rights and benefits attributed to marriages between men and women.

The argument can be made that the dynamics of marginalization or social-political effects experienced by family constellations that have been less recognized, due to dominant family perspectives, hold the potential for creating social conditions similar to those historically experienced by diverse ethnic groups within the context of white supremacy (defined as the belief or action that supports the idea that people who are white or of European descent are superior, or are the reference point in relationship to all other groups of people and should have control of resources within society). For instance, Thomas Jefferson stressed in the Declaration of Independence, "All men are created equal" during the same historical time when African slaves were considered to be only one third of a person by social dominant perspectives. Thus, the notion of "all men are created equal" excluded this community of people, in addition to, needless to say, white men and women who did not control the means of production. The idea of equality was manipulated by the power of those who controlled or had access to resources and possess power to define and influence social norms. In other words, those with power to define frequently have the power to control or at least influence the status quo.

A similar social phenomenon was observed during the period of Jim Crow laws (late 1800s to mid-1900s) where under *Plessy v. Ferguson* the legal rule of separate but equal was supported by dominant legislations, governing social norms. Looking back, it has become evident that separation between white and nonwhite Americans supported favorable physical and socioeconomic or political conditions for whites. In addition, of course, there are discriminatory experiences often encountered today by single-parenting family constellations, especially when they are headed by women, or experiences encountered by gay families. Social dominating dogmas (rigid beliefs systems) have historically promoted and perpetuated the institutionalization of hierarchal dynamics of interactions and exchanges that have given humans unnecessary pain. Therefore, in the exploration of the notion and experience of diverse family constellations, one needs to consider how the family is socially and culturally defined, as well as implications generated by such definition(s). Consciousness-raising regarding possibilities for radical transformation within current times is not only imperative but also central to the healing of the human race. We can begin by embracing and honoring the uniqueness of diverse family constellations while simultaneously assessing our individual and collective participations in the perpetuation of devastating human conditions and our commitment to restore our fundamental essence.

Another starting point for assisting in our healing is an exploration of the use of language and its power. A harmful result of the current dominant definition of family and its characteristics is the creation and use of antonyms to describe families that do not fit the expectations set by the dominant perspectives. Dominant perspectives regarding family functions and dynamics seem to promote the sense of normality that can be, and often is, translated as typical, desirable, attractive, representative, necessary, and ultimately healthy and standard. Family constellations not fitting into the dominant perspectives of family functions and dynamics are vulnerable to terms such as "maladaptive" and "dysfunctional." The meaning of the term "maladaptive" suggests that the family constellation is unable to adapt to the dominant expectation, whereas the term "dysfunctional" implies that the family is abnormal, further interpreted as atypical, nonstandard, deviant, or nonfunctional.

Current dominant definitions of the family seems to promote a notion of what is normal and what is not, and what is functional and what is dysfunctional.

Terms such as "maladaptive family" or "dysfunctional family" seem to promote disorder-based beliefs and are symbolic of fragility that is often exclusive of family resilience as well as multiple ways of being. Terms such as "maladaptive family" or "dysfunctional family" can be very damaging to the people to whom they are applied because they imply that there is something wrong with the family or its members and do not recognize behaviors and dynamics promoting different effects. These terms often come off as blaming the family and attributing any challenges they may be experiencing to personal inadequacies or poor decision-making skills.

From the point of reference of these writers, maladaptive family or dysfunctional families do not really exist. Every family is functioning within its own set of skills, knowledge, values, resources, patterns of interactions, and contexts. This is not to deny that within some specific contexts and dynamics of interactions family constellations may function in pain and unhappiness whereas within others they may function in health and joy. However, the use of terms such as "maladaptive family" or "dysfunctional family" does not honor the family's endless strengths and potentiality. One thing is to acknowledge that a family is experiencing individual or collective social adversities challenging its wellness and another is to stigmatize the family with labels that do not promote hope for transformation. As diverse family constellations deviate from the dominant interpretation(s) of the family, and terms such as "maladaptive family" or "dysfunctional family" are used, linguistic imperialism is cultivated, reflected, maintained, or perpetuated. Linguistic imperialism is viewed here as "the power to linguistically define, manipulate, and [attempt to] control [understanding of dynamics of interactions and exchanges between or among] individuals, families, groups, and communities" (Guadalupe & Lum, 2005, p. 81). In this context, the idea and use of linguistic imperialism is a demonstration of ethnocentrism, where an individual or group of individuals see the world only through their own cultural lens (made up of experiences, beliefs, values, etc., supported by their group) without the consideration or value given to other sociocultural views. Terms such as "maladaptive family" or "dysfunctional family" limit our understanding of family dynamics, and do not allow us to expand our knowledge and skills when working with diverse family constellations. The power of words cannot be underestimated.

Traditionally, dominant definitions of the family have often identified, sustained, and promoted core values, beliefs, and norms reflecting dominant social perspectives. By doing so, dominant definitions have frequently restricted our understanding of the scope of family experiences. Dominant definitions often have promoted marginalization of diverse family encounters through promotion of stereotypical perspectives—the one-size-fits-all approach. This is not to indicate that there is a problem with dominant definitions or perspectives of the family as they are indicative of some family constellations. Rather, the issue presents when dominant family definitions or understandings are used to view or evaluate as well as impose dominant values on *all* family types or forms. The time has come for a shift in perspective to one where all definitions are equally valued and understood as reflections of diverse family experiences. The writers understand that this shift in perspective will generate social–political implications as well as opportunities for social–political transformation.

Emerging Orientations within Specific Social Periods

During the 1920s and through the 1950s, the family was predominantly viewed through the lenses of psychodynamic perspectives, greatly influenced by Sigmund Freud's (1916–1917) psychoanalytic theory and Erik Erikson's (1950) psychosocial theory. Freud's and Erikson's direct work on human development and behavior focused primarily on individuals, but has been extensively applied to broader contexts, including the family. While conducting a substantial review of the literature, these authors were unable to identify a definition of the family developed by Freud or Erikson. However, Freud's and Erikson's perspectives have been used to explore and attempt to understand dynamics within diverse family constellations. Some general assumptions revealed by psychodynamic perspectives predominantly influenced by Freud and Erikson stress these points:

- Human development is deterministic. That is, childhood events and experiences shape our adult lives and pathologies. In relationship to the family, human service practitioners using this lens have stressed that adults often unconsciously seek to engage in intimate relationships that mirror those that they experienced with their parents or childhood caregivers. The reason for such unconscious determination has various rationales, including but not limited to (a) maintaining a level of familiarity with childhood learned cognitive and emotional patterns, and (b) seeking an opportunity to heal old cognitive and emotional wounds caused within the context of childhood experiences. Freud (1916–1917) suggested that human behaviors are determined by instinctual drives that have a primary purpose to satisfy unfulfilled needs.

- Our biological composition constantly influences unconscious mental processes that in turn produce and influence behaviors. All forms of behaviors can be measured and understood through an exploration of cause and effect: nothing occurs by chance. All behavioral symptoms stem from some kind of organic disorder or brain malfunction (Freud, 1916–1917). Behaviors are greatly influenced by a set of linear and predetermined stages of human growth that reflect human needs within specific developmental biological–psychological contexts. That said, human service practitioners influenced by this assumption while working with families have relied on the notion that decisions made by individuals as adults are often influenced by past biological-psychological make-ups of behavioral and relational patterns.

- People are frequently unaware of their mental processes influenced by primitive biological needs. Human service practitioners influenced by this assumption tend to believe that family dynamics and interactions can be strengthened through an exploration of unconscious psychological needs and desires with the intention of neutralizing emotional experiences.

The term "human service practitioner" is used in this text to identify individuals working within the health and human service fields, delivering services aimed to address biopsychosocial needs. These individuals may or may not have completed professional degrees in psychiatry, psychology, social work, nursing, school counseling, marriage and family counseling, and/or pastoral counseling.

One of the major critiques of psychodynamic lenses is that, although this lens (that of the psychodynamic approach) has begun to pay more attention to the effects that social or cultural environmental contexts have in the process of human development and behaviors, psychodynamic lenses continue to be heavily and primarily based on genetic, biological, and psychological influences—or should we say on intrapersonal biopsychological processes. Historically, psychodynamic lenses have not equally considered environmental factors when analyzing human behavior, decisions, and development (Schriver, 2011). Regardless of social criticism, however, psychodynamic perspectives have become one of the most powerful and influential lenses yet experienced in the field of human development and relational dynamics. Psychodynamic lenses have become the foundation for current relational theories (i.e., object relations, interpersonal theory, self-psychology, etc.) that generally perceive human relationships as a primary source for psychological change and ultimately for societal transformation.

Since the 1960s, systems theory has been heavily used to define the family as a system. Systems theory encompasses the belief that people operate within the context of a system where each aspect affects and is affected by changes in other parts of that entity. For instance, a ten-year-old female is seen as a member of several systems, one of which is her family. The birth of a new child in this family creates changes that affect the ten-year-old as well as other members of the family. Practitioners and theorists who adhere to this modality then focus on the changes that affect the functioning of the individuals as well as the family as a whole. Systems theoretical orientations and its implementation into the study of human development and behavior emerged initially as a reaction to psychodynamic perspectives, specifically Freudian's psychoanalytic theory. Ironically, contemporary systems theoretical orientations used when working with diverse family constellations have often incorporated many of the principles and assumptions produced by psychoanalytic perspectives. The many contemporary systems theories are reflected in the focus that systems theoretical orientations often place emphasis on familiar emotional relationships and psychological functions. For instance, systems theoretical orientations support the notion that human development is deterministic and that childhood encounters shape adult lives. Thus, the study of the family through the lens of systems theory, although an extension and inclusion of other areas, has been influenced by psychoanalytic assumptions.

While examining diverse written interpretations of systems theoretical orientations used to approach the family and its dynamics, one can observe the following common assumptions:

1. A system is often perceived as a set of complex living organisms interacting with and interrelated to one another. This set of living organisms interacts within individual or multiple contexts. Thus, when viewing the family through a systems lens, it is suggested that behaviors engaged by individual family members should not be examined in isolation from the entire family or from the social environment the family experiences.

2. The whole is greater than the sum of its parts. That is, although a system (i.e., a family) is a whole within itself, it is simultaneously a subsystem of a larger whole (i.e., the community or society). The notion of a subsystem, also often known as a holon, stresses that individuals-families-systems simultaneously operate and function within multiple or larger systems. (The term "holon" is used to define something that is whole as well as a part of something else at the same time. For instance, a family is whole, yet it is part of a bigger whole: a community, or a society, or a multigenerational family constellation.)

3. A system is often defined and distinguished from another system by its established and characterized norms (i.e., family standards), boundaries (i.e., family rules for interactions), structural arrangement, communication patterns and power dynamics, membership composition, members' roles, and other variables.

4. Systems are not perceived as static: they are viewed as constantly changing.

5. Change in one component of the system (i.e., family member) affects the system as a whole (i.e., the family), forcing the entire system to change or adjust to the experienced encounters.

6. Systems are in constant transactions with one another, influencing each other's sets of functional capacity, composition, structures, interaction patterns, and dynamics.

7. Systems vary in their degree of openness and closeness as dictated by their boundaries.

8. Systems have a need for input and output and tend to strive for stability and equilibrium through adaptation or changes, or both, when experiencing an imbalance. Thus, systems are goal oriented.

9. In order to function competently, systems need equilibrium.

An interesting phenomenon is observed when reflecting on various definitions of the family using a systems perspective: some definitions are more inclusive than others. Duvall (1971) defined the family as "a unity of interacting persons related by ties of marriage, birth, or adoption, whose central purpose is to create and maintain a common culture which promotes the physical, mental, emotional, and social development of each of its members" (p. 5). Duvall's definition of family generally reflects traditional systems paradigms, yet this definition seems to be in need of further clarification. For instance, Duvall speaks of a unity between family members. However, there may be multiple unities within a particular family constellation affecting its dynamics. The more members a family constellation has, the more possibilities there are for multiple relationship types within the specific family group. Furthermore, as noted by Hartman and Laird (1983), people are often simultaneously a part of multiple family groups, some that are based on biological or legal ties and others that solely stand on close personal relationship agreements to function according to characteristics often socially or culturally attributed to family constellations (i.e., a group of people supporting and looking out for the well-being of each of its members).

   Duvall's (1971) definition has potential for inclusiveness, although it is currently narrow. It is not representative of nonlegally bounded family constellations such as homosexual couples, who in general do not experience the right to marriage, or people who consider close friends to be additional family members. Duvall's definition assumes that families "maintain a common culture" when, in fact, families are constantly in a process of change. Duvall's definition also does not consider the notion that each member of a family is likely to experience family culture or subcultures differently. Guadalupe and Lum (2005, p. 8) refer to culture as "constructed ways of living or a totality of learned behaviors. These ways of living or behaviors are influenced by beliefs, values, symbols, boundaries, norms, and lifestyles that are arranged and modified. . . . Culture is based on co-creation of agreements that reveal roles and expectations for thinking, behaving, and being between those engaged through membership, whether influenced by biological ties, shared history, or social contracts." Cultures are not static and pure preservation of any particular culture over a long period of time is highly unlikely.

   Yuen (2005, p. 1) defines the family "as a system of two or more interacting persons who are either related by ties of marriage, birth, or adoption, or who have chosen to commit themselves to each other in unity for the common purpose of promoting the physical, mental, emotional, social, economic, cultural, and spiritual growth and development of the unit and each of its members. Family can be further conceptualized by its interrelated dimensions of nature, structure, and functions." This definition takes into account variables not directly addressed by Duvall's (1971) conceptualization of the family. For instance, diverse sexual orientation family constellations seem to be considered through the notion that familial commitments are not only based on marriage, birth, or adoption, but also on commitment, shared values, and possibly other characteristics. Yuen's definition stresses that families are understood in terms of transactions as well as in terms of structural or functional characteristics.

   Duvall's (1971) and Yuen's (2005) definitions reflect principles of systems theory. Both definitions perceive the family as goal-oriented with the purpose of promoting and maintaining the well-being of its members. Although ideal, not all familial relationships demonstrate the aforementioned perspective while continuing to function as a family constellation. For instance, gangs are often considered by its members to be family constellations. However, rituals, tasks, and behavioral patterns conducted by gangs and gang members may not reflect dominant notions of physical, mental, emotional, socioeconomic, cultural, or spiritual well-being. The view promoted by the aforementioned definitions seems to suggest that the family's ultimate goal is inherently the same in all families; that is, families will and do promote the well-being of its members. Although ideal, promotion of such ideas can be dangerous because they could create or reinforce a status quo, which seems to dictate what does and does not constitute a family. An inability or unwillingness of a family constellation to reflect the notion reflected by these definitions can strengthen the possibility for this family to experience marginalization. It is important to stress that contexts, historical-social times, settings, and power dynamics within a society often play a role on how a family evolves and expresses itself.

A Current Attempt at Inclusiveness

As reflected through the previous discussion, the family is a complex social phenomenon. The way the family is defined affects the nature of our professional practice. Therefore, it is important for definitions of the family to be people-centered if the intention is to honor people's unique experiences. Furthermore, it is well known that the experience of family formation, maintenance, dynamics, or termination cannot be captured by a single definition, yet definitions can open or close doors to people feeling included or excluded from specific social paradigms, privileges, and experiences.

It has not been until recent years that emerging definitions of the family as relationships that may include, but yet transcend, blood, marriage, and adoption characteristics have gained much social support. Such definitions are reflected by Yuen's (2005) conceptualization (mentioned earlier) of the family. Definitions and conceptualizations of the family, however, are works in progress when considering the uncertainties of human dynamics and evolution.

The view that as individuals we are often part of multiple family constellations has also gained recognition. An individual may be a member of a family of origin—the family through which one is raised and socialized to embrace specific cultural values, beliefs, and behaviors—not necessarily because she or he was born into this family constellation, but rather because of an adoption. Thus, this individual can be simultaneously part of a family of procreation—the family unit of which the individual was born and a family of origin. Furthermore, due to divorces and remarriages or creation of new partnerships, children within these relationships often experience reconstituted family groups, commonly referred to as stepfamilies or blended family constellations. Of course, we all have membership in multigenerational family constellations, as well.

As previously reflected, different theoretical orientations have been used to define and work with family constellations. For the purpose of this text, a social constructivist–social constructionist lens in combination with principles deriving from ecological, strengths, and feminist perspectives will be used to view and establish guidance for working with diverse family groups. Tables 1.1 through 1.4 provide a general

Table 1.1 Constructivist—Social Constructionist Orientation

General Assumptions	• Individual and collective meanings are socially constructed and grow out of daily interactions and dynamics (i.e., people often engage in co-creations of systems of meanings, called "cultures"). • Language, knowledge, and understanding are created, not discovered. • Sense of self is constructed, deconstructed, and reconstructed as core meanings or life narratives are generated, experienced, promoted, or transformed. • Contextual or personal understanding helps reduce stereotypes and marginalization of people's experiences. • There is no universal "truth," but there are different sets of subjective interpretations of constructed social "realities" (i.e., divorce emotional effects). • Language and communication patterns are sources of contextual power. • There is a relationship between language, knowledge, and power; therefore, those with power to define have power to control, or at least influence. • No universal assumptions or "facts" can explain human development or behaviors in totality. • A degree of uncertainty is always important in our human interactions; behavior cannot be completely predicted.
General Principles	• Devalues the search for universal laws and theories. • Emphasizes contextual experiences and recognizes diversity. • Advocates for recognition of the importance of language. • Social construction research stresses an analysis of human interaction, particularly conversation analysis. • Social constructions contribute to the socialization of a society's members—to the extent that social ideas are so widely shared that they become a form of truth to participants. • Rejects the notion supporting a single "reality." • The diagnosis not supported by constructivist thoughts. Standardized measures often reflect the values and culture of dominant groups and tend to pathologize people (i.e., DSM R-IV). • Does not support the notion of stage-based theories.

understanding of common assumptions and principles guiding constructivist–social constructionist, ecological, strengths, and feminist orientations.

Within the context of the United States' multicultural society, experiences and meanings regarding the family have varied from one group to another, creating a challenge in the construction of an operational definition that is inclusive of all forms of family constellation. Historically, the notion of what constitutes a family, as well as experiences influencing the construction of diverse family constellations, has reflected the importance of considering the role that context plays during the manifestation of individual roles and functions shaping dynamics within and between diverse family arrangements. It can be argued that one common denominator that all families seem to share is this: families have historically served as central socially constructed institutions that, over

Table 1.2 Ecological Orientation

General Assumptions	• An interdependent relationship exists between person and environment. This relationship is proactive, inseparable, and multisystemic. A person and his or her environment(s) shape and influence one another, although a person may experience a different degree of power within diverse contexts, settings, or time periods.
	• People connect and act simultaneously within the context of multiple systems.
	• An interdependent relationship exists between intrapersonal and interpersonal factors encountered in the process of human development. Cognitive, genetic, or other biological factors are experienced in diverse ways, reflecting a variety of transactions with the environment.
	• People as individuals and groups need to be understood within the context of their environment, and an environment needs to be understood relative to the people that are a part of it.
	• Human beings develop meanings of their environment through a process of transactions. Human beings are goal oriented and persistent in striving for competence within the context of their environment.
	• Attainment of well-being is a lifelong process.
General Principles	• Advocates for a focus on the person—environment fit with an emphasis on reciprocal exchanges and transactions between person—environment within diverse contexts and settings. Not linear focused.
	• Emphasis is on contexts, contents, and processes affecting human development. Goodness-of-fit (i.e., good match and mutual growth, or poor fit and oppression) are a primary focus.
	• Other areas of focus and relatedness, competence, role, niche (an individual's status within environment) and habitat (person's physical and social settings within a cultural context), and adaptiveness (consideration of coercive and exploitative power, stress, coping, etc.).
	• Advocate for a holistic approach (i.e., assessment and intervention must consider the whole situation of a person or community, or both).

time, have sustained, promoted, or modified individual and societal norms, beliefs, and values. Yet even this observation is misleading, because not all family constellations have experienced equal socioeconomic political power to equally influence change, nor for that matter, have all family constellations been empowered by ongoing societal modifications.

As stressed earlier, although there has never been a single-family form that has represented all family constellations, the United States' political and economic systems have historically promoted policies that view family constellations as nuclear family units. Furthermore, as will be discussed in chapter 2, what has traditionally been considered a nuclear family constellation has changed tremendously over the years. Numerous family constellations have decided not to partake in functions such as childbearing or child rearing, while others have determined to legally adopt rather than to give birth to children. Socio-

Table 1.3   Strengths Orientation

General Assumptions	• People have an inherent capability or power to transform their lives, even within the context of adversities or trauma. This capacity or power is sometimes muted, restricted, unrealized, etc. Our socioeconomic—political—cultural environmental contexts and dynamics may nurture or suppress the power of the human spirit.
	• Demanding or stressful life experiences do not automatically predetermine that people will inevitably experience vulnerability, an inability to cope, or psychopathology. Denounce the perspective that those who have suffered trauma or adversities become powerless. Adversities or trauma create not only challenges, but often opportunities as well.
	• Language and words have power. Language should not be taken for granted; human strengths should not be minimized by the language of symptom and syndrome. Identifications expressed with words often have effects (i.e., a person is suffering from schizophrenia rather than being named schizophrenic; people experience anger or fear, yet they are not angry or fearful).
	• Every environment has strengths.
	• Caring is important to human wellness.
	• This orientation stresses that theories and practices are often constructed on an idea of people becoming clients because of some type of deficit, pathology, weakness, etc. (i.e., medical model).
	• A focus on what is wrong or on psychopathologies (i.e., a deficit approach) often minimizes people's strengths or abilities to cope and promotes pessimistic expectations.
General Principles	• Practice is built on the person's, family's, or community's strengths (i.e., ability, asset, knowledge, resources, talent, competence, etc.).
	• Practice is seen as a collaborative or honesty-based process influenced by the construction of a partnership. Distance, manipulation, and inequality of power should not shape the process of serving others.
	• Psychopathologies are recognized but do not become the primary focus of assessment and interventions.
	• The "client" is the expert, and the "practitioner" is a "collaborator or consultant."
	• Advocates for practitioners' ongoing self-evaluation or awareness.
	• Respect for human diversity.
	• Using challenges as opportunities.
	• Hope, possibilities, caring, and resilience as primary principles.

economic and emotional distresses, among other factors, have had an impact on the transformation of the traditional nuclear family constellation. With this understanding in mind, it is easier to recognize that definitions of the family do not hold absolute truth, but rather create a point of reference from which to engage in a critical analysis.

Families are relationships formed, transformed, or maintained through dynamics of human interactions and exchanges. Through interactions and exchanges, a nucleus is formed, serving as the unifying form of the specific family constellation. Through time, the nucleus can

Table 1.4   Feminist Orientation

General Assumptions	• Social structures, especially within the United States, privilege or give advantages to men, and consequently oppress women.
	• Knowledge and values are interdependent.
	• There are many ways of knowing. Knowledge is holistic, not linear.
	• The personal is political. Events do not occur in isolation from the whole.
	• Inequality affects gender relationships.
	• Differences among the sexes should not promote a sense of female inferiority.
	• In order for egalitarian relationships to be promoted changes must occur at the individual and social level.
General Principles	• Ultimate goal—formation of an egalitarian society/relationships, where no one is not marginalized, but rather everyone is treated equally.
	• Consciousness-raising is used to stimulate awareness and promote change. Through consciousness-raising strategies people are supported in a process of exploring the dehumanization promoted through social structures and encouraged take actions to change social conditions.
	• A person-in-situation emphasis—considering personal, interpersonal, and social dynamics and effects. Respect for human diversity.
	• Empowerment incorporates personal and societal change.

be strengthened or altered. Dynamics of interactions—exchanges within the family constellation, as well as between the family and its surroundings—activate the nature of family constellations. Transactions also affect and are affected by the cultures, structures, functions, and roles of family constellations. These observations are demonstrated in figure 1.3.

Throughout this text, a family is viewed as a multidimensional contextual nonstatic living entity, initially constructed on the basis of a conscious or unconscious—formal or informal—relational agreement that often evolves or transforms into a more consistent commitment between two or more living beings. The experience of family is constructed, deconstructed, or reconstructed through dynamics of interactions and exchanges between and among participants within diverse contexts and settings as well as through outside influences. Family agreements or commitments are family centered: these commitments or agreements can be understood through explorations of meanings and interpretations given to dynamics of interactions and exchanges by those involved in the specific family constellation. Only the specific perceived family constellation can fully determine the depth of its meaning, its functions, and nature affecting familiar roles and possible structures. The agreement or commitment may or may not include marriage, birth, or legal or social adoption of new members. The initial agreement or commitment for the formation of a family constellation is transformed as members engage in and undergo lifespan processes; constructions, deconstructions, and reconstructions of identities and

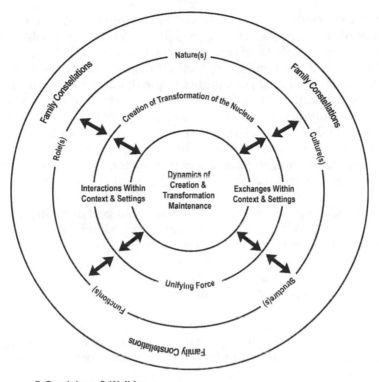

© Guadalupe & Welkley

FIGURE 1.3 *Dynamics of Family Formation and Transformation*

experiences influenced by physical or physiological events; cognitive encounters; emotional occurrences; and social contexts, as well as decision-making generated through dynamics of interactions and exchanges.

Assessment of family constellations assists in gaining an understanding of channels of communication, family composition requirements or memberships, power dynamics, and roles played by individual members, among other important family aspects. However, these alone are fragmented pieces of a larger puzzle referred to here as the nucleus. The nucleus or basic core—origin of family formation, maintenance, dynamics, or termination—is cultivated through dynamics of human interactions and exchanges. The survival of a family constellation, therefore, is not necessarily based on harmonious relations between and among its members, but rather on a conscious or unconscious decision to continue familiar interactions. In summary, families can be perceived as relationships based on specific agreements or commitments to interact in specific ways, reflecting and promoting specific purposes, structures, cultures, functions, roles, patterns, and, for that matter, dynamics. Five main premises support the aforementioned definition:

1. Family constellations are perceived as multidimensional contextual nonstatic living entities through which a variety of relationships often emerge, exist, and are reflected within family constellations: relationship with self and relationships with the notion of others. Each relationship is capable of generating unique dynamics separate and yet interdependent from the collective. The notion of family constellations as multidimensional contextual nonstatic living entities is also reflected within the context of multigenerational family constellations. In other words, families often live on through procreation or expansion, or both, and interact and exchange within various historical times and contexts affecting their sense of self and cycles.

2. As individuals, we are often simultaneously a part of multiple family constellations. We are born into a family (i.e., family of procreation), we are raised and socialized by one or more family units (i.e., family of origin that may or may not be the family of procreation); at the same time, those immediate or extended families constitute multigenerational family constellations.

3. Family constellations are constantly in a process of being and becoming (i.e., constructing, deconstructing, and reconstructing the family's identity and experiences as a continuum and through a process of interaction and exchanges within one or more physical, social, economic, political, or cultural environments).

4. The family affects and is affected by intrapersonal (micro domains), interpersonal (mezzo domains), environmental (macro domains), as well as nonordinary (magna domains). Although these domains can be addressed individually, they are interrelated and must also be considered as a collective when understanding and supporting the well-being of family constellations. The intrapersonal (micro domain) can be viewed as biocognitive patterns, processes, or experiences existing and occurring within the context of a person or a group of people's psyche, mind, inner self, or physical being. Such patterns, processes, or experiences are interconnected with the impact of beliefs, values, perceptions, thought patterns and attitudes, life orientations, and awareness or lack of awareness. These patterns in turn influence and are influenced by behaviors, decisions, and actions occurring within the interpersonal domain. The interpersonal (mezzo domain), on the other hand, is perceived as the point or interface at which individuals or the family as a whole interacts (i.e., connects and relates) and exchange (i.e., input, output, and effects generated by the interaction) with others inside or outside the family constellation. Interactions and exchanges often are guided,

fostered, perpetuated, or transformed by intrapersonal dynamics. Environment (macro domain) is viewed as physical, social, economic, political, or religious frameworks or contexts where interpersonal interactions or connections and exchanges may occur while affecting and being affected by the other domains (micro, mezzo, and magna). The nonordinary (magna domain) aspect of our existence encompasses but is not limited to experiences (or perceived encounters) or interpretations of a conventional sense of reality. The terms "nonordinary reality" or "magna domains" are used interchangeably throughout this text as an attempt to acknowledge possible experiences that one cannot understand or conceptualize in its totality by logic or reasoning. Examples of nonordinary (magna domain) include the experience of the notion of spirit, God, Great Creator, or Yahweh, and so on. The content on nonordinary (magna domains) stressed throughout this text is not meant to conclude that all family constellations engage in spiritually based practices (i.e., rituals to invoke or devote one's life to an experience of a supreme absolute truth) or have religious convictions (doctrines, system of beliefs, or dogmas guiding understanding of a supreme absolute truth). It simply means that what is called human existence cannot yet be understood in its totality by scientific evidence. Although not all families may consider themselves to be spiritual or religious, practitioners have the responsibility to be holistic when assessing families, thus identifying whether the aspect of nonordinary (magna domain) plays a significant role in the dynamics of interaction within a specific family constellation. There seems to be a realm of experience stimulating our human existence that can be categorized as the Great Unknown. Disciplinary fields of studies such as quantum physics, also known as quantum mechanics or quantum theory, have explored and continue to explore this phenomenon as interactions and interdependence between energy and matter. This well-known field of study has indicated that all matter is energy in motion, therefore encouraging us personally and professionally to consider that experiences may be more complex than can be scientifically observed. As Albert Einstein once stated, a widely regarded scientist considered to be the father of modern physics, "The eternal mystery of the world is its comprehensibility."

5. An eclectic asset-based approach is likely to enhance our practice within the context of diverse family constellations. This approach entails being inclusive of various theoretical frameworks, modalities, and skills to maximize one's understanding and practices with the uniqueness of diverse family constellations. This will be further elaborated on in chapter 4 of this text.

The aforementioned premises (see figure 1.4) are considered to be proactive, interactive, and interdependent by nature. They intend to reduce stereotypical approaches when defining or working with diverse family constellations. These aforementioned premises will be further discussed in chapters 2 through 4.

The goal of this text is to promote a family-centered approach. Therefore, human service practitioners are encouraged to honor the wisdom of uncertainty, which refers to an inner knowing or intuitive power that reveals an understanding of living experiences beyond conscious reasoning, yet which is often ignored in the name of empirical and scientific discoveries. A sense of not knowing often promotes a curiosity needed to remain respectful of new learning rather than to approach families through stereotypical lenses that tend to marginalize their experiences. Practitioners are encouraged to engage in ongoing professional self-evaluation with the intention of gaining skilled awareness, which is useful when attempting to enhance proficient competence. The family is a complex experience that requires careful and respectful attention. As human service practitioners working within the context of diverse family constellations, we have a responsibility to be mindful throughout our professional engagements. Families are great teachers when we allow ourselves to remain teachable: may we all feel honored and engaged by the reflections of truth mirrored by diverse family constellations.

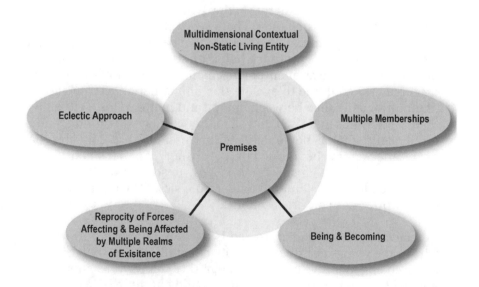

FIGURE 1.4 *Theoretical Lens*

References

Coontz, S. (2000). *The way we never were: American families and the nostalgia trap.* New York: Basic Books.

Duvall, E. M. (1971). *Family development* (4th ed.). Philadelphia: J. B. Lippincott.

Erikson, E. H. (1950). *Childhood and society* (2nd ed.). New York: W. W. Norton.

Freud, S. (1916–1917). *The standard edition of the complete psychological works of Sigmund Freud.* London: Hogarth Press.

Guadalupe, K., & Lum, D. (2005). *Multidimensional contextual practice: Diversity and transcendence.* Belmont, CA: Thomson Brooks/Cole.

Hartman, A., & Laird, J. (1983). *Family-centered social work practice.* New York: The Free Press.

Hull, G. H., Jr., & Mather, J. (2006). *Understanding generalist practice with families.* Belmont, CA: Thomson Brooks/Cole.

Saleebey, D. (2009) *The strengths perspective in social work practice* (5th ed.). Boston: Pearson Education.

Schriver, J. M. (2011). Human behavior and the social environment: Shifting paradigms in essential knowledge for social work practice (5th ed.). Boston: Pearson.

Tolle, E. (2005). *A new earth: Awakening to your life's purpose.* New York: Penguin.

Yuen, F. K. O. (Ed.). (2005). *Social work practice with children and families: A family health approach.* Binghamton, NY: The Haworth Social Work Practice Press.

CHAPTER TWO

Shifts in Family Paradigms

Krishna L. Guadalupe
Debra L. Welkley

Change is constant and inevitable.
Transformation is optional because it requires
a degree of awareness and intentionality,
which guides direction, while embracing change.

KLG

Recognizing family experiences as nonstatic occurrences can enhance our professional effectiveness. As briefly stressed in chapter 1, the family is socially and culturally constructed through interaction or connectedness and exchanges between and among human beings within one or more contexts or settings. This chapter encourages the reader to honor the family within the context of time and human evolution. It proposes an understanding of families as multidimensional contextual nonstatic living entities; where individuals can be simultaneously members of multiple family constellations. This lens reflects the first and second premise serving as the foundational framework guiding this text. Furthermore, this content stresses the importance of professional self-evaluation with the intention of strengthening professional competence.

A Brief History

Understanding of family constellations prior to or during the early colonial period is somewhat elusive and fragmented. However, there is a considerable amount of evidence that supports the view that multiple variations of family constellations as well as shared commonalities existed prior to or during this period, reflecting human diversity and common traits in terms of culture (i.e., language, customs, traditions, values, beliefs, and social norms, among others). Cultural anthropologists have suggested that, whereas for many indigenous peoples the family has historically been the largest unit, especially when they live in areas with minimal resources where collaboration has been essential for survival, for other indigenous people bands have been the largest unit, reflecting environmental demands as well as their customs, traditions, beliefs, and value systems. Unlike many European family groups, who have primarily developed and relied on patriarchal values and norms, many indigenous family constellations have valued and relied on the equal contribution of both sexes. Although daily tasks may have differed, they seemed to have been equally valued. Welch (2007) points out that during colonial times, native men often hunted and fished, and women were responsible for "growing the crops, building the houses, caring for the children, and gathering firewood. Much to the dismay of the European immigrants . . . , [some] marriages permitted considerable sexual freedom, and divorce was easy to obtain. Biracial marriages were not uncommon, as white frontiersmen sometimes married Indian [indigenous] women" (p. 9).

Many indigenous groups seemed to have experienced diverse cultural practices influenced by differences in languages, rituals and customs, educational methods, clothing styles, music, social and political systems, worldviews, and ways of life. Multiple groups often lived geographically remote from one another, resulting in the formation of diverse kinship systems—people related by blood, legal agreements or marriage, adoption, or those whom one simply considered family. The formation of diverse kinship systems reflected ways of fitting in, or adapting to, specific environmental demands.

Schwartz and Scott (2007) emphasize that the rules of descent varied among indigenous groups, influencing diverse family dynamics and forms of interactions: "Some societies, like that of the Cheyenne, were patrilineal, whereby kinship or family lineage (descent) and inheritance come through the father and his blood relatives. Others, like that of the Pueblos, were matrilineal, whereby kinship or family lineage (descent) and inheritance come through the mother and blood relatives" (p. 21).

The distinctions demonstrated by indigenous peoples reflect forma-tions of diverse family constellations. Indigenous populations, or First Nations peoples—a term gaining more social popularity to refer to North American indigenous tribes (Waller & Yellow Bird, 2002), have reflected family constellations that include the traditional notions of nuclear and extended family forms, yet this constellation of North American indigenous tribes has not been restricted to these conven-tional boundaries (John, 1988). Waller and Yellow Bird observed, "In many indigenous languages, for example, there is no term for cousin, niece, or nephew. The child is addressed by the entire clan as brother, sister, son, or daughter—terms generally reserved for immediate family in the [United States'] dominant culture" (p. 56). Devore and Schlesinger (1991) made another interesting observation when they suggested that a First Nations family "may be a network that includes several households who may live in close proximity, assuming village-type community characteristics, or it may consist of several households in each of several states, forming an interstate family structure. These families, village or interstate in structure, are active kinship networks that include parents, children, aunts, uncles, cousins, and grandparents. . . . The openness of the structures allows for the incorporation of significant nonkin as fam-ily members with responsibilities equal to those of all family members" (p. 272).

Devore and Schlesinger's (1991) observation about the structure of some First Nations family constellations can be extended to these authors' experience with various Puerto Rican family groups, in which the notion of nuclear and extended family boundaries are merged and parents, children, grandparents, aunts, uncles, and cousins are fre-quently considered part of the same family constellation. As a result of the flexibility of this type of family configuration, compadres, padrinos, madrinas—(coparents or godparents, godfather, godmother) or other significant non-kin (i.e., close friends) also are often socially or emotion-ally adopted and considered part of the family constellation. It is inter-esting to note that patterns of kinship groups also have been historically observed in many other ethnic groups including African American, Asian American, and Italian American communities, to mention a few.

History has shown that concepts of family are subject to change and that meanings given to the experience of the family are often shaped by individual experiences as well as by contextual dominant social struc-tures promoted by groups controlling the means of production (i.e., land, finance, raw materials, etc.). For instance, Welch (2007) indicates, "British immigrants brought the traditional patriarchal family structure . . . [to what is currently known as the United States]. The patriarchal family structure included the father figure, considered to be the authority over his entire household—wife, children, dependent kin, servants, slaves, and apprentices. . . . This family structure served to preserve the wealth and power of the patriarch's household and the family's lineage. When fathers died, they willed their land and property to their sons, ensuring that the family's wealth remained within the family" (p. 8). Welch's observation raises several interesting points. Within the British historic dominant model of family constellations, gender power differential often seemed to be accepted and promoted. Men who possess property or other forms of resources (i.e., finance, raw materials, etc.) often experienced attributed power—power gained through influence due to possession of resources. This attributed power often gave them the authority to rule not only members of the household (i.e., spouses, children, slaves, other individuals living in the house), but also other men and women who did not possess property and lived within the specific colony. Under the patriarchal family configuration, children often became economically dependent on their fathers for a good portion of their lives.

In contrast to a number of indigenous families that often used praise, rewards, or embarrassment for encouraging or endorsing ideal child behaviors, large numbers of British families, as well as other European groups, often relied on threats, religious guilt or shame, or physical beatings to promote desired discipline (Schwartz & Scott, 2007; Welch). In general, under the patriarchal family structure, women were expected to be submissive to their fathers or husbands. It was the father's right to withhold or give permission for a child's marriage. Although not always practiced, European women constantly faced the pressure of such expectation. According to Schwartz and Scott, "Although unmarried women had the right to own property, enter into contracts, and represented themselves in court, after marriage the English concept of *coverture* was evoked, whereby the wife's legal identity was subsumed in that of her husband, giving him the authority to make decisions for her. This doctrine was often ignored in practice, however. Records show that some colonial women, especially widows, entered into contracts and operated stores; ran taverns; and worked as millers, tanners, blacksmiths, silversmiths, shoemakers, and printers—occupations usually held by men" (p. 18). Historians indicate that during the seventeenth century and part of the eighteenth century the dominant notion of family constellation was reflected in the experience of households (i.e., people living together under the same roof). This seemed to have been perceived as the "nuclear family," a relatively modern term. This observation is particularly relevant to European groups.

The notion of the nuclear family is believed to have been a reality for large numbers of European ethnic groups including British, Dutch, Swedish, German, French, Irish, and Italians, among others. Differences between colonial and modern nuclear families have been documented, however. Schwartz and Scott (2007) write,

First, nonkin, such as orphans, apprentices, hired laborers, unmarried individuals, and children from other families, could and often did join colonial households. . . . Additionally, at times local authorities would place criminals and poor people with families. These people were to provide service to the household in return for care and rehabilitations. Second, the family formed the basic economic unit of colonial society. Women, men, and children combined their labor to meet the subsistence needs of the family. Until approximately the middle of the eighteenth century, relatively little was produced to sell. . . . Hence, as the basic economic unit of life, the family was synonymous with whoever lived and worked within the household, rather than being strictly defined by blood and marital ties. Finally, unlike today, the functions of the colonial family and larger community were deeply intertwined. (p. 17)

In other words, the notion of colonial nuclear family was often influenced by functions such as those conducted in current times by orphanages, rehabilitation houses, homeless shelters, vocational schools, hospitals, and businesses, among others. The dominant notion of family constellations sustained during the seventeenth century by most European groups seemed to have been greatly influenced by functions such as sharing of shelter, production of food, clothing, as well as provision of basic health care. During this period, European family constellations seem to have been mainly viewed as a source of reproduction and a socioeconomic productive unit. Divorces were uncommon and within many colonies even illegal. Adults in the family were morally responsible for educating its members and promoting religious values, functions currently and more formally undertaken by larger institutions.

It should be noticeable by now that when exploring family constellations, consideration needs to be given to human diversity, contexts, content, processes or dynamics, and paradigms within that particular era. For instance, the system of slavery or legal segregation established in the United States by the mid-1600s greatly differentiated experiences confronted by African American families from those encountered by European or indigenous groups, among others. As stressed by Billingsley (1988) major dynamics affecting families within these groups, included the following facts:

• African Americans did not come from Europe but from Africa.

• African Americans were removed from their cultures and families, and many were legally turned into slaves through the creation and promotion of the slavery system established in the South from the mid 1660s until it was abolished with the Thirteenth Amendment in 1865.

- African Americans have been systematically isolated from central social institutions within the United States (i.e., Jim Crow laws established after slavery had been abolished, and ongoing discrimination).

Key factors influencing diverse encounters between these families in preindustrial America were forced versus voluntary migration; colonization; power differential; unequal distribution of resources; and the experience of racial discrimination (Healey, 2011). Within the case of black or African Americans, under the system of agricultural slavery (in the South) and legal segregation and various forms of discrimination (in the North), marriages were not always politically or legally recognized. Although some slaveholders granted permission for their slaves to engage in religious marriage ceremonies, Southern laws prohibited slaves from marrying (Gutman, 1976; Healey). Slave couples did not always have the same slave owner or live in the same plantation, seeing each other only when permitted by the slaveholders. If they risked seeing each other without permission, they also risked possible inhumane punishment (i.e., beatings). The fear of forced separation was often encountered by slave families. As observed by Gutman as well as Healey, developed kinship feelings and patterns alleviated some of the distress and harsh treatments perpetuated through the slavery system, especially during the disintegration of immediate family configurations. When children of slave couples were sold and transferred to other plantations, blood relatives, or in their absence strangers residing in those plantations often engaged in parental roles. Similar to indigenous families, the notion of family within African American communities has often been inclusive beyond the traditional conventional boundaries frequently implied by the current concept of the nuclear family.

REFLECTIONS OF SOCIAL CHANGE AND FAMILY TRANSFORMATION

Evidence stresses that multiple forms of family constellations have existed throughout history. Changes in social structures (i.e., socioeconomic or political patterns and norms) and constructions of new paradigms (i.e., beliefs, values, attitudes, views, orientations), among other factors, have influenced the formation of diverse family constellations as well as the way that these have been perceived over time. An example is reflected by the industrial era of the mid 1800s to early 1900s in the United States, which generated radical transformation in the technological as well as social worlds.

Changes during the industrial period had distinctive effects for diverse family constellations. For instance, poor children were often employed at a young age, unable to experience the indulgence of a playful upbringing (Schwartz & Scott, 2007). All family constellations seemed to have been one way or another affected by these changes. The creation of new factories, technological products, railroads, and so on forced an increased wage labor movement outside the home. Private family farming was often replaced with wage labor. Distinction in gender roles and values given to those roles grew significantly (Healey, 2011). Men, specifically in European families, were more often than ever before perceived as providers or bread winners, and women were often expected to stay at home, have children, and care for the family's domestic needs. Although middle-class and upper-middle-class women often engaged in domestic roles, poor women often had to work outside their homes in unhealthy and harsh conditions and for much lower wages than their male counterparts earned. Working outside the home did not necessarily release women from domestic responsibilities (Healey; Kessler-Harris, 1981). The need of the common preindustrial household to function as a primary unit for economic production was modified, shaping families into smaller nuclear-nucleus units. The creation of hospitals, poorhouses, orphanages, and legal institutions for holding those who had broken the law relieved families from these previously accepted responsibilities. Working-class family constellations, including great numbers of indigenous, African American, Latino American, European American groups, and other immigrant groups often tended to be more fluid and rely on kinship systems in order to survive socioeconomic demands. Historical patterns of diverse populations developing kinship systems reflect multiple ways that family constellations have customized diverse characteristics, roles, and functions in order to address contextual biopsychosocial, cultural, political, and economic demands.

It is essential to stress that the industrial era reflected and promoted interpersonal and institutional oppressive patterns (i.e., racism, sexism, classism and social stratification, heterosexism, etc.), formed long before (i.e., from the arrival of the first European colonists) and having ongoing effects on family roles, patterns, and dynamics of interactions. For instance, the Chinese Exclusion Act of 1882 often made it difficult for Chinese men to maintain or build families. This act prohibited Chinese immigration to the United States and also restricted the rejoining of Chinese men, working in the construction of railroads, with their spouses back in China (Healey, 2011).

Although the system of slavery was legally abolished in 1865, black families during the industrial era often experienced the stress of socioeconomic needs and employment discrimination. Due to experiences such as racism and classism, both black men and black women were often forced to be employed in jobs with low wages and poor working conditions (Healey, 2011). Historical records indicate, "In 1900 approximately 41 percent of black women were in the labor force, compared with 16 percent of white women" (quoted in Staples, 1988, p. 307). A similar pattern of discrimination is observed when exploring experiences encountered by other groups such as Latino Americans, indigenous families, and Asian Americans, to mention a few.

Besides the industrial revolution, socioeconomic political events such as World War I, the Great Depression, World War II, social movements (i.e., women's movement, civil rights movement, gay-lesbian movement, and others), and the newer patterns of immigration, have shaped the experience of the family in ways that go beyond the scope of this book. There is also, of course, the influence that theorists have had in the way family constellations have historically been perceived including, but not limited to (a) Sigmund Freud (1916–1917) and his emphasis on psychosexual development of human personality, (b) Erik Erikson (1950) and his focus on psychosocial development through the life cycle, (c) Jean Piaget (1965) and the focus on cognitive development, (d) Lawrence Kohlberg (1979) and the emphasis on moral development, as well as (e) the emergent postmodern lenses such as ecological, feminist, constructivist, empowerment, and strengths perspectives, often formed as a reaction to the ways psychodynamic theoretical perspectives pathologized family constellations. The concept and experience of the family have undergone multiple transitions and transactions within the contexts of social, cultural, political, and economic environmental demands. Although some of the aforementioned experiences have promoted family well-being, others have challenged diverse forms of existence. Nevertheless, diverse family constellations have continued their evolution regardless of experiences with adversities, reflecting the strength of the human spirit.

FAMILY CONSTELLATIONS WITHIN THE CONTEXT OF DOMINANCE AND RESILIENCE

As explored previously in this chapter, from diverse indigenous populations, to early settlers, to more recent immigrants, the family has been an experience, which has accounted for the construction, deconstruction, and reconstruction of social orders. Family constellations have influenced as well as been influenced by formal and informal interpersonal, institutional, and environmental values, beliefs, and norms. Furthermore, multiple family experiences have mirrored an intention and active commitment to transcend conventional realities while moving into what has been previously introduced as magna domains. Martin Luther King, Jr.'s, "I Have a Dream" speech and Mahatma Gandhi's family life reflect an intention and commitment to moving beyond the status quo. These two men's lives demonstrate a strong commitment and desire to transcend the contextual cultural norms and expectations of interrelationships (individual, familial, and societal) and to honor each individual's worth and value in society. However, due to internal colonialism (a structure of socioeconomic or political dominance and power through which one group or a combination of groups of people sharing a common interest maintains or extends its control by enforcing its socioeconomic, cultural, and political establishment over other groups often considered subordinate) not all types of family constellations have equally participated in decision-making processes affecting their own lives.

History has shown that, whether by force or by choice, diverse populations have had to face degrees of assimilation into the United States' formed mainstream culture. Assimilation is viewed as a process by which individuals or groups of people gradually adopt the language, customs, traditions, rituals, values, beliefs, and norms of dominant group(s) and in so doing partially or completely abandon their own language, customs, and so on. As reflected in this definition, assimilation has a dual function: (1) the person, group, or community is motivated to merge with the dominant culture created and sustained by the dominant group(s); but (2) assimilation is not totally achieved without receiving acceptance from dominant group(s). The greater the similarities between groups, the greater the possibility for assimilation to occur; this is reflected through the experiences of European groups that immigrated to the United States during the 1700s to 1800s and early 1900s. Yet the fewer similarities between groups the lower the possibility for total assimilation. This is reflected by many immigrant groups, from the 1990s to present, coming to the United States from the Middle East (i.e., Saudi Arabia). Thus, by force or by choice, many individuals or groups of people have experienced acculturation (i.e., integration of language, customs, diets, and traditions while continuing to encounter discrimination by the dominant mainstream culture due to not being fully accepted by the dominant cultural group) and not necessarily assimilation.

The historical relationship between internal colonialism and assimilation and its effects have been reflected by different experiences encountered by indigenous populations as well as other diverse groups migrating or immigrating, voluntarily or by force, to the United States. Multiple examples of xenophobia have historically been observed in the ways that European settlers displaced indigenous groups from the land and forced them on to reservations (i.e., the Cherokee Nation relocation in 1838 to 1839, known as the Trail of Tears); the inhumane treatment that Dutch, Swedish, German, and Irish communities were exposed to by the British during the early colonial period; dominant groups' mistreatment of immigrants during the 1800s and early 1900s; the establishment and promotion of a merciless slavery or legal segregation system experienced by African populations beginning with the transportation of Africans into the new world in the 1600s; the hostility experienced by

Vietnamese and Laotian refugees during their initial arrival to this country in the late 1970s; and the discrimination historically experienced by the Japanese, Koreans, Italians, and Mexicans, among other groups. As observed by Devore and Schlesinger (1991), "While the United States claims to welcome the stranger-immigrant, history presents continual evidence of scorn and abuse of immigrant groups" (p. 5).

The experience of internal colonialism and assimilation have produced social patterns through which not all forms of family constellations are always equally considered when social policies and programs have been developed or promoted within the context of the United States. This dynamic has historically and currently produced multiple effects within diverse social settings, including educational systems and human service organizations. The way the family is defined within the powers of social structures affect the way diverse families are treated, or for that matter mistreated. A crucial example in recent years is the debate regarding gay-lesbian marriages. Dominant groups with political power have maintained the formula that a marriage can only occur between a man and a woman (i.e., a campaign supported and promoted by former President George W. Bush). As of 2010, approximately 10 percent of the fifty states had adopted legislation that permits and honors same-sex marriage (i.e., Massachusetts, Iowa), yet, there continue to be efforts to block and overturn promotion of same-sex marriages. This is exemplified by campaign efforts during the 2008 California elections regarding Proposition 8, which defines marriage as legal only if it is between a man and a woman. Proposition 8 passed in November 2008, and gay-lesbian-transgender family constellations in that state continue to struggle for socioeconomic and political recognition. For a moment, imagine the stress likely to be generated by the constant struggle to be acknowledged and integrated into an existing system that denies or rejects your existence.

In order to sustain their existence, diverse family constellations often need to acknowledge and confront diverse dominant models of normalcy constructed and perpetuated through social structures within a specific society, in this case the United States. Dominant models of normalcy, also known as models of dominance (Guadalupe & Lum, 2005), are interrelated systemic social patterns through which a dominant group(s) within a society demonstrates, maintains, or perpetuates the notion of social normality. This sense of normality is demonstrated by formal or informal social, cultural, and political norms and rules that carry on the message of what are considered to be "appropriate" ways of being, thinking, believing, or living. Dominant models of normalcy or models of dominance are infused into a society's status quo in order to promote personal and interpersonal internalization of norms and rules (see figure 2.1). As discussed by Guadalupe and Lum, the United States has cultivated various forms of models of dominance, including,

© Guadalupe & Welkley

FIGURE 2.1 *Dominant Models of Normalcy*

- The importance of white skin color and its historical association to opportunities (both individual and social privilege)

- The notion of power, control, and dominance given to masculine over feminine characteristics in their constructed social expectations

- The conviction that heterosexuality is the absolute normality and moral sexual orientation, as reflected by most social policies and homosexuals' struggle for equal treatment

- The notion that being or looking chronologically young is somehow better than looking elderly, as reflected by products of beauty advertised in the media and the common inclination toward saying, "I can't tell you my age"

- The notion that all people can become economically and socially successful and self-sufficient if they only work hard, which minimizes experiences of unequal access to quality education and other social resources, as well as discriminatory social and cultural practices (p. 84)

We would like to suggest two additional dominant models of normalcy to elaborate on the aforementioned list:

- The notion that the nuclear family constellation, often viewed as the legal union between a woman and a man, is most desirable, often considered the standard by which other family constellations are measured.

• The notion that a family constellation is smaller in membership when compared to a conventional understanding of a community, often limiting the experience of family to that of one or a combination of a few households.

While promoting a standard sense of being, thinking, believing, or living, dominant models of normalcy marginalize experiences encountered by diverse family constellations. Guadalupe and Lum (2005, p. 84) make the argument that this could be done through a "process of reinforcing a false sense of collectiveness or commonalities . . . , thus human *oppression* [that is, power used to diminish accessibility to significant resources important for sustaining well-being] seem inevitable when such models are in operation. It seems impossible to escape *oppressive forces* [means used to cultivate and reinforce oppression—racism, sexism, heterosexism, classism, etc.] in a socioeconomic-political system in which daily human relationships are, to one degree or another, shaped by models of dominance" (emphasis in original).

Yet the human spirit has always demonstrated endurance.

Family resilience (an innate individual or collective essence that promotes "an ability to maintain, recover, or regain a level of control, intention, and direction before, during, or after an encounter with adversity"; Guadalupe & Lum, 2005, p. 39) has been reflected throughout history within or in the absence of adversity. Family resilience exists beyond simply surviving social adversities and harsh conditions. Resilience has enabled individuals and families to heal and transcend wounded painful experiences as well as the image of victimization that can keep family members in a vicious cycle of hatefulness, guilt, shame, or blame.

Within historical and current contexts, multiple family constellations have demonstrated resilient traits—characteristics that have strengthened their abilities to interact and cope successfully with diverse physical, social, economic, and political environments. Some of these traits have been a sense of self-efficacy and self-direction (Rutter, 1985), persistent attitude (Murphy, 1987), and actions guided by a sense of faith—hope (Andrews, Guadalupe, & Bolden, 2003). While relating to family constellations, it becomes important to recognize that resilience cannot be forced, but rather encouraged and supported through what are often considered protective factors (i.e., supportive relationships, resources, and environments). Therefore, human service practitioners working with diverse family constellations must maintain a family-centered approach, making the well-being of the family the primary focus of any assessment and intervention.

A New Voice: Nonstatic Living Entities and Multiple Memberships (Premises One and Two)

The premise for approaching families as multidimensional contextual nonstatic living entities and the principle of multiple memberships is intended to expand traditional approaches that seem to promote the notion of families as monodimensional (a look at family constellations in terms of single units while neglecting the experience of multiple family affiliations). The premise of multidimensionality and contextualization of the family as well as the principle of multiple memberships advocate for consideration of practices that transcend traditional stereotypical perspectives that promote the notion of "one model fits all." These two premises encourage assessment and intervention that consider family constellations as multisystemic and proactive entities. The aforementioned principles support the position that family units do not necessarily live in isolation, but instead often form part of larger social occurrences.

Frequently, a variety of relationships (i.e., with self and others) are cultivated and reflected in family constellations while these interact and exchange within multiple contexts and settings. Each relationship is unique in its dynamics and character, but it can be interdependent to other relationships established within the collective (i.e., relationship between and among adults and children). Through the dynamics of procreation, adoption, transactions, relatedness, and culturalization the sense of familial relationship persists; it is promoted, expanded, perpetuated or transformed. Although it may seem that a child is born into a family unit, and that this is the primary or only way a person enters a family unit, assessment of family constellations within contexts can reveal that what appears to be a family unit is in fact a multisystemic nonstatic living entity.

Although diverse family constellations have existed historically, they seem increasingly visible and acknowledged in society. Diverse forms of family constellation, as reflected in figure 2.2, include multigenerational family constellations, transitional family arrangements, multipartner family groups, step or blended family units, foster family systems, communal family structures, spiritually based family forms, cohabitation, single-parenting family units, families without children, same-sex family constellations, and opposite-sex family groups, which are traditionally viewed as nuclear families. (A number of these family constellations will be further discussed in other chapters.) It is important to recognize that most family constellations can reflect a combination of two or more of the aforementioned family structures. Furthermore, it also seems important to acknowledge that it is misleading to refer to only one type of family constellation as the nuclear family

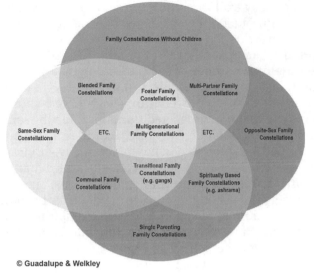

Family Constellations Without Children

Blended Family Constellations

Foster Family Constellations

Multi-Partner Family Constellations

Same-Sex Family Constellations

ETC.

Multigenerational Family Constellations

ETC.

Opposite-Sex Family Constellations

Transitional Family Constellations (e.g. gangs)

Communal Family Constellations

Spiritually Based Family Constellations (e.g. ashrams)

Single Parenting Family Constellations

© Guadalupe & Welkley

FIGURE 2.2 *Multidimensional Contextual Nonstatic Living Entities and Multiple Memberships*

when the nucleus is a central and essential component serving as a core unifying force for diverse individuals participating in unique family constellations.

Ongoing immigration and blending of multiple cultural experiences have influenced the way family constellations are experienced as well as arrangements in the roles and functions that the family, and members within the family, adopt. The visual and current demonstration of diverse family constellations in the United States reflects changes in the dominant paradigms historically referred to as the nuclear family. These transitions provide an opportunity to encourage social receptivity into the complexity of the family and to honor the fact that no one single family form has represented, or ever will represent, all variations of family constellations. As observed by Gillis (1996),

> If history has a lesson for us, it is that no one family form has ever been able to satisfy the human need for love, comfort, and security. . . . We must keep our family cultures diverse, fluid, and unresolved, open to the input of everyone who has a stake in their future. . . . Our rituals, myths and images must therefore be open to perpetual revision, never allowed to come under the sway of any orthodoxy or to serve the interests of any one class, gender, or generation. We must recognize that families are worlds of our own making and accept responsibility for our own creations. (p. 240)

When historically exploring the experience of the family, one thing seems consistent. The family has never been a static experience, but rather consists of forms of relationships that are constantly transforming.

The multidimensional nature of the family is reflected by its complexity and multiple components constituting its formation, maintenance, and transformation. As reflected in figure 2.3, the multidimensional nature of family constellations encourages human service practitioners to explore multifaceted domains affecting family dynamics (i.e., family essence or life-giving force; culture and subcultures—the totality of learned and practiced behavior; ethnicity–ethnic group affiliation (s); experiences within the social–cultural dynamics of race; socioeconomic status; geographical living locations; ages of members; type of membership—child, parents, immediate and extended family members, adopted members; genders and sexual orientations within the family group; family structure, roles, functions, and processes; religious or spiritual practices; physical, cognitive, and mental factors; individual and collective identities, including the meaning of existence; life spans; mechanism for making decisions; sense of direction, etc.). The multidimensional nature of family constellations stresses that people within family constellations are not simply bodies that have biophysical experiences or minds that engage in cognitive and emotional processes. As Guadalupe and Lum (2005, p. 3) stress, "The interdependence of body, mind, and spirit within human experiences is recognized and explored through the lens of multidimensionality."

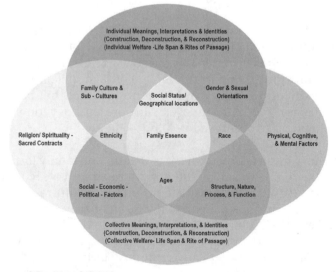

© Guadalupe & Welkley

FIGURE 2.3 *Multidimensional–Contextual Family Factors*

Within the space of the multidimensional nature of family constellations exist contextual interactions and exchanges. Thus, the contextual nature of family constellations encourages us to recognize the interplay of the family-in-environments (physical, social–interactional, institutional–organizational, cultural, sociopolitical; and religious surroundings). Environmental surroundings can be natural (i.e., forests) or built (i.e., diverse religious orientations or spiritual convections). Thus, the lens of families as a multidimensional contextual nonstatic living entity encourages human service practitioners to consider context (i.e., the interface or intersection in which transactions of family-in-environments occur) and dimensions of interactions and exchanges (i.e., magnitude or scope of the interdependence of variables and effects involved) throughout their assessments and interventions with diverse family constellations (see figure 2.3). The premises regarding multidimensionality and contextualization of the family and multiple memberships encourage human service practitioners to engage and remain active in an ongoing process of professional self-evaluation. The intention of professional self-evaluation is to promote and strengthen professional competence within the context of working with diverse family constellations, which is the focus of the next chapter.

References

Andrews, A. B., Guadalupe, J. L., & Bolden, E. (2003). Faith, hope, and mutual support: Paths to empowerment as perceived by women in poverty. *Journal of Social Work Research and Evaluation*, 4(1), 5–18.

Billingsley, A. (1988). *Black families in white America*. Clearwater, FL: Touchstone Books.

Devore, W., & Schlesinger, E. G. (1991). *Ethnic-sensitive social work practice* (3rd ed.). New York: Macmillan.

Erikson, E. H. (1950). *Childhood and society* (2nd ed.). New York: W. W. Norton.

Freud, S. (1916–1917). *The standard edition of the complete psychological works of Sigmund Freud*. London: Hogarth Press.

Gillis, J. (1996). *A world of their own making: Myth, ritual, and the quest for family values*. New York: Basic Books.

Guadalupe, K., & Lum, D. (2005). *Multidimensional contextual practice: Diversity and transcendence*. Belmont, CA: Thomson Brooks/Cole.

Gutman, H. G. (1976). *The black family in slavery and freedom: 1750–1925*. New York: Vintage Books.

Healey, J. F. (2011). *Race, ethnicity, gender, and class: The sociological of group conflict and change* (5th ed.). Thousand Oaks, CA: Pine Forge Press.

John, R. (1988). The Native American family. In C. H. Mindel, R. W. Habenstein, & R. Wright, Jr. (Eds.), *Ethnic families in America: Patterns and variations* (3rd ed.; pp. 325–363). New York: Elsevier.

Kessler-Harris, A. (1981). *Women have always worked: A historical overview.* New York: Feminist Press.

Kohlberg, L. (1979). Revisions in the theory and practice of moral development. New Directions for child development. San Francisco, CA: Jossey-Bass.

Murphy, L. (1987). Further reflections on resilience. In E. J. Anthony & B. Cohler (Eds.), *The invulnerable child.* New York: Guilford.

Piaget, J. (1965). *The moral judgment of the child.* New York: The Free Press.

Rutter, M. (1985). Resilience in the face of adversity: Protective factors and resistance to psychiatric disorder. *British Journal of Psychiatry, 147,* 598–611.

Schwartz, M. A., & Scott, B. M. (2007). *Marriages and families: Diversity and change* (5th ed.). Upper Saddle River, NJ: Pearson Education.

Staples, R. (1988). The black American family. In C. H. Mindel, R. Habenstein, & R. Wright, Jr. (Eds.), *Ethnic families in America: Patterns and variations* (pp. 303–324). New York: Elsevier.

Waller, M., & Yellow Bird, M. (2002). Strengths of First Nations peoples. In D. Saleebey (Ed.), *The strengths perspectives in social work practice* (3rd ed.). Boston: Allyn & Bacon.

Welch, K. J. (2007). *Family life now: A conversation about marriages, families, and relationships.* Boston: Pearson Education.

CHAPTER THREE

The Family in Constant Transition and Transaction

Krishna L. Guadalupe
Debra L. Welkley

Our beingness transcends
glimpses of understanding.
Let's remain open to the infinite.

KLG

Family transitions reflect multiple levels of family's existence and seem to be reciprocally affected by the realms of family essence (i.e., the central core of the family constellation that influences its nature, function, and activities fundamental to ways through which families interact and exchange within the family itself as well as with other entities outside the family), and conventional consciousness (i.e., socialization regarding societal ways of knowing, doing, and being that are either acceptable or not acceptable). The family is a miraculous experience often reflecting a multitude of worldly manifestations, ranging from joy, love, compassion, caring, and potential, to pain, suffering, challenges, resilience, and opportunities for healing. The absolute beingness of each family constellation and individual members, although it can be understood partially within context, is vast and transcends logical comprehension. The family essence exists beyond all human imagination or the mind's ability to reason. As human service practitioners, we are encouraged to move beyond our human-imposed limits that tend to categorize interpretations of family and family dynamics as absolute truths. Thus, human service practitioners are encouraged to honor, through a degree of "not knowing," the complexity and infinite depth of family dimensions and experiences. This practice can assist practitioners to maintain a sense of humility and receptivity that reaches beyond the context of thoughts and dogmatic ethnocentric (the rigid use of one's own cultural norms, values, and beliefs as the yardstick to judge other's ways of doing and being) conventional structures of understanding. Such practice can stimulate the development and use of assessment and intervention modalities that are not based on moral superiority influenced by socially dominant paradigms, but rather are fostered by the desire to employ family-centered approaches.

The third premise describing the family as being and becoming (Fromm, 1955), as an entity constantly undergoing a process of construction, deconstruction, and reconstruction of identities and experiences, is elaborated on in this chapter. Potential dynamics generated from the process of construction, deconstruction, and reconstruction within the context of possible family basic needs, strengths, and challenges also are examined. Furthermore, the fourth premise of the family being affected by and affecting intrapersonal (micro) domains, interpersonal (mezzo) domains, environmental (macro) domains, and the family's experience/interpretations of a nonordinary sense of realities (magna domains) is also further explored. The content looks at the sociopolitical, economic, and spiritual contexts of the family as well as implications for practice. Additionally, this chapter investigates families as resources versus only looking at what the family is lacking. This content should not be considered by the reader as the way things truly are, but rather as possibilities for further exploration and consideration.

Two Major Approaches

While exploring current literature regarding the family, one can observe that two major approaches (i.e., "family life-cycle perspectives" and "family-centered orientations") have emerged, both of them attempting to explore and understand dynamics of change within and between family constellations. Whereas family life-cycle perspectives tend to focus on a sequence of developmental stages and tasks affecting chronological changes that an individual or family may encounter from birth to death, family-centered orientations encourage exploration of the family through an analysis of family transactions within its immediate and extended surroundings. Family life-cycle perspectives often explore human behavior as constructed patterns of interactions and

exchanges influenced through generational dynamics, moral development, and construction of meanings passed on from one generation to
another. Family life-cycle perspectives often perceive family constellations as being widely shaped by particular family structures and nature
in constant search for stability (i.e., adaptability–homeostasis) within
the context of generational and sociohistorical changes. Although to a
certain extent inclusive of social contexts, Demo and Allen (1996) stress
that the family life-cycle perspective "does not challenge the status quo,
does not explain the marginalization of certain family types and does
not recognize the influence of intersecting power hierarchies (e.g., race,
gender, and sexual orientation)" (p. 427). The aforementioned notion is
identified as one of the goals of family-centered approaches.

A family-centered approach considers a multitude of nonordinary
dynamics and experiences in which the family may be a participant. An
example of nonordinary experiences are spiritual rituals (i.e., ceremonies and practices that provide the family with a sense of connectedness with a notion of a supreme being, serve as opportunities for sacred
expression, or aid in decision-making processes). In some cultures,
families have used the ritual of sacrificing an animal in order to create
harmony with what they perceive as the Spirit or Great Creator (however
that might be defined within their understanding). It is essential to recognize that not all families engage in what we have presented here as a
spiritual ritual. However, family-centered orientations present human
service practitioners with opportunities to be mindfully present, which
can allow for the trusting of family processes through the lens of multiple ways of knowing, doing, and being. This observation is frequently
not observed in life-cycle perspectives.

A specific example of a life-cycle perspective is briefly illustrated in
table 3.1 by Erik Erikson's eight stages of psychosocial development.
Erikson (1950, 1968, 1982) viewed human development as occurring
through a series of eight universal predetermined developmental
stages, through which individuals need to address and resolve specific
psychosocial tasks or crises in order to progressively reach full development. According to Erikson, each crisis or task experienced throughout
his conceptualized developmental stages serves as a turning point
marked by a degree of vulnerability and potentiality or opportunity.

Erikson stressed that each of his developmental stages is interdependent, and that one stage of development builds on how successfully
individuals have resolved the crisis or tasks presented in the previous
stage(s). Unsuccessful results of crises or tasks presented in earlier
stages are likely to determine psychological issues in later stages. Thus,
new opportunities to revisit and resolve early stage crises are presented
at different times throughout the life cycle.

Table 3.1 Erikson's Developmental Stages

Developmental stages	Psychosocial Tasks—Crises
Infancy: birth to 2 years	Trust vs. Mistrust Strength: HOPE Children's major task is the development of trust influenced by physical well-being and minimization of fear. A sense of hope increases, the more the child experiences trusting relationships.
Early childhood: 2 to 4 years	Autonomy vs. Shame Strength: WILL Children's major task is the achievement of autonomy without shame. The child manifests and strengthens self-will.
Play age: 4 to 6 years	Initiative vs. Guilt Strength: PURPOSE Children's major task is the development of an ability to take initiative without feeling guilty. Children learn to be purposeful. A restriction of individual initiative while they attempt to experience their independence is likely to influence feelings of guilt.
School age: 6 to 12 years	Industry vs. Inferiority Strength: COMPETENCE Children's major task is the development of knowledge and skills to perform competently within his or her environment. Constant criticism is likely to influence a sense of inferiority in a child.
Adolescence: 12 to 22 years	Identity vs. Role confusion Strength: FIDELITY Youngsters' major task is to gradually develop a strong sense of self-maturity and integration with the outer world, without being forced to do so. Low or lack of sense of self is likely to influence self-esteem and sense of direction.
Young adulthood: 22 to 34 years	Intimacy vs. Isolation Strength: LOVE Young adults' major task is to demonstrate an ability to risk intimacy rather than become isolated from close relationships due to fear of losing oneself or fear that something will go wrong.
Adulthood: 34 to 60 years	Generatively vs. Stagnation Strength: CARE Older adults' major task is being productive at work while raising children to avoid a sense of stagnation.
Old age: 60 to death	Integrity vs. Despair Strength: WISDOM An individual's major task is to confront his or her own death with integrity. Despair emerges as one perceives one's life has been incomplete and fears not having enough time to achieve desired accomplishments.

Although useful within context, Erikson's (1950, 1968, 1982) approach to the life span does not include significant experiences encountered by diverse family constellations. For example, it does not consider the impact or role of ethnicity, sexual orientation, socioeconomic status, or spiritually based orientations within the context and process of human development, interactions, and exchanges. Erikson's life-cycle perspective, as it is the case with many others, is based on an assumption that all humans are alike and that human behavior is somehow predictable regardless of varying social or environmental conditions.

Family life-cycle perspectives, through which a number of practice models have been constructed, tend to divide the life span of a family into a series of significant events or life changes. Family life-cycle models, such as the one created by Duvall and Hill in the late 1940s (Schriver, 2004) tend to focus on children as the center for family development and transformation. Duvall and Hill's original eight stages of a family life cycle are as follows:

Stage 1: Establishment (newly married, childless)

Stage 2: New Parents (infant–3 years)

Stage 3: Preschool family (3–6 years and possible younger siblings)

Stage 4: School-age family (oldest child 6–12 years, possibly younger siblings)

Stage 5: Family with adolescent (oldest child 13–19, possible younger siblings)

Stage 6: Family with young adult (oldest 20, until first child leaves home)

Stage 7: Family as launching center (from departure of first to last child)

Stage 8: Post-parenting family, the middle years (after children have left home until father retires). (Schriver, p. 318)

As reflected by Duvall and Hill's eight stages of family development and dynamics, traditional models of family life cycle assume that children are a central part of what constitutes a family and that child rearing, or parenting, is the main focus of most family life. Furthermore, these types of models tend to assume that children are born within wedlock and that the parents of the children have been living independently for some time before the birth of their first child. As observed, Duvall and Hill's conceptualization does not include issues of children being raised by grandparents or in foster homes, and the familial relationship between the two married adults is considered to be heterosexual.

Carter and McGoldrick (1999) constructed a different family life-cycle model. Their initial model was very similar to the one structured by Duvall and Hill. Its six stages are briefly listed below:

Stage 1: Leaving home: single young adult

Stage 2: The joining of families through marriage: the new couple

Stage 3: Families with young children

Stage 4: Families with adolescents

Stage 5: Launching children and moving on

Stage 6: Families in later life (p. 2)

Although continuing with a traditional focus on family life cycles, Carter and McGoldrick (1999) have recognized the impact that culture has on family dynamics. They wrote, "Not only do cultural groups vary greatly in their breakdown of family life cycle stages and definitions of the tasks at each stage, but it is clear that even several generations after immigration, the family life cycle patterns of groups differ markedly. . . . Furthermore, families' motion through the life cycle is profoundly influenced by the era in history at which they are living. . . . Family members' world views, including their attitudes toward life cycle transitions, are profoundly influenced by the time in history in which they have grown up" (p. 3). Carter and McGoldrick also recognize the impact that individual and social oppressions have on diverse family constellations. They have stressed that oppressive social forces such as racism, sexism, homophobia, and classism, to mention a few such forces, influence the way individuals and families experience family life-cycle patterns.

Carter and McGoldrick (2005) stressed that many changes have occurred in the family. The expansion of their new life-cycle model demonstrates an inclusion of divorce and remarriage as part of the life cycle of some family constellations. Although the new model is more representational than that of Duvall and Hill, it continues to assume that being a family means having children and that those children are generally assumed to be born within marriage, even if that marriage fails to last. It is also generally assumed that the parents of the children reach a level of emotional and financial responsibility before having children. It can be found that in current times these assumptions are in fact rarely the case.

After a decrease in the number of teenage pregnancies in the United States in the mid- to late-1990s, a rise was observed in 2004 and 2005 (Welch, 2007). Infants continue to be born to unwed parents and many of these parents choose never to marry or to marry someone who is not the biological parent of the child. This can mean that many children are being born to parents who are not emotionally or financially ready to raise a child. This is likely to lead to the formation of new family dynamics in which the child may be raised by someone other than their biological parents, perhaps by a relative or by a foster or adoptive family. There are also many more family dynamics to consider. Examples of these are interracial–multiethnic couples, cohabitations, homosexual couples, families in which one or more members live with a disability, and families in which traditional gender roles are challenged. Taking a family-centered approach means allowing the family constellation to define what family is to them. This means accepting cohabitation or couples living together as a family unit as well as single individuals who may experience family as their group of close friends.

It is important to understand that, while traditional life-cycle models such as those created by Erikson, Duvall, and Hill, as well as Carter and McGoldrick are limited because they do not seem to apply to the many unique family constellations present in today's society, these models are neither good nor bad. The model is not necessarily the issue, but rather a professional and/or social attempt to make diverse family constellations fit into a model that does not represent or take unique families' experiences into consideration. It can be detrimental to expect a family to change and conform to fit into a model. As observed in previous chapters, the family is a unique and individual experience that needs to be honored, recognized, and endorsed if the overall intention is to promote family wellness and optimal health. It is important for today's human service practitioners to keep an open mind about the diverse possibilities of what may constitute a family and to allow family constellations to identify and describe family dynamics in their own terms.

Along with the aforementioned observation, human service practitioners must realize that multiple family experiences are rarely strictly linear. The traditional linear approach depicts families as moving through a series of predictable stages and changes. This description of families as definitive and uniform creates problems because it does not allow for the appreciation of diversity or acknowledge that each family is unique in its own way. Instead of celebrating individuality, this view establishes expectations that many family constellations will never meet due to their diverse natures.

The linear stage–based approach can be dangerous if used exclusively as the standard of what is normal or acceptable and what is not. Traditional family life-cycle models describe the family as moving together through the children's developmental changes as they grow older. A family who has a child with developmental disabilities may not follow the predictive tasks, which could produce feelings of guilt and shame on the part of the family as they feel or are perceived by dominant paradigms as abnormal. Other families may not have children at all or a child may die, bringing the family through changes based on grief and coping that are unique to the family dynamic and that are not described in the life-cycle models of traditional theorists.

Although content regarding the family life-cycle perspective is important and often useful within context, this perspective should not be treated as universal. Perhaps one of the most important concepts for human service practitioners to consider is diversity within diversity (Guadalupe & Lum, 2005; Schriver, 2011). This reminds us that although people can be placed in groups based on commonalities such as gender, ethnicity, or type of family constellation, the actual life experiences of each individual in that group may be very unique and distinctive. It is important to remember how each person's unique life experience may affect the way in which he or she develops as a person and the processes that are encountered in order to understand who and how he or she is and relates to the world (Guadalupe & Lum; Schriver).

Another area that human service practitioners need to consider when providing inclusive services to diverse families, especially those consti- tuted by opposite-sex partnerships, is the possible dynamics promoted through socialized and emerging gender and sex roles. It is critical to understand that many families do not conform to traditional ideas about men as the head of the household and the sole wage earner. More and more women are working outside their homes and financially pro- viding for their families. In many occasions, when a woman becomes employed full time, she continues to perform the bulk of work in the family, including household chores and child care, in addition to her paid profession. According to social statistics (Welch, 2007), women are much more likely to hold the responsibilities of single parenting com- pared to men, adding to their need to work both professionally and domestically. These experiences cannot be ignored because they affect familial dynamics of interactions and exchanges.

When working with families, it is important to acknowledge that the way in which a human service practitioner personally defines the family or perceives familial dynamics will affect the way he or she relates to family constellations. Thus, it is important to understand the broad experiences of family life and to be accepting of nontraditional and con- ventional experiences of family. Understanding that a family can include nonrelatives or people who are outside a person's physical home may allow a human service practitioner to help the family con- stellation find support and resources within a broader context and set- ting. Furthermore, it is important for practitioners to make the connec- tion between a societal dominant definition of family and its impact on laws surrounding marriage, child custody, employee benefits, and adoption. Clearly, the understanding of family is a subject that can generate much discussion and analysis; it is important for human service practitioners to take part in that discussion.

Basic Human Needs Within the Context of Uniqueness

It can be stated that people, regardless of ethnicity, age, gender, or sexual orientation, have basic or common human needs, among other forms of human uniqueness. Nevertheless, such needs often are distinctively experienced by diverse family constellations or family members. For instance, a basic or common human need is food. The food we consume, or do not consume, is likely to reflect a sense of preference, life orientation, medical circumstances, or socioeconomic experiences, and so on. It is important to stress that the ways we experience basic or common human needs can, and often does, promote family strengths or challenges. Thus, human service practitioners are encouraged to consider basic or common human needs not necessarily as universally the same, but rather how these relate to, affect, or are affected by the specific family constellation and members within. Although, this might seem as obvious, it is often not considered when using a family theoretical lens(es) that promotes exclusiveness.

Multiple individuals have identified and written about perceived basic or common human needs. Guadalupe and Lum (2005) stress that "needs represent wants, desires, and demands shaped by human interactions, exchanges, and conditions" (p. 66). We would like to add that basic human needs also exemplify a call for remembrance to connect to and rely on our essence and resilience. As stated in another context, "A metaphor to help us better understand this conceptualization of the relationship between essence and resilience is the following: Essence exists within the seed (the human being) and is activated through the care given by soil, water, and sun (supportive factors), manifesting the flower (resilience). The relationship between resilience and essence, then, can be understood as one of nature and nurture" (Guadalupe & Lum, p. 39). Expanding the view of basic human needs helps us to remember that individuals, families, and communities are more than can be perceived through logic or reasoning. It brings our attention to a possible relationship between the physical and nonordinary realms, which will be further discussed later in this chapter.

A number of writers have conceptualized basic or common human needs as a continuum within the context of physical, emotional, cognitive, social–economic, and spiritual realms. For instance, Towle (1945) stresses that all individuals, families, and communities have physical needs (i.e., the need for food, health, shelter, etc.); cognitive needs (i.e., the need to understand one's life, identity, belonging, direction, emotional stability, etc.); and social needs (i.e., social networks and safety, recreation, employment, etc.). We would like to add emotional needs (i.e., subjective expressions of sensations or feelings such as the manifestation of anger, fear, love, remorse, or contentment) as well as spiritual needs (i.e., the constant search for and construction of meaning and interpretation of esoteric experiences, often with the intention to foster a sense of connectedness with spirit—the infinite of all life). Towle goes on to point out that fear of the unknown is not uncommon within human experiences and that lack of satisfaction of basic human needs can harm human functions, accomplishments, capabilities, and ultimate wellness.

Among other human needs, Fromm (1955) spoke about the need that human beings have to develop meaningful relationships with self and others, the need for love and compassion, the need to revisit our past as a mechanism to address conflictive experiences with the intention of promoting new ways of being, and the need to assess our present moments in order to plan for future possibilities. While addressing the aforementioned needs, Fromm reminds us that human beings are in a constant process of being and becoming and that we can be presented with opportunities to create a society where priority is given to people over profit or personal gains. He emphasizes that honoring, embracing, and respecting basic human needs are initial steps toward the creation of harmonious socioeconomic–political environments.

Brill and Levine (2002) address basic human needs with the intention of assisting human service practitioners in the process of strengthening their competence when delivering professional services. In their writing, Brill and Levine encourage practitioners to recognize and address their own basic human needs while understanding what they call recognition of the human condition, which affects practice and circumstances experienced by diverse communities of people. In general, Brill and Levine recognize the needs addressed by both Towle and Fromm. However, their primary focus of discussion is more on cognitive development. Brill and Levine posted the following questions as areas that human beings are constantly exploring:

• What kind of creature am I?

• Where do I come from, and where do I go?

• How can I understand and control myself, my own behavior, my relationships with others, my life, and my future? (p. 19)

Within the context of this text, basic human needs, although interactive and often interdependent, are not linear. People may experience what are commonly known as basic human needs at different times, within diverse contexts or settings, and through distinctive degrees of intensity or severity. A number of people may not even experience some of these needs. Consideration of context, historical time, individual resources or lack of, diversity within and between family constellations, and interactions and exchanges of families within the society as a whole is important when attempting to gain glimpses of understanding regarding familial basic needs manifesting in the space of being and becoming.

Third Premise: Being and Becoming

Throughout the life span, family constellations are likely to experience diverse and interrelated strengths (i.e., intrapersonal and interpersonal abilities, assets, talents, potentiality, essence–resilience, access to resources, etc.) as well as demands or challenges:

- Physical stresses—the need for shelter and food, the need for resources such as a job and financial revenues, physical disabilities within a family constellation, the aging process, biological needs, issues of procreation, etc.

- Cognitive, mental, and emotional pressures—the need for a sense of connectedness, love, caring, acceptance, sense of direction and empowerment, growth and possible transformation in patterns of communication and relatedness in order to create harmonious interactions and exchanges, mental disabilities within a family constellation, emotional disturbance within a family constellation, possible childbearing, etc.

- Social and cultural tensions—the need for recreation and collaboration, the need for affiliation and sense of community, discriminative experiences, etc.

- Spiritual experiences—the need for connectedness with transcending realities beyond the context of logic and reasoning, the need for experiencing one's own essence, the need to create meaning out of experiences that are esoteric by nature, etc.

Strengths and challenges possibly encountered by diverse family constellations are perceived as a cyclical expanding continuum (similar to a funnel) through which their appearances and degree of intensity and severity can differ from context to context and setting to setting throughout the family life span. This observation gives birth to the third premise influencing the content of this text. As reflected in figure 3.1, family constellations are believed to be in a constant process of being and becoming.

The lens of family constellations as multidimensional contextual nonstatic living entities encourages human service practitioners to approach families as a moving target (first premise). The family is constantly participating in a process of construction, deconstruction, and reconstruction of its identity (perceptions of individual and collective self marked by expectations) and experience as they interact within diverse context and settings. The process of being and becoming reflects multiple forms of knowing, doing, and being (Guadalupe & Lum, 2005). Assuming that all family constellations are the same within the context

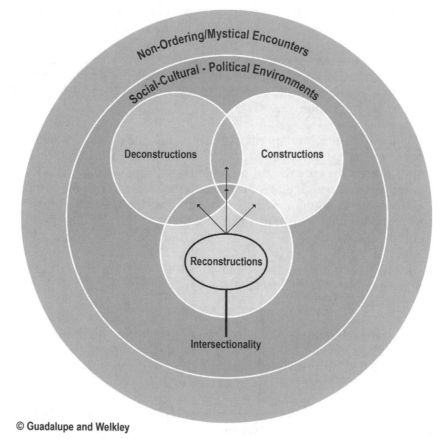

FIGURE 3.1 *Being and Becoming*

of worldly experiences tends to minimize the power and effects of dominant paradigms.

As demonstrated by figure 3.1, family constellations are in constant transition and transaction through a process of construction, deconstruction, and reconstruction of identities and experiences which are affected and being affected by social, cultural, and political encounters and nonordinary encounters (i.e., God, the transcendent, the Great Unknown, the realm of spirit). The continual nonstatic interface or intersectionality of change is what we refer to as being and becoming. Construction of a familial experience is frequently influenced by preexisting human occurrences in a constant process of transformation. For instance, cohabitations or couples living together with familial agreements or commitments are likely to have constructed a sense of identity influenced by what may have been perceived as family life. If choosing to give birth to children, such children will be born into a preexisting family culture operating under specific norms, beliefs, values, behaviors, religious or spiritual principles, social and economic circumstances, and familial dynamics. Furthermore, the birth of a child is likely to initiate additional changes in the initial familial identity. These observations demonstrate various encounters with construction of an experience (i.e., the initial agreement or commitment of the partners as a family constellation, decision to give birth to a child, the actual birth, etc.).

The culture influencing the nature, structure, function, roles, dynamics of interactions, and exchanges within the aforementioned family constellations is likely to undergo a degree of change and adjustments: as new members are adopted into the family unit, if a family member develops a physical or mental disability, if the relationship ends and new familial relationships are established, or if transformation in the religious or spiritual orientation occurs, among other possible processes. The process of deconstruction and reconstruction is likely to be activated by unplanned happenings or conscious decisions. The intersectionality with encounters and possible changes can reflect the deconstruction of initial identity or experiences reflected in the example presented above as well as reconstruction of others ways of knowing, doing things, and being in the world. Life experiences, options, conscious determination or unconscious processes stimulate the process of construction, deconstruction, or reconstruction reflected throughout the family life span and its members.

The process of being and becoming occurs throughout the life span of an individual, family constellation, community, society, or nation, yet this process is not necessarily shaped by predetermined or predictive linear developmental stages. The process is proactively generated by human interactions and exchanges demonstrating a continuum in human evolution.

A question that may arrive in the reader's mind is, Why do specific family constellations seem to repeat or promote the same interactional patterns, creating similar results? The brief answer to this important question is that there are no two experiences that are indeed the same. In taking domestic violence as an example, we observe that part of the cycle is that an incident leads to built-up tension (where the abuse eventually occurs) which then results in a make-up phase and in turn a calm state (where participants act as if nothing transpired) (Walker, 1979, 2009). In the domestic violence literature it has been observed that as the cycle proceeds and progresses, the cycle is intensified, which creates a difference in the process and in the result (i.e., a push, to a punch, to ultimately death). It is important for practitioners to recognize that the cycle of violence may not occur in the same way within all family constellations or that not all family constellations will experience the cycle as described in the literature.

The magnitude or scope of changes that a family constellation can reflect may be considered insignificant or nonexistent when approached through the lens of immediate gratification or an evidence-based mentality. However, as proposed by biological and neurological findings, as human beings we are not the same from moment to moment and some changes occurring in our biopsychosocial lives take time to be clearly revealed. From a philosophical standpoint, one may argue that what we resist persists. There seems to be some validity in this statement. For instance, ignoring an issue (i.e., not making decisions considered imperative due to fear of the unknown, the need to avoid painful experiences, etc.) may not make it go away. Nevertheless, the premise of being and becoming supports the awareness that issues may dissolve due to degrees of importance or may be perpetuated due to its magnitude. Even if issues are perpetuated these cannot be considered within the lens of sameness, however, due to its changing nature (i.e., they may increase or decrease in levels of intensity and severity).

The premise of being and becoming is reflected in transactions and effects between families and their immediate and extended surroundings. It seems important, however, to state that the family's evolutional progression does not necessarily mean development of ways of knowing, doing, and being that promotes personal and collective wellness. This observation has been reflected by multigenerational family constellations that have used dynamics of familial interactions and exchanges to promote hatred toward specific ethnic groups (i.e., family constellations involved in the Ku Klux Klan movement or those continuing to promote a belief in white superiority). These types of family constellations have clearly reflected the role of the family as a social institution that attempts to promote the internalization of beliefs, values, life orientations, and behaviors, in this case oppressive forces, that progressively evolve through an ongoing process of culturalization, as reflected in figure 3.2.

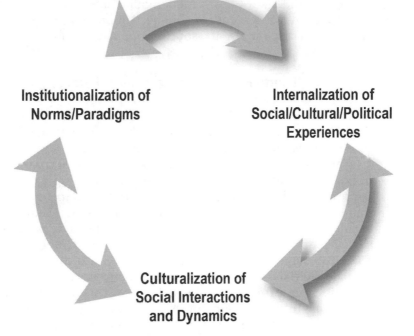

© Guadalupe & Welkley

FIGURE 3.2 *Interactive and Independent Cognitive and Social-Cultural Phenomena*

The aforementioned process of institutionalization of norms and paradigms, internalization of social, cultural, and political experiences, and culturalization of social interactions and dynamics, often reflected within family constellations and societies, can be more easily demonstrated through an example of raising a child. Let's take a child who was born or adopted into a family constellation. Depending on the age and developmental process of this child, through family dynamics of interactions and exchanges the child is likely to internalize all or part of the belief and value system, attitudes, orientations, communication, and behavioral patterns consciously or unconsciously being promoted by the family constellation. The type of internalization can be manifested externally within the context of interpersonal relationships (i.e., relationships with peers in school or on the playground) and reinforced through cultural influences or culturalization promoted through ongoing dynamics of interactions and exchanges between the child and different participants within different contexts or settings. An important phenomenon revealed through our work with diverse family constellations is that everything that is learned and perpetuated through the process of institutionalization, internalization, and culturalization can be altered, modified, or transformed. Again, families are not static, but rather proactive living agents of change. Although families experience vulnerabilities, they are also the source of transformation.

Fourth Premise: Reciprocity of Forces: Affecting and Being Affected

The family is a powerful nonstatic multidimensional living entity (first premise) that is often experienced through multiple family member-ships (second premise). Families undergo a continual process of con-struction, deconstruction, or reconstruction or being and becoming (third premise) that can generate opportunities to foster wellness or human tenderness. Recognition of the exchange between the family being affected by and the family affecting interdependent and interac-tive occurrences (fourth premise), existing at the intrapersonal, inter-personal, social, cultural, environmental, or nonordinary realms can encourage the view of the family as actively participating in the process of evolution and promotion of its existence. This observation can be called the institutionalization, internalization, or culturalization of and by the family. This process of evolutional progression, viewed as a cycli-cal expanding continuum (again, similar to a funnel), illustrates the fourth premise prevailing throughout this text, reflected in figure 3.3. The premise of being affected by and affecting intrapersonal, interper-sonal, social, cultural, environmental, or nonordinary senses of reality recognizes that the family is not exclusively imprisoned by constructed human conditions (i.e., oppressive social forces such as sexism; racism; heterosexism; classism; cultural, social, or linguistic imperialism, etc.) or cognitive patterns (i.e., internalization of beliefs, values, and social norms that promote unhealthy and destructive behaviors), but that the family has the fundamental essence to transform or to perpetuate pain. That is, the family is in a constant paradox between cultural influences and cultural choices (or culturalization of and by the family).

The relationship between cultural influence and cultural choice can be described as proactive, interactive, and interdependent. Guadalupe and Lum (2005) view cultural influence as "conscious or unconscious systems of beliefs, values, and ways of thinking, believing, and behaving that are perpetuated through human encounters and reinforcements" and perceive cultural choice as "conscious identification and explo-ration of beliefs, values, and ways of thinking, [believing,] and behaving, followed by a determination to embrace these or to actively engage in conscious change" (p. 9). Again, one cannot disregard that the degree of participation and influence that a family has is likely to be affected by the family status within an environment, family habitat (physical and social settings within a cultural context), and degree of integration within social dominant or emerging paradigms, as well as family consciousness and resilience.

As reflected in figure 3.3, although interrelated and interactive at various degrees, uniqueness exists within each of the dimensions affecting and being affected by the family. The premise of family being affected by and affecting the four domains described in chapter 1 (intrapersonal [micro], interpersonal [mezzo], environmental [macro], nonordinary [magna]) has gained more support and recognition in recent years. Traditional paradigms (i.e., the medical model, which has historically concentrated on how to fix what is broken) have begun to be a bit more inclusive of ways to address family needs and challenges (Schriver, 2011). Traditional paradigms have primarily focused on what the family lacks while confronting vulnerability, rather than perceiving the family as a source of transformation. These lenses have often promoted an "either/or" mentality. The notion of family as monodimensional has the potential to view the family as powerless or a victim of circumstances. Being affected by societal dynamics is different from identifying the family as the victim. It makes a difference when a group of people are categorized as people experiencing oppression rather than oppressed people. The notion of oppressed people seems to belittle the power that people often demonstrate within the context of vulnerability, especially when families' resilience is activated. Guadalupe and Lum (2005) refer to resilience as an innate source "that promote[s] an ability to maintain, recover, or regain a level of control, intention, and direction before, during, or after an encounter with adversity" (p. 15).

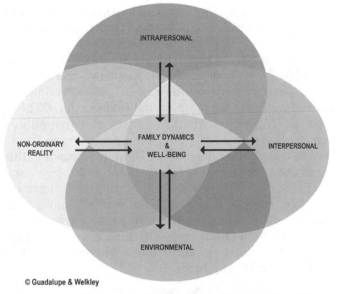

© Guadalupe & Welkley

FIGURE 3.3 *Affecting and Being Affected: Reciprocity of Force*

An essential part of families' processes toward engaging in transformation is the acknowledgement and embracing of their own strengths (i.e., assets, abilities, etc.). Too often families who seek services are seen as victims and treated as if they do not have the resources and strengths to meet their goals on their own, promoting the impression that what will make the difference in the family's solutions to confronted circumstances will be professional intervention. Although it is accurate to say that families seeking social services have needs and challenges, it is important to remember that this does not mean that they do not have the capacity within themselves to engage in the steps necessary to meet their own needs and overcome their challenges. This statement is not attempting to romanticize human pain, but rather to honor and embrace the endless power of the human spirit.

Families are making their own changes and helping themselves every day. Everyone has the capacity for transformation within themselves, although some may need guidance in realizing this capacity. Others may be aware of their personal strengths, but need to be connected to resources through which those strengths can be nurtured (Saleebey, 2009). Sometimes all that a family may need is a reminder to tune into its own essence. It is the human service practitioner's responsibility to guide families in identifying their own strengths and link them with the resources necessary for them to gain or strengthen their sense of empowerment and direction. Empowerment can be briefly defined as people's ability to discover and foster their own strengths and to use these to meet personal goals and overcome challenges. No one can empower someone else. However, one person can provide the encouragement necessary to bring another to a place of self-empowerment. We should never underestimate the power of families and their abilities to be resourceful beyond logical understanding.

When assessing recent literature regarding the family, there is a tendency to view family constellations as systems being affected by intrapersonal, interpersonal, environmental, or societal challenges, constantly generating a need for professional interventions. This tendency seems to promote the notion of family constellations as simply receivers of outcomes created through dynamics of cognitive and social interactions and exchanges. The observation of family constellations being affected by multiple phenomena is important and needs considerable attention. However, making it the heart for understanding family dynamics and experiences is likely to minimize a family's possible participation in the creation or perpetuation of challenges. It is important to assess ways in which family constellations may contribute to their challenges as well as to their resourcefulness when engaging in solution-focused or client-centered approaches.

Viewing the family as an entity that can be vulnerable and yet powerful within or among diverse contexts in itself means understanding the profound affect a family may have on an individual. To begin to use the family as a source, one must identify the many strengths and challenges present within the family constellation. For some, a family may be a source of strength providing the support and encouragement needed to complete difficult tasks or pull through personal challenges. Others may find that the many difficulties and hardships they have experienced within their family have become the catalyst for understanding the need for transformation. There are endless ways that a family may be a source unique to each member or other family units, especially when examining multigenerational family constellations. Minimizing the multiple aspects affecting and being affected by family constellations promotes professional practices that are fragmented. One must never forget that families create and are created, or vice versa.

Although the experience of family in interactions and exchanges with a nonordinary sense of reality (the Great Unknown, Spirit, Magna, etc.) is socially–culturally reflected within our society (i.e., families engaging in spiritual-oriented practices), many individuals or interest groups hesitate to encourage the total integration of this experience into current conventional or traditional educational institutions. Many social phenomena can account for this observation, including the notion and importance given to the sense of total professional objectivity, the view that experiences that cannot be measured do not exist, the emphasis on empirically based practices, and the movement and legal separation between church and state, to mention a few. However, to ignore or minimize possible family spiritual encounters can marginalize family experiences. This can be especially the case for individuals and families who consider themselves spiritual beings living human experiences. (These authors understand that a difference exists between religiosity and spirituality. Whereas religiosity could be perceived as an experience based on doctrines and indoctrination, spirituality may not. Spirituality involves a sense of connectedness and beingness, which transcends religious beliefs and rituals. Thus, this content is focused on that sense of connectedness and beingness influencing family dynamics, a sense that may or may not be found through religious activities.)

The lens of multidimensionality honors the family, not exclusively as a nonstatic living entity that has a past, present, and future within the context of its humanity, but as an entity whose spirit or essence simultaneously lives beyond time. Although the abstractness of this view may be confronted with skepticism and cynicism, the reader is reminded that "spirituality is about honoring the presence of endless possibilities;

it is about recognizing and transcending constructed senses of conventional realities/consciousness" (J. Guadalupe, 2005, p. 151). The aforementioned observation is furthered elaborated by Faiver, Ingersoll, O'Brien, and McNally (2001) who wrote, "Spirituality may be described as a deep sense of wholeness, connectedness, and openness to the infinite. . . . We believe spirituality is an innate human quality. Not only is it our vital life force, but at the same time it is also our experience of the vital life force. Although this life force is deeply part of us, it also transcends us. It is what connects us to other people, nature, and the source of life. The experience of spirituality is greater than ourselves and helps us transcend and embrace life situations" (p. 2). We would like to add that through the lens of multidimensionality, spirituality exceeds ordinary intellectual, logical, and physical boundaries. The content presented here represents only glimpses of understanding in order to stress the vast complexity of family existence and its members. Lerner (2000) stressed that our human lives are connected by the realms of the physical world and spirit or nonordinary realities: "The deepest spiritual thinkers warn us that the realm of Spirit is the realm of the ineffable. It simply can't be adequately expressed in language. The best we can get is poetry and song, not prepositional knowledge. Again Abraham Joshua Herschel: 'The heart of being confronts me as enigmatic, incompatible with my categories, sheer mystery. All we have is a sense of awe and radical amazement in the face of a mystery that staggers our ability to sense.'" (p. 32). Words and language fall short when attempting to describe interactions and exchanges of families within the context of what we have been referring to as a nonordinary sense of reality. Two things we can do: impeccably listen and learn from the experiences of family constellations. We may discover that families' interactions and exchanges with the realm of spirit often reinforce their resilience in times of crises or when facing human adversities (Andrews, Guadalupe, & Bolden, 2003). Thus, human service practitioners are invited to practice trusting the wisdom of uncertainty, "an inner knowing or innate intuitive power that reveals understanding of living experiences beyond conscious reasoning, yet it is often ignored in the name of empirical and scientific discoveries" (Guadalupe & Lum, 2005, p. 16). Wisdom of uncertainty represents trust in the unknown.

As observed, the family is a complex living entity and must be addressed with care. The four premises discussed so far illustrate possible implications when defining and working with diverse family constellations. The initial four premises give birth to a fifth premise that advocates for the use of an eclectic approach when conducting professional assessment and intervention. An example of an eclectic approach will be introduced in the next chapter.

References

Andrews, A. B., Guadalupe, J. L., & Bolden, E. (2003). Faith, hope, and mutual support: Paths to empowerment as perceived by women in poverty. *Journal of Social Work Research and Evaluation, 4*(1), 5–18.

Brill, N. I., & Levine, J. (2002). *Working with people: The helping process* (7th ed.). Boston: Allyn & Bacon.

Carter, B., & McGoldrick, M. (Eds.). (1999). *The expanded family life cycle: Individual, family, and social perspectives* (2nd ed.). Boston: Allyn & Bacon.

Carter, B., & McGoldrick, M. (Eds.). (2005). *The expanded family life cycle: Individual, family, and social perspectives* (3rd ed.). Boston: Allyn & Bacon.

Demo, D. H., & Allen, K. R. (1996). Diversity within lesbian and gay families: Challenges and implications for family theory and research. *Journal of Social and Personal Relationships, 13*(3), 415–434.

Erikson, E. H. (1950). *Childhood and society* (2nd ed.). New York: W. W. Norton.

Erikson, E. H. (1968). *Identity: Youth and crisis.* New York: W. W. Norton.

Erikson, E. H. (1982). *The life cycle completed: A review.* New York: W. W. Norton.

Faiver, C., Ingersoll, B. E., O'Brien, E., & McNally, C. (2001). *Explorations in counseling and spirituality: Philosophical, practical, and personal reflections.* Belmont, CA: Wadsworth/Thomson Learning.

Fromm, E. (1955). *The sane society.* New York: Rinehart.

Guadalupe, J. A. (2005). Spirituality and multidimensionality. In K. Guadalupe & D. Lum, *Multidimensional contextual practice: Diversity and transcendence.* Belmont, CA: Thomson Brooks/Cole.

Guadalupe, K., & Lum, D. (2005). *Multidimensional contextual practice: Diversity and transcendence.* Belmont, CA: Thomson Brooks/Cole.

Lerner, M. (2000). *Spirit matters.* Charlottesville, VA: Hampton Roads.

Saleebey, D. (2009). *Strengths perspective in social work practice* (5th ed.). Boston: Pearson.

Schriver, J. M. (2004). *Human behavior and the social environment: Shifting paradigms in essential knowledge for social work practice* (4th ed.). Boston: Pearson/Allyn & Bacon.

Schriver, J. M. (2011). *Human behavior and the social environment: Shifting paradigms in essential knowledge for social work practice* (5th ed.). Boston: Pearson.

Towle, C. (1945). *Common human needs.* Silver Spring, MD: NASW Press.

Walker, L. (1979). *The battered woman syndrome.* New York: Harper Perennial Library.

Walker, L. (2009). *The battered woman syndrome* (3rd ed.). New York: Springer.

Welch, K. J. (2007). *Family life now: A conversation about marriages, families, and relationships.* Boston: Pearson Education.

CHAPTER FOUR

An Eclectic Approach

The Power of Inclusiveness

Krishna L. Guadalupe
Debra L. Welkley

Embrace the infinite, even
when it seems unreachable.

KLG

An eclectic approach to working with diverse family constellations (fifth premise) honors and attempts to embrace the vastness of family dynamics of interactions and exchanges, contexts, settings, definitions, possibilities, experiences, as well as ways of knowing, doing, and being. An eclectic approach to practice does not claim that one specific theoretical lens or model is more effective than another. However, it is constructed and guided through diverse orientations, strategies, techniques, and methods derived from the strengths of multiple conventional and nonconventional lenses. The primary goal of most eclectic approaches is to honor and embrace the power of inclusiveness and by so doing to move our attention from possible stereotypical or dogmatic paradigms to realms of exploration where the mind may have not gone. Eclectic approaches, however, can be perceived as too general or abstract. This may be the case with the eclectic practice template introduced and addressed in this chapter. With that in mind, however, these writers will attempt to be mindful while being descriptive in their explanations. Although there are restrictions in the spoken and written words, these writers are committed to engaging the reader in a journey of possibilities.

The eclectic practice template discussed here is built on the four premises addressed in the previous chapters (i.e., the family as a multi-dimensional contextual nonstatic living entity, existing and journeying through diverse realms of perceived or constructed realities; multiple memberships; the family in a constant space of being and becoming; the family as affecting and being affected by, or reciprocity of forces). The template presented here becomes the fifth premise guiding this text—"An eclectic asset-based approach is likely to enhance our practice within the context of diverse family constellations." This eclectic practice template is perceived as a changing phenomenon. That is, it is not absolute or ever completed. It is presented here as a baseline from where human service practitioners can begin their assessment and work with diverse family constellations. This eclectic practice template should not be perceived as one model fits all. Through the lens presented in this text, the family is the expert and the practitioner can serve as a protective factor—a supportive and caring resource.

Human service practitioners construct knowledge and skills through the process of education and direct experience. However, the practitioner continues to be a learner and thus is encouraged to tune into the family's uniqueness and wisdom. That said, it is recommended for human service practitioners to add experiences perceived as crucial to the eclectic practice template explored in this chapter or to delete areas that seem unnecessary while honoring and embracing family constellations within diverse contexts and settings. A major goal of the eclectic practice template presented here is to support or preserve the well-being of family constellations while fostering professional competence.

Challenging One's Lens in the Context of Family Practice

An important aspect of strengthening professional competence is a commitment to engage in a continuous process of professional self-evaluation. Professional self-evaluation can be perceived as a willingness and ongoing commitment to reflect on one's own professional strengths and restrictions within the context of service development and delivery. During the process of ongoing professional self-assessment, the human service practitioner is encouraged to sincerely examine his or her skills or capability to serve others, as well as possible values, beliefs, assumptions, norms, and experiences encouraging or disrupting professional effectiveness. This means understanding how a practitioner's own process of believing, thinking, and behaving affects his or her ability to provide services intended to promote the well-being of the people he or she works with, in this case diverse individuals and family constellations. One needs to remember that human service practitioners are not excluded from painful human experiences and personal human wounds can promote multiple responses and biases. By exploring ways in which we work with clients and by acknowledging our strengths and restrictions, an opportunity for possible healing, growth, and ongoing professional development is likely to occur. A committed human service practitioner can be perceived as one who is in a constant process of learning and growing in knowledge and skills as well as engaging in individual or family-centered approaches.

Although much can be learned from mentors and study materials, perhaps some of the most valuable lessons come from within one's self and one's own receptivity to opportunities to learn and grow. This can be reflected by how we perceive and practice with family constellations we serve. To begin to understand and engage in the process of professional self-evaluation, there are many different areas to be considered, including, but not limited to, beliefs, values, theoretical paradigms, social and cultural norms, and personal living experiences. For a moment reflect on your initial conceptualization of the family prior to being exposed to this text's content. Contemplate on what informed your understanding and perception of what constitutes a family, what problems face families, which theoretical frameworks demonstrate your view(s) of family, which modalities you think are best to use when working with families. Addressing these arenas relative to past and current learning will help your professional growth and competence.

Working with diverse family constellations is not simple. Although multiple theoretical orientations (i.e., psychodynamic perspectives, ecological lenses, empowerment, strengths, constructivist orientations, etc.) have been developed to explore human development and behavior, no one single theoretical orientation can explain or predict human growth and changes with absolute certainty. It is safe to say that our human development and behavior unfolds through a degree of mystery not completely understood by logic or reasoning. Therefore, professional competence is never totally achieved, although degrees of professional competence can be observed, maintained, and further strengthened through ongoing professional self-exploration, which can in fact influence our professional decision-making process. In attempting to conceptualize professional competence, Guadalupe and Lum (2005) stress that it can be viewed as an

> ability to skillfully serve diverse individuals[, families,] and communities within different contexts without engaging in stereotypical or immediately gratifying approaches that promote marginalization of important attributes or disempower-

ment of those being served. Professional competence often requires a balance between learned skills and cultivated values of respect regarding human diversity/uniqueness, a degree of professional self-awareness and evaluation, confrontation of discriminative cognitive patterns and actions promoted in the name of professionalism, as well as a level of trust in the wisdom of uncertainty. (Wisdom of uncertainty refers to an inner knowing or innate intuitive power that reveals understanding of living experiences beyond conscious reasoning, yet it is often ignored in the name of empirical and scientific discoveries.) An individual with professional competence is able to assess, distinguish, and simultaneously embrace commonalities, differences, and controversies within and between diverse groups of people. Professional interventions, whether conducted at the micro-intrapersonal, meso-interpersonal, macro-environmental, or magna-spiritual level, or a combination of these, are not mechanically facilitated. They are [can be] planned and carried out with a degree of mindfulness. While cultivating professional competence, risk taking beyond professional comfort zones becomes vital in order for ongoing professional development to be broadened; yet, decisions involving risk must be evaluated as much as possible prior to their implementation in order to ensure client well-being. (p. 16)

In other words, professional competence requires a degree of professional intentionality, self-awareness, and an active commitment to promote individuals and families' well-being as it may relate to biopsychosocial–cultural–spiritual health. Through ongoing professional self-evaluation, an opportunity is created for self awareness to emerge. Guadalupe and Lum (2005) describe self-awareness as "practitioners' cultivated understanding of how their paradigms, encounters, sense of 'normality,' and expertise may affect the process of client-worker interactions, exchanges, and success" (p. 50). Such awareness, although not sufficient to guarantee change, is essential for practitioners to strengthen their professional competence or effectiveness. Guadalupe and Lum go on to indicate that awareness generated from ongoing professional self-evaluation is useful when confronting "the possibility of conflicts that could be generated because of clients' unique experiences and practitioners' inaccurate assumptions influenced by elements such as practitioners' lack of familiarity with encounters clients have experienced, cognitive rigidity, and inflexibility. Self-awareness can be the practitioner's initial step in the process of analyzing and solving such conflicts, while constant self-evaluation can serve as a building block in

© Guadalupe & Welkley

FIGURE 4.1 *Interactive and Independent Realms*

the search for alternatives and in strengthening competency" (p. 50). Professional self-evaluation is a tool for promoting professional awareness essential when engaging in decision making that will have an impact on a family's life (see figure 4.1).

A major aspect of professional self-evaluation is to answer the following two questions:

• Who am I within the context of my professional world?

• How do my personal life experiences, beliefs, and values influence my professional choices?

To begin to answer these questions, human service practitioners may consider the various roles they play in the agency they work for and in their relationships with diverse family constellations. With this in mind, one is likely to gain a better understanding of how one reacts to different people and different situations and to understand whether these reactions are appropriate or ideal. Some examples of roles that are often seen in human services are those of educator, counselor, social activist, advocate, and mediator (see figure 4.2).

Professional roles are not positive or negative. However, the way we perform within those roles can encourage or harm the well-being of individuals or families with whom we work. For instance, one may be an educator: educators are consistently researching services and opportunities in the community and sharing them with clients and coworkers. This role could be helpful in that it can mutually benefit the human service practitioner as well as those who are learning from him or her. However, this role could have harmful effects in relationships

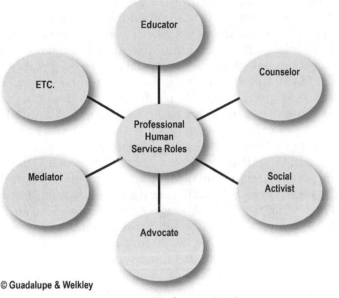

© Guadalupe & Welkley

FIGURE 4.2 *Professional Roles*

where those learning from the educator may feel patronized or develop a dependence on the educator to the degree where they see themselves unable to gather the information themselves.

Another role the practitioner can engage in is counselor, delivering therapeutic services to individuals and families facing adversities. The caring and support promoted through the counseling role could be just what an individual or family needs. However, it is important to consider whether the counselor is beginning to feel emotionally drained, if this role enables an individual or family to remain in a state of dependency rather than encouraging self-empowerment.

A final example to reflect on is that of the mediator. This role can be reflected as human service practitioners engage in a process of arbitration to help create common ground among family members experiencing conflicts or disagreements. Here, the mediator may want to think about whether he or she is truly helping family members by mediating: Would it be more effective to step back and allow them to talk through their presented challenge?

Overall, a human service practitioner is likely to take on many roles throughout his or her career. Many times these roles are a necessary and effective part of the job. However, it is important to identify and analyze these roles as part of the process of developing a stronger professional sense of self. Also, the practitioner must seek to understand whether these roles are appropriate and effective in reaching his or her desired goals, or whether an alternative approach could be applied.

Also necessary in working toward a greater sense of self-awareness and professional competency is considering one's own biases and stereotypical thinking. Personal biases are understood as encouraging or harmful mental inclinations, often sustained through beliefs and values affecting our choices. On the other hand, stereotypes are viewed as "generalized assumptions, beliefs, opinions, and images held and perpetuated toward specific individuals, groups, families, and communities. Stereotypes disregard information available that contradicts or is more inclusive of variables influencing the identities or experiences of those being stereotyped" (Guadalupe & Lum, 2005, p. 13). Biases and stereotypes can be difficult to acknowledge, but recognition of them is an integral part of growing and developing, both personally and professionally. To begin, a practitioner may consider interactions he or she has had with individuals and diverse family constellations who are from different backgrounds (i.e., cultural, ethnical, economic, sexual orientations, etc.) from his or her own. It is important to acknowledge and explore assumptions based on the aforementioned differences in order to minimize insensitive practices.

Biases and stereotypical thinking are usually subconscious, and assumptions made as a result of these are generally unintentional. However, to create comfortable and trusting relationships with families from diverse backgrounds, human service practitioners must continue to evaluate their own competency while transforming biases or stereotypes they may hold. Through professional self-evaluation, human service practitioners can develop the ability to note when biases and stereotypes have arisen in their work and begin to confront them. In this way, the human service practitioner could constantly work to develop sensitive approaches that are not predetermined by preconceived assumptions, but rather a mindful ability to address individuals' and families' strengths and challenges. As a result, a practitioner can create more meaningful relationships with the people she serves.

Another extremely important part of self-evaluation is related to ethics. The term "ethics" refers to a set of principles—standards guiding conduct. The argument can be made that at least three sets of codes of ethics are in constant interaction and influence professional decisions: the societal code of ethics, the professional code of ethics, and the personal code of ethics (see figure 4.3). Human service practitioners are encouraged to assess the degree through which these codes of ethics connect or disconnect as well as possible implications for practice.

Part of considering and preventing possible ethical dilemmas is to explore and recognize differences between the family constellation as client and the practitioner within the context of the environment in which services are being developed, delivered, and evaluated. It is also important for human service practitioners to identify any professional biases they may hold. By reexamining a situation from a different point

© Guadalupe & Welkley

FIGURE 4.3 *Interactive and Interdependent Codes*

of view or within the context of a different cultural or personal experience, the practitioner may be able to identify and avoid making professional decisions that could hurt or offend others. For instance, as
emphasized previously, we live in a society that does not necessarily
support gay marriages. Are the dominant societal norms and beliefs
part of the practitioner's personal ethics? Regardless of the practitioner's
personal ethics in this context, it is important that he recognize how
those ethics may affect his or her application of theory and skills with
this family constellation being served.

In order to promote growth and development, the human service
practitioner also must consider the theoretical orientations applied to
the work. For instance, if a human service practitioner has a tendency to
work from a feminist perspective, it is recommended that she or he analyze whether this is the most effective theory to apply to all areas of
work. The same is recommended for any other theoretical orientation
being applied, such as a psychodynamic perspective. In understanding
the strengths and restrictions of a theoretical orientation, the practitioner can consider the time and context within which the theory was
developed and determine its appropriateness to the current environment in which he or she is working.

As human service practitioners, we are responsible to provide services that are based on conscious consideration of families' unique and
collective experiences, and that do not marginalize through the effects
of personal biases, stereotypes, unethical practices, and unsuitable theoretical orientations. It is our responsibility to recognize others' uniqueness and gifts to the human experience.

An Eclectic Practice Template

As stressed in previous chapters, the family is in a constant space of transitions and transactions within multiple realms: intrapersonal, interpersonal, social–cultural–environmental–political, and nonordinary. These realms of family existence, although they may be separated for the purpose of an analysis, are considered proactive, interactive, and interdependent. These realms, identified more specifically in figure 4.4, are also believed to provide practitioners with opportunities to more comprehensively identify and attempt to address potential families' strengths and challenges.

The eclectic practice template as identified in figure 4.4 has as its primary intention to enhance the delivery of services that are inclusive and with the ultimate purpose of fostering ongoing family wellness. Family wellness or well-being "refers to the attainment and maintenance of various domains of human functioning that promote optimal health, including, but not limited to, one's physical, cognitive, emotional, spiritual, social, and economic stability" (Guadalupe & Lum, 2005, p. 13).

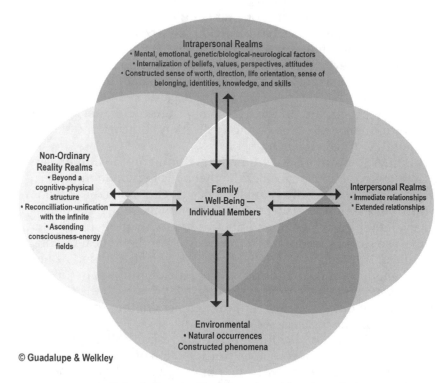

© Guadalupe & Welkley

FIGURE 4.4 *Eclectic Practice Template: Consideration of Diverse and Interconnected Realms of Existence*

This eclectic template encourages human service practitioners to assess, and if necessary conduct an intervention of, areas reciprocally affecting and being affected by individual–family dynamics of interactions and exchanges.

It is essential to briefly elaborate on each of the areas considered by the eclectic practice template exemplified in figure 4.4. It is also important to remind the reader that the realms represented in this diagram are not linear or predetermined. They do not follow a hierarchal order. However, they stimulate unique dynamics of interactions and exchanges within and outside family constellations. It is also important to remind the reader that the intention of this eclectic template is not to propose that all families are equally experiencing the dimensions identified, but rather to encourage practitioners to be inclusive of possible experiences, influencing family dynamics.

The intrapersonal realms represent mental, emotional, genetic or biological, and neurological factors, as well as the internalization of beliefs, values, perceptions, and attitudes affecting and reflecting cognitive processes within a family and its individual members. Intrapersonal realms are uniquely experienced and outwardly manifested. Cognitive processes can be illustrated by an individual or family's constructed sense of worth, direction, life orientation, and cognitive–emotional need for belonging or connectedness, as well as perceived notions of knowledge and skills. In general, the intrapersonal realms often reflect a picture of an individual or family's conceptualization of self and others (the construction, deconstruction, or reconstruction of individual or collective identities). Conceptualization of self and others often plays a role in the manifestation of learned behaviors generated through human interactions and exchanges and demonstrated within and between diverse interpersonal relationships.

The eclectic practice template presented in figure 4.4 promotes the view that what can be perceived as our human external experiences occurring within the interpersonal and social–cultural–environmental–political realms are moderately influenced by intrapersonal processes and vice versa. This observation is briefly reflected in diverse parenting styles. Parents tend to use parenting strategies that they have learned and believe are appropriate, valuable, useful, and practical. Although externally manifested, such strategies seem to be internally reinforced. Furthermore, through ongoing interactions and exchanges at the interpersonal realms, parental strategies can be altered or perpetuated. This reciprocal dynamic between realms again reflects the interface between cultural influence and cultural choices discussed earlier.

The interpersonal realms are constituted by multiple relationships that are formed within and outside the family through direct or indirect transactions. These include immediate relationships (i.e., relationships with close cousins, aunts, uncles, grandparents, godparents, friends, and social or legally adopted family members) and extended relationships (i.e., relatives not closely connected to the specific family constellation or members, relationships with acquaintances).

The diagram illustrated in figure 4.4 encourages human service practitioners to assess intrapersonal and interpersonal realms without neglecting or minimizing the role(s) played by the social–cultural–political–environmental realms, as well as the realms of nonordinary reality. All the realms are perceived as equally important and, although interdependent, each can play a significant role in a family's inner dynamics (transactions among and between family members) and interactions and exchanges.

The social–cultural–political–environmental realms symbolize natural occurrences (i.e., forest, rivers, oceans, oxygen, gravity, etc.) or constructed phenomena (i.e., social clubs, recreational programs, social service organizations, educational systems, political institutions, global warming, religious establishments, societies, and nations, to mention a few). These realms often mirror human conditions (i.e., poverty, homelessness, violence, addictions, greed, illnesses, oppressive or discriminative forces, and sense of separation—the paradigm of "them and us"), as well as relational resilience (collective ability to be caring, supportive, and compassionate) generated through human interactions and exchanges. Interpersonal interactions and exchanges observed during family transactions with immediate and extended relationships are intensified when seen through the lens of social–cultural–political–environmental realms. The family directly or indirectly forms what we call society–nation (multiple groups in constant transactions, connecting or disengaging through experiences of ethnic or gender affiliations, sexual orientations, socioeconomic stratifications, among other forms through which we, as human beings, tend to associate or to build walls of separation). Thus, what is often perceived as foreign affairs (harmonious or conflictive interactions and exchanges between nations within the context of world relationships) has a direct or indirect impact on family functioning and wellness, and vice versa. For instance, the terrorist incidents occurring on September 11, 2001, in this country and the subsequent war in Iraq have directly affected family constellations in the United States and around the world. Furthermore, how families and members approach their experiences can perpetuate or assist with the transformation of similar occurrences. The social–cultural–political–environmental realms often mirror what can be referred to as the cocreation of experience. Guadalupe and Lum (2005) wrote, "co-creation emphasizes that although social and cultural [and we would like to add environmental and political] power is not equally distributed, participation [in the construction of experiences] occurs at different levels, for different reasons, and is a compilation of different efforts. Participation to promote or change a status quo, for instance, may come from a conscious effort that is made after people or communities have evaluated their choices . . . , by promotion of indirect input, or by ignorance likely to influence a decision without evaluating possible outcomes" (p. 79). The power of family dynamics, within the context of social–cultural–political–environmental realms, cannot be marginalized or ignored. Family dynamics, if observed carefully, can help us develop glimpses of understanding regarding the magnitude of human experiences—vulnerability and power.

The physical realms of reality are clearly reflected in cultural–social–political–environmental areas (i.e., societal demands, conditions, and options), but realms of nonordinary reality are frequently revealed through what can be called energy fields (i.e., dimensional arenas that are experienced through vibrational or gravitational frequencies, often beyond the intellect, logic, reasoning, and physical world). The development of the notion of energy fields is an attempt to acknowledge the multidimensionality of family constellations within and outside the space of conventional—empirical debates because this notion is not always measurable. As stressed in this context, the notion of energy fields pays attention to the phenomenon scientifically recognized as kinetic energy (energy in motion), which these authors perceive as an underlying family constellation's ability to experience their existence, functions, and dynamics of interactions within their possible physical structures and beyond. The field of physics has provided us with an opportunity, or should we say a gateway, to explore the notion of energy reflected in multiple forms, including thoughts, emotions, vibrations, and particles, among others. In the study of physics, it is well understood that as an experience (i.e., a family constellation) is formed, maintained, or altered, such experience generates and holds potential energy (energy that represents the innate ability of such phenomenon). The notion of nonordinary realms of reality stresses that families hold and experience potential energy, or should we call it energy fields, that reflect vibrational frequencies influencing relationships and ways of relating as well as a variety of gravitational energy patterns (frequencies often encouraging or promoting energy to move in specific directions).

Vibrational frequencies and gravitational energy patterns can be reflected in ways that a family constellation and its members may engage during the process of exchanges. For instance, whereas members in some family constellations may frequently relate from a constant space of individualism influenced by internalized notions of separation with all that exist (i.e., the me, mine, and I), others may engage in exchanges from a constant space of collectivism based on an internalized sense of oneness (i.e., the notion that all human beings are connected and interdependent). Ways through which individuals and family constellations relate or interact reflects energetic vibrational frequencies as well as gravitational energy patterns. Of course, diverse vibrational frequencies and gravitational energy patterns generate diverse outcomes. One could argue, for instance, that vibrational frequency based solely on the gravitational energy patterns that we can call the notion of individualism is likely to generate a sense of emotional and social isolation or dismissal of collective responsibilities, whereas vibrational frequency based on the gravitational energy patterns that we can view as the notion of collectivism can promote a sense of emotional and societal belonging or collaboration. These are the extremes, though: in a constant process of being and becoming family constellations can experience opportunities for equilibrium as well as opportunities for a variety of encounters.

It is scientifically understood that the variables affecting and being affected by the creation, preservation, or transformation of an experience are not totally definable. That is, science does not totally understand or explain our human existence or experiences. As human beings, however, we have attempted and continue to explore the possibilities of meanings and substance of experiences that we encounter. In doing so, we are constantly reminded that the mind is limited to its own boundaries, and science is restricted by its own rules. That is, although science provides a gateway into the unknown, that we attempt to understand with our human mind, energy fields within the context of nonordinary realms of reality addressed here are vast and boundless. Thus, language is limited when we use it to attempt to conceptualize the realms of nonordinary reality that are perceived to be inclusive of what can be viewed as spiritual experiences beyond the scope of a measurable concept.

The realms of nonordinary reality generally symbolize the realization that human beings are more than cognitive or physical structures (Renard, 2006). These realms represent our unification or reconciliation with an infinite, immeasurable, and absolute force(s). Our realization that we are more than cognitive and physical structures serves as a remembrance of our vastness and infinite nature.

The realms of nonordinary reality assist us, while we encounter human experiences, to be open to the realization that our beingness transcends multidimensional constraints of the physical realms (Rasha, 2003). The realms of nonordinary reality represent our ascending consciousness and energy fields. These realms can be demonstrated by spiritual practices and rituals (i.e., prayers, meditations, vision quests, etc.) that are used as tools by multiple family constellations, to connect or reconnect with our life force or essence.

It is essential to stress that even the terms or words used here to attempt to articulate the realms of nonordinary reality are limited, reflecting a human inability to capture the vastness of the infinite. It is well understood that the infinite cannot be compartmentalized.

However, these authors hope that glimpses of understanding or further curiosity can be generated in the reader through the content presented here, allowing for ongoing exploration and commitment to be present to the Great Unknown. Families are vast and complex entities. They are personal and political within the physical realms. They are concrete and abstract within the space of being and becoming. They have histories within the earthly planet and yet they extend into the realm of infinite. We are families. We make families. We live through families. Wherever we go as individuals, family is there.

Families are in existence within and out of the physical realms. This is illustrated by multigenerational family constellations that have physically departed; we refer to them as ancestors. They do not exist within a physical structure, yet, due to their influences and significant marks in the human existence, these families often live in the hearts, memories, or through the experiences of those currently living in the human form.

The realms of existence through which the family engages in dynamics of interactions and exchanges encompasses and yet transcends the limitations of reasoning. It can be said that what we perceive as knowledge regarding the family is simply glimpses of understanding of diverse constructed perspectives. As reflected in figure 4.5, families constitute and at the same time participate in multiple relationships as relatives, friends, acquaintances, small groups, neighborhoods, communities, societies, nations, and the world. These relationships are in direct and

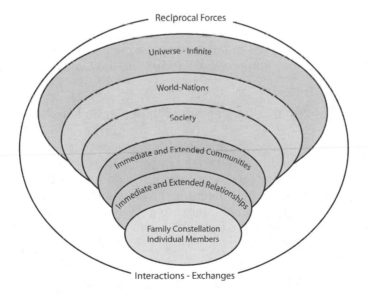

© Guadalupe & Welkley

FIGURE 4.5 *Family Constellation Within Multidimensional and Contextual Interactions and Exchanges*

indirect transactions and are embraced by the context of a universal or the infinite, which as human beings we only experience glimpses of understanding.

The family is not an experience that can be taken for granted. When we think we have absolute knowledge of families we lose, because the experience of the family cannot be compartmentalized to one perspective. Therefore, as human service practitioners, our assessments and opportunities to work with diverse family constellations are sacred moments in which we can offer concrete tools and practical resources while holding the space that allows for miracles or the unexpected to occur: as human service practitioners, let's allow ourselves to be surprised by a family or family member's creativity, courage, and resilience.

Before continuing, the reader is encouraged to take a moment to respond to the following questions:

- To what degree can I relate to the areas presented by the aforementioned eclectic practice template?

- What do I perceive are major strengths and restrictions of this template?

- What can I do to strengthen its application or personalize it to fit my approach?

Answering these questions can help human service practitioners further explore their interpretations of the content presented in figure 4.4. It also can further assist practitioners to tune into the complexity of working with diverse family constellations and the family's members.

Further Enhancement of the Eclectic Lens

It may have already become obvious to the reader that assessment and intervention are not perceived by the introduced eclectic lens as a simple task, but rather a process that is complex and needs to be handled with mindfulness and care. Therefore, the following content is intended to assist human service practitioners to gain additional understanding of practical skills believed to be useful when using the aforementioned eclectic practice lens.

THE ROLE OF AUTHENTIC LISTENING AND IMPECCABLE SHARING

Although each of the areas addressed by the aforementioned eclectic practice template is considered important, the practitioner's ability to engage in a process of authentic listening and impeccable sharing is invaluable. Such capability can assist in the process of reciprocal rapport building likely to foster empowering trust-based partnerships between the practitioner and diverse family constellations. Authentic listening simply means being attentive without judgment regarding the information presented by the family, paying attention to details concerning the meanings and interpretations of experiences encountered while allowing for the voice of the family and its members to be heard, acknowledged, and embraced. Impeccable sharing, on the other hand, represents the practitioner's ability to mindfully communicate his or her understanding of the information presented. It does not require a sense of perfection, but rather an ability to be honest and trustworthy when sharing about his or her assessment, strengths, and restrictions. The idea behind authentic listening and impeccable sharing is to enhance an opportunity for reciprocal rapport building (i.e., a sense of mutual connectedness between a family and practitioner) strengthening the likelihood of an empowering trust-based partnership (i.e., a relationship that is intimate, genuine, caring, supportive, proactive, and based on truth, while identifying and addressing the family strengths, challenges, potential, and options). This phenomenon is viewed in this context as a sacred occurrence (a moment-to-moment opportunity for a family practitioner to develop an alliance that would encourage and allow the establishment and consent of an empowering working relationship). This phenomenon is briefly reflected in figure 4.6.

Nicholas M. Tschense, a nine-year-old boy, wrote, "In my own personal experience, when I feel deeply heard, I feel a relaxation in every cell of my body. This relaxation is most amazing to bring change. I have learned in my own life, living as a child of the universe, yet in a unique

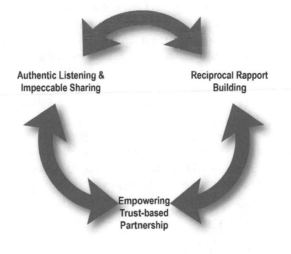

Authentic Listening &
Impeccable Sharing

Reciprocal Rapport
Building

Empowering
Trust-based
Partnership

© Guadalupe & Welkley

FIGURE 4.6 *Sacred Occurrence*

body with its own mind, that I feel the most supported with the relaxation that comes from deep listening" (in Losey, 2007, p. 18). Tschense seems very mature for his age as he reminds us of the importance of authentic listening and impeccable sharing. Being aware of how we listen, as well as how and what we communicate regarding that which is observed, is important because it is very likely to affect families' initial or ongoing interpretations and decisions regarding what we represent to them (i.e., a resource or barrier). This awareness is especially imperative if the family has had wounding experiences with one or a number of human service practitioners through previous encounters.

While attempting to tune in with a family or member, a practitioner may use the technique of paraphrasing (rephrasing a statement with the intention of exploring if what the individual or family is communicating is clearly understood by the practitioner). Paraphrasing gives the individual or family an opportunity to further clarify content being communicated, and can be used by practitioners as a way of seeking feedback. For example, while working with a family constellation, a family member may state, "I feel like an outsider when relating to my siblings and parents. They don't share my beliefs and value things that I am against. They think that all people receiving federal assistance are lazy." A paraphrasing example may be "I hear that your siblings and parents feel that individuals receiving federal support are lazy and what they believe and value makes you feel like an outsider when relating to your family. Is that accurate?" Besides tuning in with a family or member's meaning and interpretation, the use of paraphrasing also provides an opportunity for clients to reflect, feel heard, and not judged. Paraphrasing is a technique that, although useful throughout the course of working with a family constellation, is extremely important during the process of rapport building. Techniques such as paraphrasing and unconditional positive regard (i.e., demonstration of understanding without ignoring or condoning harmful behaviors) can assist with the establishment of relationships that are based on respect, empathy, and honesty, and that are open to growth.

Our moments of interactions and exchanges with diverse family constellations cannot be taken for granted. Mindful attention is highly recommended in our communication efforts. In order to enhance the practical application of the eclectic lens discussed in this chapter, practitioners are presented here with a set of ideas to be considered during an assessment or possible intervention.

STRATEGIES FOR ASSESSMENT

Assessment represents one or multiple ways through which human service practitioners gather data that identify and clarify strengths and challenges encountered by a family constellation and/or its members. Assessment can be viewed as a product (i.e., the creation of a baseline formed through initial data collection), process (i.e., ongoing gathering of data and monitoring of processes, interventions, and results), or outcome (i.e., evaluation of dynamics of interactions and exchanges as well as the effects that have unfolded in the helping process from initial assessment—the creation of a baseline—throughout intervention processes to the completion of the client-practitioner relationship). This idea is reflected in figure 4.7.

While assessment as a product assists practitioners to develop and implement an initial plan of action for intervention, assessment as a process helps practitioners evaluate what is working or not working with the plan executed during the active course of intervention. Assessment as an outcome, on the other hand, often needs to respond to the following questions:

- Overall, what happened?

- How did it happen?

- What affected the specific outcomes?

- To what degree were the overarching goals accomplished?

- Is there a need for continuation, termination, referral, or follow up?

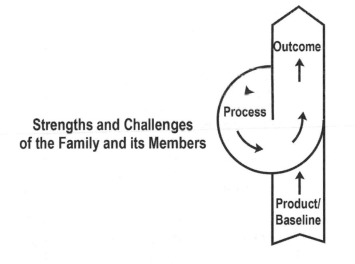

© **Guadalupe & Welkley**

FIGURE 4.7 *Cyclical Continuum Assessment*

Assessment may be considered to be a cyclical continuum phenomenon. Practitioners begin and end their relationships with family constellations and its members through an assessment. Assessment as an ongoing process considers constant transformations occurring within family constellations as well as the helping process. It recognizes that the baseline initially established by a practitioner may be proven to be inaccurate if the information provided by a family or members is incomplete or false due to issues of trust or if the initial perceptions of the practitioner were limited. Potential inaccuracies creates the need for the construction of a new baseline through assessment as a process. Ongoing assessment embraces the possibility of new issues emerging as the family continues its transactions within the realms of intrapersonal, interpersonal, social–cultural–political–environmental, and nonordinary realities.

Assessment procedures can, and often do, become direct or indirect interventions, especially when questions asked to assess a family's experience with a specific issue activate the process of expanding awareness. This may be the case within the context of a practitioner who is attempting to ask questions to familiarize himself or herself with a family's past experiences with issues of grief and loss. While responding to the questions, the family or individual members can begin to recognize effective coping skills and strengths previously experienced.

Human service practitioners are encouraged to assess the realms of intrapersonal, interpersonal, social–cultural–political–environmental, and nonordinary realities in order to develop a comprehensive plan for working with diverse family constellations. Again, consideration of each of these areas is intended to enhance the inclusiveness of possible factors strengthening or challenging family experiences. While assessing the aforementioned realms, the practitioner is encouraged to examine

- family resourcefulness and strengths;

- family beliefs, values, norms, rituals, customs, identities, or culture(s), a totality of learned behaviors;

- family roles, social status, boundaries;

- the family communication patterns, and decision-making and coping skills;

- dynamics of power within the family and within the boundaries of its transactions;

- family risks or challenges (i.e., experiences likely to increase the degree of family vulnerability) and protective factors (i.e., experiences that enhance family's resilience);

- personal and social adversities or issues faced by the family or its members (i.e., domestic violence, drug or alcohol dependency, disabilities, poverty, homelessness, oppressive forces, grief and loss issues, etc.); and

- the family's previous and current experiences within diverse contexts and settings, among others.

Multiple assessment techniques already exist to support human service practitioners when assessing the realms considered by the eclectic practice lens discussed previously. These include the use of closed and open-ended questions, narratives and family history, genograms, ecomaps, self-reports, and professional observation and intuitive guidance. Although the magnitude of these assessment techniques is beyond the scope of this chapter, brief discussions of each follow.

Use of Closed and Open-ended Questions   Assessments are meaningfully guided through questions we construct and use. Such questions can be clustered into two major groups: closed and open-ended questions. Whereas closed questions are useful to promote responses that are condensed and specific (i.e., Do you have any children? How many children do you have? Do you consider yourself a Christian? a Muslim? a skeptic?), open-ended questions provide the opportunity for elaboration and depth (i.e., What do you perceive happens after death? What do you mean when you stated that you had a vision? What were causes of your divorce? How may I support you?). These two groups of questions can be used interchangeably during an assessment in order to enhance concrete and elaborative data collection.

Both closed and open-ended questions can serve multiple purposes. Open-ended questions, for instance, can be used to solicit or promote exploration of an area(s) of focus, elaborate on or ask for clarification of statement or observations or interpretations, encourage family self-reflection, and encourage the family or members to identify possible strategies that they may find useful for addressing their presented circumstances. Among open-ended questions, solicitation–exploration question can be reflected by the following inquiries: "What would you consider effective communication?" and "How would you describe your relationship with your partner?," followed by an elaboration–clarification question: "Can you elaborate on your answer?" Furthermore, reflection questions tend to explore meanings and interpretations (i.e., a sense of perceived reality), beliefs (i.e., viewpoints, paradigms), values (i.e., life principles and ethics), feelings or emotions (i.e., anger, fear, sadness, guilt, shame, joy, caring, compassion, kindness, love, etc.), thought patterns (i.e., frequencies of ideas), perceptions (i.e., discernment), or attitudes (mind-sets), among other phenomena. Reflection questions can also be used to encourage the family or members to engage in a process of identifying possible skills, strategies, or solutions for addressing and confronting life demands. Examples of questions promoting self-reflection and a search for options through which one can base and encourage decisions are these:

• What effects have your experiences with alcohol or drugs have had in your life?

• Do you consider yourself skillful when communicating your emotions? Explain.

• How do you tend to behave when feeling ignored?

• What would you have done differently if presented with another opportunity?

• What have been your experiences when confronting adversities?

• What have been your major strengths when confronting this illness?

• What skills or approaches do you perceive useful to address your current situation?

• What have been some of your spiritual experiences?

• Please describe your view of a spiritual orientation.

• Can you share about your spiritual practice or religious rituals?

This list can go on and on. The point here is that questions are used to support and promote the process of working with diverse family constellations.

Through the use of questions, authentic listening, and impeccable sharing, human service practitioners support the construction of what these authors refer to as a blueprint, a dialogue that is intended to navigate the multiple faces of language or communication (see figure 4.8) in order to enhance understanding of family experiences while forming a structure for interactions and exchanges between the family, its members, and the practitioner. Although this dialogue can be initiated by the practitioner, the channel of communication constructed through the use of questions can be reciprocal, and families can be encouraged to also use questions to generate understanding of practitioner's roles, competence, and approaches. Through formation of a blueprint, the family, its members, and the practitioner can identify the

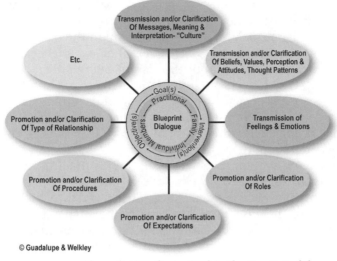

© Guadalupe & Welkley

FIGURE 4.8 *Blueprint Dialogue Within the Context of the Multiple Faces of Language-Communication*

goal(s) (overarching purpose of the family–practitioner working relationship), objective(s) (measurable tasks or procedures for achieving overarching purpose), and interventions (practical approaches, methods, tactics, techniques, and strategies used to support the objective while reaching the overarching purpose). The goal(s), objective(s), and intervention(s) give focus to the transactions occurring within the helping process.

Although not all communication is verbal (i.e., it can be reflected by gestures, facial expressions, body movements, energetic exchanges, etc.), questions constructed and used during the helping process can assist practitioners to search for concreteness beyond preconceived ideas, stereotypes, biases, or assumptions. Cultural uniqueness can, and often is, misinterpreted when assumptions (i.e., interpretations of facial expressions or gestures, intuitive urges or feelings) go unquestioned. Honoring experiences encountered by diverse family constellations and members encourages human service practitioners to be mindful about assumptions. Still, the mind is conditioned to assume. Thus, transforming our assumptions into questions is likely to assist human service practitioners to remain in a space of curiosity, integrity, and respect.

Use of Narratives and Family Histories   As stressed earlier, throughout their life span families and family members are in a constant space of being and becoming. Through transactions within diverse contexts and settings, families develop, promote, maintain, or transform meanings given to experiences. Through their transactions and transitions, families construct narratives or stories that symbolize their interpretations of encountered experiences (Fisher, 1984, 1987; Miller, 2005). Constructed narratives generate families' expectations for interactions and exchanges and guide decision-making processes. Through the use of a narrative approach, families are encouraged to share their experiences, interpretations, and perspectives without the risk of being judged, blamed, or pathologized. Practitioners attempt to understand and honor the family experiences as they engage in authentic listening and impeccably share without a chronic need to search for evidence to construct a diagnosis. The family is considered the expert of its own experiences and practitioners become supportive agents.

Using a narrative approach to assessment, practitioners have an opportunity to explore family constellations' notions of reality as a notion that is constructed, deconstructed, or reconstructed through interactions and exchanges. There is no one way of knowing, doing, and being. Each individual or family, though, has dominant stories—meanings and interpretations of life events that carry personal significance and are likely to influence family wellness. A narrative approach frequently focuses its attention on meanings attributed by the family or members to the encountered strengths, needs, issues, and challenges. Assessment is not concerned with diagnosis or classification, but rather with the family's strengths and nurturing of possible solutions. Language is not taken for granted, because it can assist in the process of understanding family experiences while promoting a family-centered approach.

A narrative approach as reflected in various writings (Andersen, 1991; Hoffman, 1992; White & Epston, 1990) often promotes a set of steps while assessing and intervening with individuals and families. These steps include, but are not limited to the following:

- Use of closed and open-ended questions to guide the assessment while encouraging the family or members to openly share about their experiences, meanings, expectations, and effects.

- Identified issues, needs, or challenges are often given names in order to promote an externalization of the experience through which the family can briefly distance itself in order to less stressfully begin to address the situation presented. The externalization of issues, needs, or challenges reflects the view that a family's encounters do not represent who the family truly is. The family's beingness, as discussed within the realms of nonordinary reality, transcends constraints observed within the physical realms.

- Through the use of questions, the effect or influence that the issues, needs, or challenges has on the family and members and how the family and members may have contributed to the creation of the presented situation is explored.

- The identified strengths, needs, or challenges are examined within the context of an evolutionary process (i.e., from its possible origin as identified by the family or family members and through the context of time).

- Through the assessment of narratives, families are encouraged to explore and participate in identification of solutions to the presented situations while considering possible setbacks. Identification and application of solutions are intended to assist the family and its members in the process of construction, deconstruction, and reconstruction of narratives, expectations, decision-making skills, and effects. An overarching objective of a narrative approach can be said to assist the family and members to conscious awareness of its constant dynamics of being and becoming.

The questions presented and asked during an assessment process that employs a narrative approach takes into consideration, at a minimum, the aforementioned steps. Common questions used in a narrative assessment (de Shazer, et al., 1986) include, but are not limited to

- Exceptional questions (i.e., that focus on situations of successful outcome: What has aided in achieving successful outcomes? What have been some of the times when you have resisted . . . ? What have been barriers to successful outcomes?)

- History of exceptional questions (i.e., How did you come to this perspective?)

- Significant questions (i.e., What does discovery of this perspective mean to you?)

- Coping questions (i.e., that assist families and family members to identify and explore times when they have coped successfully with similar situations: What did you do that was different? What worked that time?)

- Action questions (i.e., Where do you think you should go from here? Knowing what you know now, what do you think may be a good approach for addressing . . . ?)

Again, questions have the intention to encourage the family and family members to share their narrative(s), explore reciprocal effects or influences between the family and situation presented, examine previous successes, and deconstruct and reconstruct narratives as the family is guided to continue nurturing and strengthening its well-being.

Use of Genograms   Genograms are generational diagrams developed through a collaborative effort between a family or family members and a practitioner. Genograms are useful to examine family experiences and possible patterns of interactions and exchanges passed on from one generation to another (Hartman, 1978). A family member's date of birth, age, gender, sexual orientation, and intrapersonal and interpersonal experiences can be demonstrated through the use of a genogram. Genograms are valuable for exploring common and diverse life orientations and decision-making processes reflected within and between family constellations as well as a variety of family structures and occurrences evolving throughout time. In summary, genograms can illustrate a graphic picture of familial relationships and their transactions, transitions, and experiences throughout the life span.

It is important to consider that genograms were initially developed to be used within the context of traditional heterosexual family paradigms (i.e., male–female family constellations). Therefore, historically the genogram as a tool for assessment does not sufficiently encompass diverse family experiences. The emerging acceptance of the family as a complex and nonstatic living entity provides an opportunity to broaden the genogram's scheme beyond traditionally used symbols and rules (i.e., a box symbolizes a male while a circle represents a female; a horizontal straight line connecting two people means marriage; a straight horizontal line intersected by a short line means divorce). See figure 4.9 for different samples of genogram symbols (some traditionally used and new ones proposed) and meanings.

An important aspect of any genogram is that it needs to be family-centered and symbols used need to be understood by all the participants involved (the family, its members, and the practitioner). Thus, although human service practitioners are encouraged to be creative when constructing a genogram with a family, symbols used need to be operationalized. Genograms can help human service practitioners to move away from the idea of family as monodimensional, and can present family chronologies within the context of diverse experiences, transactions, and transitions. A family must be given the space to identify its own individual strengths, needs, and challenges. Understanding the family as a multidimensional contextual nonstatic living entity means acknowledging that every family is unique and each individual member provides a distinctive and necessary element to the development of the family group as a whole.

Use of Ecomaps   Ecomaps are another useful tool to assess family within interpersonal transactions and transitions (Hartman, 1978). As reflected in figure 4.10, ecomaps explore the family's ecological systems

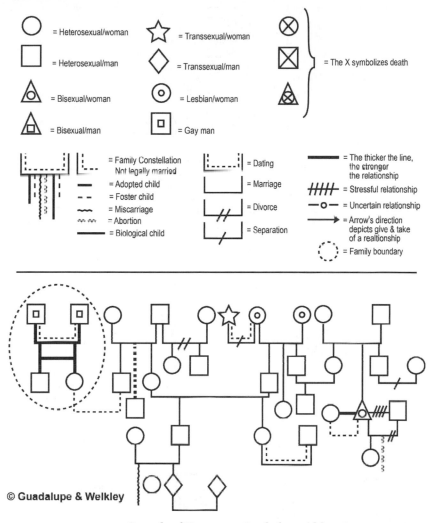

FIGURE 4.9 *Sample of Genogram Symbols and Meanings (Traditional and Emerging)*

and type of relationships (i.e., its immediate and extended relationships with entities such as school programs, employment, religious institutions, neighborhoods, the sociopolitical environment, etc.). An ecomap can assist practitioners to help families identify strengths (i.e., assets, resources, etc.) and challenges (i.e., stressful relationships) within its surroundings. Ecomaps also can help the family to mindfully observe the social networks that it has created, as well as the reliability and frequency through which those networks are used.

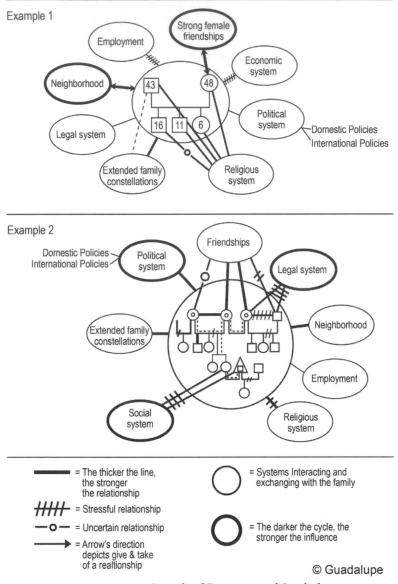

FIGURE 4.10 *Sample of Ecomaps and Symbols*

Similar to genograms, ecomaps are constructed through the use of symbols reflecting unique dynamics of interaction and exchange. Again, practitioners are encouraged to be creative while remembering to operationalize the use of symbols.

Use of Self-Reports   Self-reports are constituted by information directly provided by the family or its individual members. Such information can be generated through informal dialogues (i.e., the process of checking in at the beginning of each session: How did it go this week?) or through the use of structurally constructed standardized instruments (i.e., standardized scales regarding a child's level of functioning, such as the Child Behavior Checklist; Achenbach, 1991); child abuse, such as the Trauma Symptom Checklist for Children (Briere, 1996); magnitude of family violence, such as the Revised Conflict Tactics Scales (Straus, Hamby, Boney-McCoy, & Sugarman, 1996); or building blocks for healthy children and youth development, such as the Search Institute's 40 Developmental Assets (www.search-institute.org/). While standardized tools provide guidelines, informal dialogue allows for the family to lead the focus of conversation. When used interchangeably, these standardized tools can be a useful.

Use of Professional Observation and Intuitive Guidance   Professional observations can take multiple forms. They can range from abstract to concrete observations. Professional observations can be made during assessment as a baseline, process, or outcome. An overall intention of professional observations, however, is to encourage practitioners to continue to engage in reflective practices. That is, once observations are generated, possible constructed assumptions are directly explored with the family or its members. For instance, a practitioner may observe incongruence between what a family member is verbalizing and the behaviors in which he or she is engaging. The practitioner can immediately choose to ask a reflective question: "Do you perceive incongruence between your words and behavior?" A practitioner may also observe that during a dialogue, subgroups within the family constellation(s) are reflected. This becomes an opportunity to discuss and explore types of interactions, exchanges, and relationships among family members.

Professional observations can vary from cognitive–behavioral observations to the emergence of intuitive guidance. (Intuitive guidance is insightful sensations of occurrences—gut feelings—encouraging a direction[s] to be considered, and is not necessarily based on rational reasoning.) Choquotte (2007) stresses that being intuitive is one's "birthright to expect extraordinary levels of insight at any given time—from subtle impulses to full-blown psychic experiences such as clairaudience, clairvoyance, telepathy and even precognition" (p. 1). Although not directly verbalized, a practitioner may intuitively sense that a family or a family member's fears of the unknown (i.e., life after a divorce) are discouraging the family or member's ability to confront current hurtful dynamics (i.e., domestic violence). When directly asked, the family or family member may stress that there is no fear. The practitioner's sensation of the role of fear continues to be energetically revealed, however. At this point, the practitioner may consider, if he or she is qualified, encouraging the family or members to engage in a combination of self-reflection techniques, such as these:

- Journal writing. Responding to questions such as, For what reasons would I stay in this relationship? What are possible effects of continuing or ending this partnership? What is preventing me from making a decision?

- Creative visualization techniques (i.e., creating possible results through the power of conscious attention and intention). Briefly explained, this technique encourages the family or members to create a mental image or picture of a desired outcome (i.e., Close your eyes and imagine how it would feel to have a harmonious relationship. What would it be like to communicate authentically and in harmony with one another? How can you contribute to the creation of such a relationship?). The family or members can be encouraged to practice this technique regularly and observe the possible outcomes. This technique can help the family or member to recognize that the current relationship may not be the appropriate one for experiencing harmonious relational interactions and exchanges. Creative visualization relies on the power of thought, perception, and imagination. It can help in the process of recognizing ways through which we, as human beings, develop comfort zones that can restrict us from growing and transforming. As stated by Shakti Gawain (1985),

  > The process of change does not occur on superficial levels, through mere "positive thinking." It involves exploring, discovering, and changing our deepest, most basic attitudes toward life. That is why learning to use creative visualization can become a process of deep and meaningful growth. In the process we often discover ways in which we have been holding ourselves back, blocking ourselves from achieving satisfaction and fulfillment in life through our fears and negative concepts. Once seen clearly, these limiting attitudes can be dissolved through the creative visualization process, leaving space for us to find and live our natural state of happiness, fulfillment, and love. (p. 7)

- A gratitude list to identify and reflect on experiences or people that are supportive and encouraging.

- The use of various meditation techniques or relaxation approaches (i.e., yoga, music, breathing methods), prayer or other spiritual rituals (depending on the family or family member's religious–spiritual orientation as well as the practitioner's competence in these areas). The family can be encouraged and supported to use cognitive–behavioral observations as well as intuitive guidance. The practitioner may support the family or members by asking questions such as

a. What kind of transformations have you observed in your life so far?

b. Looking back, would you have predicted such transformations?

c. What has given meaning to your life in the time of crisis?

d. What do you understand about intuitive guidance? gut feelings? inner knowing?

e. How has intuition been reflected in your life decisions or experiences?

f. How may you strengthen your intuition?

Families' direct observations and intuitive guidance can be an asset when being mindfully present of its transactions and connectedness with the realms of ordinary and nonordinary realities. For instance, a family or a family member confronting social adversities such as unemployment may rely on prayer and meditation as a way to alleviate mental–physical anxiety. Prayer or meditation may be used as tools to strengthen a family or member's faith and trust that, as they take the necessary steps, a job or financial resources will become available.

The interdependence of body, mind, and spirit can be more comprehensively addressed as families and members are supported through the development or maintenance of their intuition. A major purpose of developing or maintaining our direct experience with intuitive guidance is to sustain an alliance with our beingness or life force. The notion here is that the more we are aligned with our intuitive guidance, the more likely we are to connect with our infinite creative abilities and potential to transform—or assist others to transform—cognitive and physical restrictions. A family or family members' remembrance that their existence transcends a cognitive–physical structure is likely to affect their approach when addressing a personal or social challenge.

While supporting a family and members to nurture and strengthen their intuitive guidance, a family and members can be encouraged to develop a sanctuary (a mental or physical space of relaxation–meditation–tranquility—safety) where each can practice daily silence, conscious breathing, or reflection for a period of time (Hanh, 2007; Sky, 1990). A daily silence, meditation, or breathing practice can enhance individuals and families' intuitive guidance as well as support family members in their process of increasing their awareness prior to engaging in a specific decision-making process(es).

A number of diverse assessment strategies have been briefly addressed. The intention has been to assist human service practitioners while supporting diverse family constellations to explore the realms of intrapersonal, interpersonal, social–cultural–political–environmental, as well as of nonordinary realities. At this time, we introduce some intervention ideas for consideration when servicing diverse family constellations.

INTERVENTION STRATEGIES

A major purpose for professional interventions is to promote, strengthen, or preserve the well-being of families and their members. In order to bring the purpose to fruition, professional interventions are guided by a variety of interdependent goals:

- Prevention of behaviors, experiences, activities, or events that put at risk the well-being of the family and its members

- Transformation of behaviors, experiences, activities or events that have been affecting the well-being of the family and its members

- Promotion or maintenance of behavior, experiences, activities or events that foster well-being (see figure 4.11)

Although the aforementioned goals can be established and addressed independently, they mutually affect one another. For instance, while

© Guadalupe & Welkley

FIGURE 4.11 *Intervention Goals*

preventing specific behaviors or experiences that may put the family's wellness at risk, other particular behaviors or experiences that will support the family's wellness need to be simultaneously promoted. While working directly with diverse family constellations, human service practitioners are encouraged to clearly identify the goal(s) of the professional relationship and tune into the family's expectations, understanding, and level of consent. Again, the use of questions, authentic listening, and impeccable sharing can serve as a baseline.

Intervention approaches often have, at minimum, one or more of the following objectives:

- Consciousness raising: Increasing or expanding awareness considered useful to promote intended transformation or for maintaining a level of stability in family functioning

- Skill development or enhancement: Often necessary to support or strengthen family essence, sense of direction, or competence when addressing life circumstances or demands

- To honor and support the family within its transitions and transactions (see figure 4.12)

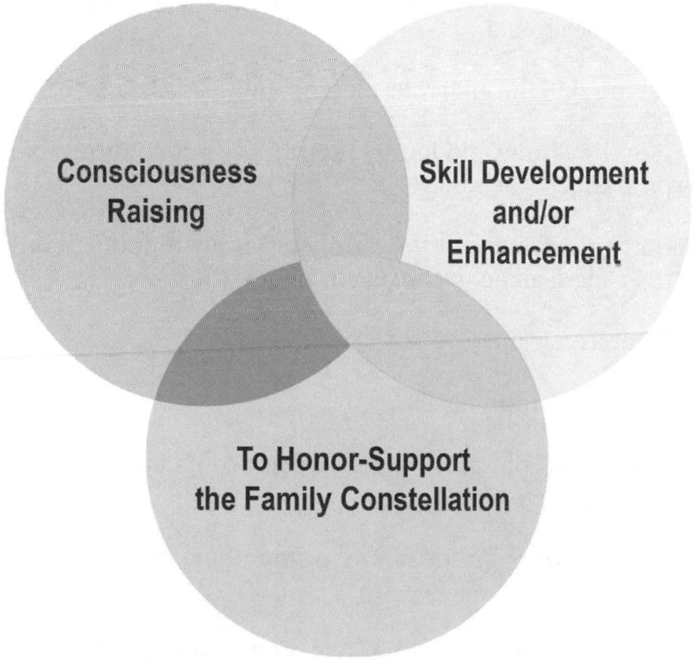

© Guadalupe & Welkley

FIGURE 4.12 *Common Intervention Objectives*

In order to increase the possibility for successfully accomplishing the aforementioned objectives, human service practitioners are encouraged to employ a variety of intervention methods or approaches, including, but not limited to

- Dissemination of information: Use of didactic presentations, discussions, lectures, films, articles, books, analysis of narratives or case studies, and so on.

- Development or strengthening of skills: Needed skills may vary from coping to communication skills, conflict management to decision making, assertiveness to relaxation-stress management and breathing techniques, and so on. While teaching a skill, the following steps can be useful:

  - Identify the major components of the skill as well as its strengths and restrictions.

  - Discuss the skill in detail with the family and family member.

  - Discuss the rationale for the skill.

  - Together brainstorm about life circumstances when and where the skills can be crucial.

  - Model the skill through role-playing and discussion.

  - Provide the family and family members opportunities to evaluate the potential of the skill.

  - Encourage and support the family or family member while applying the skill in an actual life event or situation.

  - Together assess the results.

  - Task-oriented approaches.

  - Modeling and role-playing a task prior to its application in a real life situation.

  - Use of homework for the family or members to complete between sessions.

  - Capacity-building methods: Assistance provided to the family while supporting family members to build resources and enhance the ability to network (i.e., linking the family with community resources; helping the family to organize a community family support group, etc.).

- Mobilization approaches: that is, the worker serving as a catalyst for change, organizing and mobilizing the family or its members to take action. Common mobilizing strategies are networking, lobbying, or advocacy within the family and between family and social systems.

- Social action strategies. Active collaborative efforts taken by families or family members to explore issues affecting their lives as well as actions needed to effectively address, confront, and transform circumstances or presented situations. Through social actions families and family members' network(s), lobby, and advocate on their behalf. (For more detailed content on assessment and interventions within diverse contexts and settings refer to Hepworth, R. Rooney, G. Rooney, K. Strom-Gottfried, & J. Larsen, 2010.)

Professional interventions can be strengthened through the use of professional guidelines, identifying areas believed to be important for consideration. The eclectic template discussed in this chapter encourages the consideration of intrapersonal, interpersonal, environmental, and nonordinary realities. One way for honoring and considering these domains is to directly ask and engage the family and its members in dialogues—creating a blueprint. Family constellations and members can be encouraged to share their perspectives and experiences. For instance, a family can be asked, "What do you understand about culture?," "What is culture to you?," "Please share about some of your cultural traditions, beliefs, customs, experiences, and so on . . . ," and "How do your beliefs about the different genders, sexual orientations, spirituality, and so on . . . influence your life choices and decisions?" Exploring a family's uniqueness, as well as the practitioner's ability to be receptive and open to learning can promote and enhance a family-centered approach. Each family and member needs to be considered and honored. As practitioners we are being asked to think outside the box. This is briefly reflected in the following poem:

> See Me
> No, I am not the image printed in the mind,
> for the mind is limited by its own perceptions and conditions.
> No, I am not solely a reflection of a time in history,
> for change is constant, transformative, and ultimately time is
>   an illusion.

No, I am not exclusively a mirror of a culture, family system, a
    collective identity,
for to see me like that is like seeing the forest while failing to
    remember the
uniqueness and lifeness of each of the trees.
No, I am not my name, profession, human roles,
for those are boundaries through which we can begin com-
    munication.
No, I am not my pains, sorrows, glories, healings,
for these are only manifestations of my human experiences.
I am the emptiness which is whole.
I am the uncertainty which is certain.
I am the spaceless which is filled with possibilities.
Please, don't diminish my existence.

                                                                    KLG

Multiple approaches, ranging from conventional to nonconventional, are available for working with families: narrative, feminist,
strengths and empowerment, psychodynamic or psychoanalytic, structural, cognitive or behavioral, vision quests, soul retrieval sessions,
sweat lodges, as well as storytelling; life-review, and forgiveness. However, before using any of these approaches human service practitioners
need training and experience. Intervention approaches are vast and
transcend the limitations of this chapter. Practitioners are encouraged
to become aware and embrace an eclectic approach when learning and
gaining competence in the use of a variety of practice intervention
approaches. This chapter presented an eclectic practice template to be
considered when addressing diverse family constellations within the
context of professional social–health–human services. This chapter presented ideas for consideration within the process of assessment and
intervention. Part 2 of this text focuses on a more comprehensive application of the concepts addressed in chapters 1 through 4 within the context of diverse family constellations. Enjoy the journey.

References

Achenbach, T. M. (1991). *Manual for the child behavior checklist*. Burlington: Uni-
    versity of Vermont Department of Psychiatry.
Andersen, T. (1991). *The reflecting team: Dialogue and dialogues about the dia-
    logues*. New York: W. W. Norton.
Briere, J. (1996). A self-trauma model for treating adult survivors of severe child
    abuse. In J. Briere & L. Berliner (Eds.), *The APSAC handbook on child mal-
    treatment* (pp. 140–157). Thousand Oaks, CA: Sage.

Choquotte, S. (2007). *The intuitive spark: Bringing intuition home to your child, your family, and you.* Carlsbad, CA: Hay House.

de Shazer, S., Berg, I. K., Lipchik, E., Nunnally, E., Molnar, A., Gingerich, W., & Weiner-Davis, M. (1986). Brief therapy: focused solution development. *Family Process, 25,* 207–222.

Fisher, W. R. (1984). Narration as a human communication paradigm: The case of public moral argument. *Communication Monographs, 52,* 347–367.

Fisher, W. R. (1987). *Human communication as a narration: Toward a philosophy of reason, value, and action.* Columbia, SC: University of South Carolina Press.

Gawain, S. (1985). *Creative visualization.* Mill Valley, CA: A Bantam Book.

Guadalupe, K., & Lum, D. (2005). *Multidimensional contextual practice: Diversity and transcendence.* Belmont, CA: Thomson Brooks/Cole.

Hanh, T. N. (2007). *Chanting from the heart: Buddhist ceremonies and daily practice, for diverse meditation techniques.* Berkeley, CA: Parallax Press.

Hartman, A. (1978). Diagrammatic assessment of family relationships. *Social Casework, 59,* 465–474.

Hepworth, D. H., Rooney, R. H., Rooney, G. D., Strom-Gottfried, K., & Larsen, J. A. (2010). *Direct social work practice: Theory and skills* (8th ed.). Belmont, CA: Cengage Learning.

Hoffman, L. (1992). A reflective stance for family therapy. In S. McNamee & K. J. Gergen (Eds.), *Therapy as a social construction* (pp. 2–24). Newbury Park, CA: Sage.

Losey, M. B. (2007). *The children of now.* Franklin Lakes, NJ: New Page Books.

Miller, K. (2005). *Communication theories: Perspectives, processes, and contexts.* New York: McGraw-Hill.

Rasha. (2003). *Oneness: The teachings.* San Diego, CA: Jodere Group.

Renard, G. R. (2006). *The disappearance of the universe: Straight talk about illusions, past lives, religion, sex, politics, and the miracle of forgiveness* (8th ed.). Carlsbad, CA: Hay House.

Sky, M. (1990). *Breathing: Expanding your power and energy, for specific breathing exercises.* Rochester, VT: Bear and Company.

Straus, M., Hamby, S., Boney-McCoy, S., & Sugarman, D. (1996). The revised conflict tactics scales (CTS2). *Journal of Family Issues, 17,* 283–316.

White, M., & Epston, D. (1990). *Narrative means to therapeutic ends.* New York: W. W. Norton.

PART II

A Closer Look at Diverse Family Constellations

Throughout part 2 the reader will be exposed to diverse family constellations and experiences, including an exploration into the notion of nuclear families, lesbian and gay families, single-family constellations, multigenerational family constellations, blended family groups, and foster family systems. This list of family constellations is not exhaustive, but rather provides a foundation for applying the lenses presented throughout the text. The chapters that follow are an elaboration of the five premises introduced in part 1 of this text: (1) the family as a multidimensional contextual nonstatic living entity, (2) individuals constantly experiencing multiple family memberships, (3) the family in a constant space of being and becoming, (4) reciprocity of forces or realms of existence affecting and being affected by the family, and (5) the importance of an eclectic approach to family practice. Readers are encouraged to reflect on their perceptions regarding the family constellations addressed here in order to enhance their ongoing professional development.

CHAPTER FIVE

Language, Law, and the Supremacy of the Opposite-Sex Family Ideal

Myles Montgomery

> Employing this language . . .
> excludes other valid family
> arrangements.
>
> MM

As addressed by Guadalupe and Welkley in previous chapters of this book, the family is a complex experience affecting and being affected by "intrapersonal (micro domains), interpersonal (mezzo domains), environmental (macro domains), as well as nonordinary (magna domains)" (p. 22). Language greatly influences our understanding of family constellations and can be used to expand or narrow, accept or reject, our views of what may or may not constitute a family experience. According to Abrams (2000), attorneys interested in pursuing a career in family law are encouraged to first answer "the deceptively simple question, 'What is a family?' " (p. 165). Such a question is deceptively simple because, to many people, a family is exclusively an arrangement of persons who fit a prescribed norm of married heterosexual couples, usually with children. For the purposes of this chapter, such relationships will be referred to as opposite-sex family constellations or the opposite-sex family ideal. Abrams goes on to correctly note that "today's family members negotiate a web of relationships far more complex than those depicted by the ever cheerful step-family on *The Brady Bunch*. . . . [Instead] families may include birth parents and adoptive parents, gay and lesbian partners, and step-siblings from multiple families" (p. 165). Although Abram's definition of families is progressive for the field of law, it is still relatively limited: it does not include multigenerational members, nonrelated members, and so on. Nonetheless, her question underscores the tension that exists between the legal process and modern family constellations.

While supporting the premises addressed in previous chapters (i.e., families as multidimensional contextual nonstatic living entities, individuals constantly experiencing numerous family memberships, families continuously engaging in the process of being and becoming, family constellations affected and being affected by diverse realms of existence, and an eclectic practice approach vital to advance our work with diverse family groups), this chapter primarily explores the family experience in the United States through a legal lens: law, language, and effects. The contrast between the traditional (i.e., the notion of man-woman-child nuclear family system) and multidimensional contextual (i.e., families as multidimensional nonstatic living entities) perspectives becomes especially visible in the area of law, where the way the concept of family is understood and defined has the power to affect millions. This chapter demonstrates the power of perspective in understanding definitions. Moreover, this chapter thoroughly examines the tension between definitions created through the legal process, on the one hand, and through observations of actual family constellations on the other. Throughout this chapter, attention is given to how notions about family, according to the law, often differ from the ways in which family membership is experienced. Discussion about this contrast is significant, since the law regulates and governs numerous aspects of social life. Another theme in this chapter involves the flexible character of families in their construction, reconstruction, and deconstruction. Special emphasis is given to how inclusive ideas and language regarding families may be instrumental in accurately reflecting and honoring families as they actually exist.

In order to navigate the complex tension that exists between actual family arrangements and the law, this chapter is divided into four separate but interrelated sections. The first section examines how the traditional perspectives of opposite-sex family constellations dominate legal thinking. Moreover, this section examines how the opposite-sex family constellation is understood as a normative baseline, which has been challenged, but only through landmark cases. This section also observes the underlying prescriptive norms with regard to race, gender, and sexuality contained in opposite-sex family forms.

The second section begins with a brief survey of the legal process and illustrates how the process of creating laws moves much slower than the fluid movement of actual family constellations. One of the greatest sources of tension between the legal process and actual family forms arises from this difference: whereas the legal process can be slow, rigid, and exclusive, families can be elastic, flexible, and inclusive. In general, this section attends to how the legal process can exclude or include notions of family, and how ideas and language influence the creation of laws.

In the third section, attention is given to the United States Constitution and the language in Supreme Court cases that have shaped its interpretation and expectations regarding families. The Constitution is the source from which all other U.S. laws and legal structures flow, so the perspectives used in its interpretation are a subject of great importance. In this chapter, several seminal cases are reviewed to show how the underlying reasoning of cases can translate into the regulation of family constellations. Two particular cases analyzed are *Moore vs. the City of East Cleveland*, where the Supreme Court struck down a city ordinance that threatened to separate a grandmother and her two grandchildren, and *Lawrence v. Texas*, the landmark case in which the privacy rights of two homosexual men were honored. These cases demonstrate a significant shift in perspective with regard to how the Constitution is interpreted, from a traditional to a multidimensional contextual perspective. Thus, the trajectory of cases in this section and the shift in perspectives reflect some changes in beliefs about families as the membership of the Court has changed.

The fourth (final) section offers a new approach to Constitutional interpretation of families. Specifically, this chapter argues that the First Amendment right to assemble could be a more appropriate safeguard for modern arrangements of families than the amendments used in the past. The idea here is that the right to assemble may be more effective than the current right to privacy and more reflective of family structures as they actually exist.

FAMILY CONSTELLATIONS

The word "family" instantly invokes definite but varied ideas. Nonetheless, the importance of this word cannot be overstated, because it recognizes the basic unit of survival for human beings. It could be argued that without the ability to form families humans would not have been able to withstand the harsh forces of nature. As described in the first chapter of this text, families often provide crucial support for the individuals of which they are composed. Often, this means meeting the members' basic material needs—food, clothing, shelter, and so on. Equally important, families often provide a sense of safety, protection, and belonging, even when some or many of the material needs are absent. Although the word "family" has such important connotations, in modern times "family" is a highly politicized term, with different notions fighting for supremacy under the color of law.

For this section, the metaphor of family as constellation fits well because, as mentioned in previous chapters, the concept of a family tends to be more fluid than static. Implied by this metaphor are three assumptions described below. In reading this section, it should be observed that a family as a constellation metaphor aligns more with a multidimensional contextual perspective than with the traditional perspective.

The first assumption of a family-as-constellation metaphor is that as the needs of its members change, so do families. Put more accurately, families sometimes gain or lose members over time, depending on known and unknown circumstances. Families range in size and even in variations of biological relations. Over the course of one lifetime, one may be a member of several families simultaneously—with varying traditions, customs, languages, and social expectations.

The second assumption holds that to accurately reflect and honor the diversity in actual family constellations, inclusive rather than exclusive language is preferable. Since the construction, reconstruction, and deconstruction of a family is fluid, inclusive language—language that remains open and flexible—more accurately mirrors the structure of real families. By contrast, defining families only in terms of immediate bloodlines—as the law often does—neglects many other valid arrangements, such as adoptions, blended families resulting in stepchildren, fictive kinships, and so on. Thus, narrowly defining family only as those who share a common bloodline fails to account for the actual arrangements in which many families form. Nonetheless, stereotypical notions of what a family is or should be are deeply rooted in language and the law. This concept is made clear in the examples of Constitutional cases in the third section.

The third and final assumption is that pervasive ideas about how people are arranged in families are presented and reified through media, such as news reports, television shows, popular literature, and educational institutions. Perhaps the most ubiquitously presented construction of family structure is that of the opposite-sex family constellation. In this section, the definition and impact of this ideal are discussed. Following this discussion, further attention is given to the roles of marriage and sexuality in the common definition of family in the United States.

THE OPPOSITE-SEX FAMILY IDEAL

The opposite-sex family form, traditionally known as the nuclear family, has become a default basis for understanding (and even expecting) who belongs to a family. Its basic premise is that families are predictably (or expectedly) arranged in dyads of husbands and wives, often with children. From the traditional perspective, the opposite-sex family constellation has defined what many people have come to understand and believe as the exclusive ideal family. Consequently, many other notions of family constellations have been disregarded, ignored, or disparaged. For example, extended families—those with several generations cohabiting together—are viewed as the exception to the rule. Similarly, implied in many court decisions and statutes is the underlying assumption that family indicates the opposite-sex constellation: courts define family as based on unions between heterosexual couples, usually married and with children.

It should be noted that, whereas the opposite-sex family system is held as the ideal under the traditional perspective, that system is understood from the multidimensional contextual perspective as one possible family form. Instead of preferring an ideal arrangement, this perspective recognizes the variety of constellations that have emerged over history. This perspective also remains open about possible family arrangements in the future.

SEXUALITY, MARRIAGE, AND FAMILY

Further complicating the definition of family are the topics of sexuality and marriage. As characterized from the traditional perspective, the opposite-sex constellation typically indicates married, heterosexual couples. Many Supreme Court decisions reflect a preference for this traditional perspective by exclusively defining the parameters of a family through a limited list of intimate interpersonal activities, mainly marriage, heterosexual sexuality, procreation, and contraception. In other words, when the Court takes on an issue related to family it is usually in one of these areas, reducing notions of family to this short list of intimate activities. Proof for this claim is found in the language of many Supreme Court decisions discussed in the next section.

By definition, the opposite-sex family constellation does not include families composed of gay, lesbian, or transgender members, for whom the legal institution of marriage is often denied. This issue was illustrated in 2004, when the mayor of San Francisco, Gavin Newsome, declared that marriage between same-sex couples would be recognized there. The reaction to this news was varied and broad: whereas some vigorously supported this idea, others vehemently opposed it. The political response, however, was unequivocal. In his 2004 State of the Union address, President George W. Bush emphatically concluded, "Our Nation must defend the sanctity of marriage." Building up to this end, President Bush disparaged the attempt of so-called activist judges who "have begun redefining marriage by court order, without the will of the people and their elected representatives." In this portion of his speech,

President Bush referenced the 1996 Defense of Marriage Act, which is a federal law that defines marriage as "a union of a man and a woman."

Two significant issues are gleaned from this speech. First, in the United States, notions of family are closely tied to the concept of marriage. Second, only family forms that resemble the opposite-sex family structure, as understood by the traditional perspective, are deemed legitimate. Reasoning from this premise, unmarried, same-sex, and unconventional family constellations are not valid. The fact that marriage legitimizes the composition of a family demonstrates how the law affects notions of family. But marriage is simply one point of entry into this discussion: the law has also been used to affect basic living arrangements. However, to appreciate how the law and notions about family interact, it is first appropriate to define and understand the legal process.

THE LEGAL PROCESS

The two pillars of discussion in this section are (1) the process by which laws are created and (2) the various functions of and perspectives on laws that have been created and enacted. After covering these two major points, the discussion turns to how the legal process in its entirety often conflicts with actual family arrangements.

The Creation of Laws   In the United States, two layers of law coexist— the federal law and laws of each state in the union. The Constitution holds that the former is to be narrow, while the latter shall be broad. However, as a check and balance, whereas federal law is narrow in its scope, it contains the power to preempt state laws that conflict with it. By contrast, unless preempted by federal law, each state has absolute power to create its own laws and lawfully use its police power to enforce them.

On the state level, both houses of the legislature convene and draft bills that are supported and signed into law, or that are not signed or vetoed by the state's governor. This process, of course, mirrors the federal system, where both houses of Congress draft bills that will be signed into law, be left unsigned, or vetoed by the president.

When states do not legislate and enact specific laws to govern a particular issue, most state courts adopt the American Common Law, which is chiefly derived from the English Common Law. For instance, if a state chooses not to draft a specific definition of the act of murder, that state's courts will apply the Common Law definition in order to decide a case.

Moreover, most courts, including the Supreme Court, follow the Doctrine of *Stare Decisis*, which binds courts to follow the precedent of previously decided cases. Therefore, courts are not typically allowed to make novel decisions if the law has been decided and has been well established in a given area. Nonetheless, the law builds on itself—and may take new directions—when cases are similar in context, but unique on their facts. In this way, courts have some leeway to accommodate new situations.

Whether talking about the drafting of bills or rulings by courts, typically, the law is a slow-moving vehicle in adjusting to social trends: only after human behavior has already changed and conflicts begin to emerge do courts address specific issues. This is because someone must file a claim and the court must agree to hear the case. Even then, after appeals and a final ruling, implementation of new policy often occurs with a great degree of resistance. Take, for example, the 1954 seminal case *Brown v. The Board of Education of Topeka*. In *Brown*, the Supreme Court determined that segregated education was far from equal education. The Court, thus, ruled that African American students must be allowed to attend public school with European American children. In spite of this decision, many years passed before racially integrated school systems began to be the norm. In fact, it was not until the 1980s that a majority of schools in the United States were considered integrated. By that time, the membership of the Supreme Court had shifted to a group of justices who were less concerned about racial integration as a priority.

Because the law addresses social issues slowly, it infrequently represents the social structure of life as it exists in the current moment. However, when the Supreme Court finally does choose to act, it frequently derives conflicting outcomes regarding the same subject matter. The history of Supreme Court decisions regarding the treatment of families, for example, is illustrative of this process. The cases below demonstrate how conflicting outcomes arise out of similar subjects. For the most part, these conflicting outcomes arise when the Court alters its rationale in reaching its decision. Thus, it is important to study the language of seminal cases, since all other lower court decisions shall not transcend or deviate too far from the decision handed down by the Supreme Court. It is also important to realize that, as seen in the example of *Brown*, not all states immediately act on a Supreme Court ruling.

Functions of and Perspectives on Law   Once a law is enacted or a court makes a ruling, the character of the law begins to take shape. Most laws function for one of three purposes—protection, declaration, or prescription. Sometimes, however, a law may perform multiple functions. At other times, a law may be primarily intended for one purpose but ultimately may achieve another purpose. Before beginning this discussion, it is appropriate to define each of these purposes in detail.

Laws that are intended for protection use language identifying a protected class of persons or the public, in general. For example, a law prohibiting child labor is intended to protect a specific group of persons— those persons under the age of eighteen—whereas a law prohibiting arson is intended to protect the public from a particular behavior. In both of these examples, the law prohibiting a specific behavior has the primary function of protection.

Laws created for the purpose of declaration are typically intended for conflict resolution between two parties. A common example of this kind of law is the legal action of quiet title in a dispute regarding the ownership of a particular piece of property. Under this doctrine, the court hears evidence from both parties and then, based on the weight of the evidence, declares that lawful title to the land belonging with one of the parties.

The third purpose of laws is prescription. More specifically, these are laws that govern and regulate the social norms of human conduct. For instance, a law that prevents the marriage of adults of different races would fall under this category. Another example would be a law that prevents any further laws, those that would protect the rights of homosexuals. Both of these examples are from actual cases and both of these cases involve the creation of laws based on ideas about how humans should and should not interact with one another. In deciding these cases, the terms "community standards" and "morality" are frequently found in the court's reasoning. The remainder of this chapter is most concerned with this variety of laws, because laws that prescribe and regulate human behaviors are often those that have the greatest effect on families.

As mentioned above, the initial purpose of a law may differ from its ultimate effect. In fact, many laws that are intended to promote a particular purpose end up achieving a significantly different one. Other times, how a law functions is a matter of opinion. For example, whereas some would argue that a law prohibiting mixed-race marriage is prescriptive in character because it freezes the ability of two consenting adults to marry, others would argue that such a law is protective, in that it protects racial purity. Furthermore, this dichotomy illustrates one source of tension between law and social arrangements—those promoting a particular law for one purpose are not always aware of how its purpose may change when the law is implemented. However, once this conflict is realized, another process—through the courts or legislature—must be enacted in order to remedy the problem.

Ideas, Language, and Law   Before prescriptive laws become laws, they are usually specific ideas about social norms. After being captured and codified in the language of a bill, these ideas gain the power to regulate human conduct, prescribing which behaviors are acceptable and which are not. As a result, the formation of prelaw ideas are worth considering. Ideas gain their working form only through the medium of language (written or oral). Consequently, the connotations and denotations of language play a significant role in the formation of the ideas that ultimately become laws. Unless a term is highly technical, most judges apply a plain meaning analysis and adopt the popular or dictionary interpretations of a given word. When courts struggle to understand the meaning behind the language of a particular law—when the law is unclear on its face— they look to the legislative process and how the legislature defined specific terms. Here, they attempt to glean from various sources what was meant by certain words in the law. Remember, legislators rely on their staff members and lobbyists to draft pieces of legislation.

With regard to the term "family," either path of the above-mentioned process yields similar meanings, usually rooted in stereotypes, traditions, or vague notions. Consider the first level of scrutiny—when a judge uses the plain language definition of a word. In this scenario, a judge simply accepts a word's popular or common meaning. Applied to the term "family," a plain meaning analysis usually results in the opposite-sex family constellation.

If, on the other hand, a judge combs through the legislative history of a piece of legislation, the result is largely the same. This is because, as stated above, unless a term is highly technical, legislators also adopt the plain meaning of words. With the pervasiveness of the opposite-sex family form, it is unlikely that legislators would understand this term in any other way. Thus, when the term "family" is used in legislation, it simply codifies the popular and often stereotypical meaning.

PAST CONSTITUTIONAL APPROACHES TO FAMILY

The United States Constitution contains seven articles and twenty-seven amendments, as of this writing. The first three articles lay out the three coordinate branches of government—the legislative, the executive, and the judicial, respectively. By contrast, the first ten amendments, also known as the Bill of Rights, describe specific freedoms that citizens may enjoy and that may not be infringed upon by the federal government. Most of these same amendments are also applied to the states through the Fourteenth Amendment. Constitutional law books refer to the application of these amendments to state governments as the Doctrine of Incorporation. For instance, the First Amendment, which bars prohibitions against speech, applies to the federal government as an amendment, and to the governments of all fifty states and the District of Columbia. through the Doctrine of Incorporation.

Although the Constitution does not use the word "family," the Supreme Court has ruled on a number of issues related to the arrangements and interactions among groups of people that concern the ability of governments to interfere with families. For example, although sexuality does not exist exclusively within the realm of families, it is certainly a significant part of many relationships among people who view themselves as part of a family. As such, Court rulings on the issue of sex and sexuality affect the ways in which people are allowed to interact on an intimate basis. When sexuality is defined only through the opposite-sex family constellation, any other family form can, and often does, become marginalized and, thus, unprotected by law. Moreover, any ruling regarding such an intimate subject runs the risk of creating social norms that are inclusive of some practices and exclusive of others. As discussed in the sections above, social prohibition of a specific behavior can lead to the formation of accepted stereotypes and, thus, alienation for excluded members.

PRIVACY VS. MORALITY

Seeking an appropriate basis to interpret the Constitution with regard to family relations, the Supreme Court has seemingly followed two concepts in different cases: privacy or morality. In some cases, privacy has served as a basis for protecting the decisions of individuals to behave and to arrange themselves in relationships free from the intervention of government regulation. In other cases, the Court has preferred morality to govern statutes and regulations concerned with prescribing relationships among humans. These arguments usually rely on an articulation by the Court of the pervasiveness of a particular belief system and why it contains a compelling merit.

During the 1960s and 1970s, the Supreme Court recognized the principle of privacy from government intrusion with regard to certain issues, such as abortion, procreation, marriage, and contraception. Each of these activities the Court viewed as existing in a domain too intimate for government intervention, because each involved decisions specific to an individual's identity or physical being. It was also exclusively with reference to these concepts that the Court predominantly ruled on notions of family. Through a number of seminal cases, each of these areas was determined to be off limits to government regulation without a compelling and necessary reason—a burden few states were able to meet. As a result, attempts by state governments to regulate in any of these areas were generally struck down by the Supreme Court. The concept of privacy arose from the Supreme Court's interpretation of privacy interest implied in the Bill of Rights. Although not spelled out in those amendments, the Court reasoned that a privacy interest exists to protect specific human interactions against government meddling. However, how and when this privacy interest applies has been the subject of much debate throughout a vast number of decisions.

In contrast to the Court's privacy reasoning stands the reasoning of morality as a valid basis for primarily prescriptive state laws. Essentially, the morality reasoning holds that conventional or religious morality embodies the standards established within a given community or state. Thus, in a case where a state enacts a prescriptive law, the morality argument holds that the law may be found valid if it comports with that state's accepted moral standards, which represents the majority view of that state's inhabitants. This argument relies heavily on the power of a state to create its own laws and exercise its police power under the Constitution. Consequently, when the Court is arguing from the basis of privacy, it is usually referring to the federal power—implied in the Bill of Rights—to protect individual rights against the regulation by a state. By contrast, when the Court takes the morality position, it generally argues in favor of a state's ability to enforce its own laws. These two strands of reasoning are found intertwined among a vast majority of cases involving aspects of family arrangements.

Arguably the best illustration of the privacy–morality dichotomy comes from the contrast between the cases of *Bowers v. Hardwick* and *Lawrence v. Texas*. In the former case, the court relied on morality as a basis to restrict relationships between homosexual partners. In this decision, a Georgia statute criminalizing homosexual conduct between adults was upheld. Language in the majority decision of *Bowers* written by Justice White separates sexual interactions between homosexual men from the concepts of family, marriage, and procreation—concepts that have been afforded Constitutional protection under the basis of privacy. Moreover, in his concurring opinion, Chief Justice Burger proclaims, "Decisions of individuals relating to homosexual conduct have been subject to intervention throughout the history of Western Civilization. Condemnation of those practices is firmly rooted in Judeo-Christian moral and ethical standards." Notice that the former opinion divorces ideas of homosexuality from accepted notions of family, whereas the latter opinion offers morality as the rationale for this separation. Taken together, these opinions seem to suggest that because homosexual behavior does not conform to an accepted social norm (i.e., "Judeo-Christian moral and ethical standards"), it is not a practice that should receive the constitutional protection of privacy, which is afforded to other issues involving family and marriage.

In his dissenting opinion, Justice Blackmun, joined by Justices Brennan, Marshall, and Stevens, argues that "[the] fact that individuals define themselves in a significant way through their intimate sexual relationships with others suggests, in a Nation as diverse as ours, that there may be many "right" ways of conducting those relationships, and that much of the richness of a relationship will come from the freedom an individual has to choose the form and nature of these intensely personal bonds[W]hat . . . the Court really has failed to recognize is the fundamental interest all individuals have in controlling the nature of their intimate associations with others" (Stone, Seidman, Sunstein, Tushnet, and Karlan, 2005, p. 933). Later in this same opinion, Justice Blackmun argues that Judeo-Christian values "cannot provide an adequate justification for [the statute]" (ibid.). This dissenting perspective widely differs from the majority opinion in an important way: it recognizes sexuality as a process by which certain relationships are defined. In addition, it honors the notion that arrangements in human relationships are broader than the opposite-sex family constellation. Notice that the majority opinion uses a more traditional perspective in understanding notions about family whereas the dissenting opinion more closely reflects the multidimensional contextual perspective.

Seventeen years later, *Bowers* was overturned in the landmark case of *Lawrence v. Texas*. In *Lawrence*, the Court found privacy from government intervention in homosexual relations to be a more compelling argument. The majority decision, written by Justice Kennedy, begins, "[L]iberty presumes an autonomy of self that includes freedom of thought, belief and certain intimate conduct" (Stone et al., 2005, p. 935). In challenging the validity of a Texas statute, which prohibited homosexual conduct, the opinion proceeds, "When sexuality finds overt expression in intimate conduct with another person, the conduct can be but one element in a personal bond that is more enduring. The liberty protected by the Constitution allows homosexual persons the right to make this choice" (ibid., p. 937). Following this reasoning, statutes prohibiting this choice encroach on the exercise of liberty under the Due Process Clause of the Fourteenth Amendment. Therefore, the Texas statute was struck down. A clear departure from the reasoning of *Bowers*, this decision understands sexuality as a personal decision of significant importance in a relationship between two persons—regardless of sexual orientation. Notice that the language describing the right of privacy is more inclusive of notions of family outside the opposite-sex family constellation. Furthermore, the court adopts a more multidimensional contextual reasoning over the traditional perspective.

Whereas the language of *Lawrence* applies the protection of privacy beyond the opposite-sex family structure, it follows the Constitutional pattern of defining families through the narrow lens of sexuality. By contrast, in an earlier case, *Moore v. City of East Cleveland*, the Court directly confronted an ordinance regulating untraditional family arrangements. Specifically, in *Moore*, a city ordinance limited the occupancy of any dwelling to members of the same family, which was defined by "a few categories of related individuals." The appellant in this case, a grandmother living with her two biologically unrelated grandsons, argued that the ordinance was unconstitutional. The Court agreed with her and offered the following reasoning to support its decision:

> This Court has long recognized that freedom of personal choice in matters of marriage and family life is one of the liberties protected by the Due Process Clause of the Fourteenth Amendment. [When] government intrudes on choices concerning family living arrangements, this Court must examine carefully the importance of the governmental interest

advanced and the extent to which they are served by the challenged regulation. When thus examined, this ordinance cannot survive. The city seeks to justify it as a means of preventing overcrowding, minimizing traffic and parking congestion,
and avoiding an undue financial burden on [the] school system. Although these are legitimate goals, the ordinance
[serves] them marginally, at best. (Stone et al., 2005, p. 918)

In the language of this decision, a few important points stand out. First,
it should be observed that the Court here recognizes family life and marriage as two distinct but equally important concepts. The separation of
these two concepts is significant because, in many other decisions, marriage and family life are viewed as one and the same.

Second, the language of this decision illustrates the earlier point that
the purpose of certain laws may differ from its ultimate effect. In this
case, the Court recognized that, even if the original purpose of the ordinance was protective (e.g., against overcrowding, traffic and parking
congestion, and undue financial burdens on the school system) its
effect was prescriptive, because it violated the implied right of families
to arrange themselves.

Finally, this case again illustrates the tension between traditional
beliefs about family, often contained in the law, and the actual forma-
tions that arise naturally. Although the city ordinance defined family
exclusively—individuals related only through blood, adoption, or marriage—the Court recognized protection for a broader spectrum of
arrangements: "The tradition of uncles, aunts, cousins, and especially
grandparents sharing a household along with parents has roots equally
venerable and equally deserving of constitutional recognition. [Out] of
choice, necessity or a sense of family responsibility, it has been common
for close relatives to draw [together]. Especially in times of adversity
[the] choice of relatives in this degree of kinship to live together may not
lightly be denied by the state" (Stone et al., 2005, p. 918). This language
still principally defines family as connections between related persons,
but expands notions of family beyond simply the opposite-sex family
constellation. Although *Moore* is a landmark case, it is unique; few cases
have replicated its internal logic that the language of the legal process
should respect and reflect the natural variety of family forms.

Coupled with the holding of *Lawrence*, *Moore* demonstrates an
expression of legal reasoning that contains language of expanding
notions of family constellations and a layer of constitutional protection
to preserve it. However, as demonstrated by the trajectory of cases following the *Brown* decision, how the reasoning of a Court proceeds is
often dependent on the composition of the Court's justices. Since the
Lawrence decision in 2003, Justice Sandra Day O'Connor has retired and
Chief Justice William Rehnquist has died. Filling these vacancies were

Bush appointees Justice Samuel Alito and Chief Justice John Roberts. Even more recently, President Barack Obama appointed Justice Sonia Sotomayor to replace retiring Justice David Souter and Elena Kagan to replace retiring Justice John Paul Stevens. Whether the court moves in the direction of privacy or morality with regard to family issues will continue to be decided by this new group of justices.

As of this writing, the issue of whether gays and lesbians have a right to marry is still under hot debate. So far, the morality argument seems to be prevailing, as state legislatures are urged to protect notions of the traditional family and the Supreme Court has not performed a Constitutional analysis on the subject. Thus, currently, the issue is confined by the decisions of state legislatures and court systems. This is reflected in the Massachusetts Supreme Court, which holds that a prohibition against the marriage of gay and lesbian persons is unconstitutional. Should this issue continue to escalate, the next logical step would be for the U.S. Supreme Court to review the Constitution and consider whether the marriage of gay and lesbian persons should be treated as a privacy right, protected by the Fourteenth Amendment, or as an issue of morality, to be handled state by state.

CONTEMPORARY ISSUE: GAY MARRIAGE AS FUNDAMENTAL RIGHT

As of this writing, an issue being debated in the state of California is the recognition of marriage for gay and lesbian couples. A dispute over the constitutionality of Proposition 8, a referendum passed in November 2008 that disallows the recognition of gay and lesbian unions as marriages, was taken to the state court level in March of 2009. In many ways, the arguments around the issue of Proposition 8 reflect the tension mentioned in the cases above.

The main issue in this debate recapitulates many of the themes and content already addressed in this chapter. That is, the debate about Proposition 8 centers on whether marriage is considered a fundamental right, available for all people. Proponents for the proposition argue that marriage is historically and traditionally reserved for opposite-sex unions. Such language, again, mirrors the opposite-sex family ideal from a traditional perspective. By contrast, opponents of Proposition 8 hold that marriage is a fundamental right that should be enjoyed by more than just opposite-sex family constellations. This argument appears to be more akin to the multidimensional contextual perspective, recognizing opposite-sex family structures as simply one possibility of a valid marriage.

Although this issue has not yet been resolved (and will not likely be resolved in the near future), it illustrates the ongoing tension between language, law, and the role of the opposite-sex family ideal. It is significant to note that, in this debate, the perspective used to understand notions of and definitions of family ultimately lends itself to the position that one takes on either side of the debate.

ALTERNATIVE THEORY OF CONSTITUTIONAL PROTECTION

In the majority of cases involving notions of family, when the Supreme Court finds protection of a definition of family outside the opposite-sex family ideal, it does so by recognizing a privacy right through the Due Process Clause of the Fourteenth Amendment. However, it could be argued that an alternative reasoning exists under the First Amendment right of assembly. In the future, the latter may provide a more enduring and less vulnerable basis for the natural arrangements of families. To properly address this hypothesis, this chapter analyzes some key differences between the right of privacy and the right to assemble in relation to the formation of families.

DUE PROCESS CLAUSE OF THE FOURTEENTH AMENDMENT

As noted above, the Supreme Court has had no difficulty discovering in the Bill of Rights a privacy interest that applies to all fifty states through the Fourteenth Amendment. The Court refers to this right as substantive due process and, when applied, triggers a closer scrutiny by the Court with regard to the actions of a state. Behind the reasoning of privacy is the principle that state intervention offends the constitutional recognition of certain decisions made by an individual. Moreover, the term "privacy" implies a sphere of autonomy in which individuals are allowed to arrange their lives without unnecessary government regulation.

On the one hand, the strength of this argument seems to lie in its recognition of certain liberties that should be left up to individuals first and only to the government in severe cases where the health, safety, or welfare of the public is placed in jeopardy. Historically, this argument is compelling: the United States Constitution was largely based on the reaction by English colonists against the invasive and arbitrary rule by English kings. In addition, the notion of privacy divides human life into separate spheres between the government and the individual, each operating on its own terms. Although this paradigm has remained the basis for many Court decisions expanding notions of family, it is also vulnerable to attack.

The major weakness of the privacy basis of Constitutional protection is that it does not actually appear in the Constitution. The term "privacy," as it is used in the Fourteenth Amendment, does not guarantee a right in the same way that the First Amendment guarantees the right of free speech. In fact, neither the Fourteenth Amendment nor any other part of the Constitution even mentions the word "privacy." Instead, privacy is a judicial invention that was inferred by a particular group of justices roughly forty years ago. Thus, if the current or future Courts decide to chip away at the power of privacy, they may strongly argue that the plain language of the Constitution does not honor such a right and that the lowered expectation of privacy with the increase in interactive technologies makes this notion less relevant anyway. During debates such as these, command of the text of the Constitution is indispensible. Consequently, since privacy is not listed as a right under the text of the Constitution, notions of family may need to be protected through other parts of the Constitution, where actual language exists.

RIGHT TO ASSEMBLY UNDER THE FIRST AMENDMENT

The term "assembly" is highly inclusive. That is, it is not a term that is bound by definite conventions and understandings of human arrangements. An assembly could occur among related or unrelated individuals. Furthermore, there are fewer built-in expectations for the composition of an assembly of persons the way that there exists for notions of the opposite-sex family constellation.

Opponents of this reasoning may argue that the term "assembly" must be read in the context of the First Amendment, so it should be viewed only as it relates to speech or religion, not construed broadly, as with families. This kind of reasoning, however, ignores the fact that rarely do Courts read a general concept narrowly. For instance, the word "speech" under the First Amendment refers to written, oral, symbolic, and novel means of communication; it does not refer to only one means. Analogizing to notions of assembly, it naturally follows that this general term should be treated in the same way: assembly does not refer to simple arrangements between two people of a particular sex or racial composition. Instead, it refers to interactions of an infinite number of people, without regard to gender, sexual orientation, ethnicity, languages spoken, or age. In many ways, families behave the same way; essentially, modern families are assemblies formed of individuals who are related and nonrelated, same-sex and opposite sex, with children and without children, old and young. Furthermore, assemblies can be fluid, and are not fixed in time or space—much like the nature of families. Finally, much like speech, the assemblies of families are inherently expressions of self-identification and shared values, which may be unique.

In sum, the term "assembly" has received little treatment in Constitutional discussions. Nonetheless, perhaps its time has come as a more accurate reflection of contemporary arrangements among families. Understanding integral terms, such as marriage and sexuality, from the perspective of a right to assemble also seems more inclusive and less attached to the opposite-sex family constellation. As indicated above, it may also be argued that with whom and how an individual chooses to interact is an expression at least as important as speech. Thus, it is appropriate that speech and assembly, however defined, should be protected as a right under the First Amendment.

Summary

This chapter began with the premise that defining a family is a deceptively simple task, since actual family arrangements transcend traditional categories, such as bloodlines, adoptions, and so on. Nonetheless, the opposite-sex family constellation ideal remains ubiquitous and has infiltrated even expectations under the law. That is, the opposite-sex family structure—composed of married, heterosexual couples, typically with children—has been established as the default position for many people when they are asked to consider notions of family.

Language regarding the concept of family in legal decisions often favors the opposite-sex family form, and even Constitutional analysis has reduced protection of family interests to issues involving marriage, sexuality, procreation, and abortion—concepts that are primarily slanted toward the concerns of families composed of heterosexual pairs. Employing this language, which concerns only this limited range of interests, excludes other valid family arrangements—gay and lesbian partners, multigenerational family membership, and fictive kinships, to name a few. Furthermore, the legal process that generates laws remains slower and more rigid than the process by which families are constructed, deconstructed, and reconstructed.

In terms of seminal Supreme Court cases, whereas many cases demonstrate a bias toward the opposite-sex family constellation, some changes have been made over the last forty years. In studying the cases, presented in this chapter a pattern emerges: when the Supreme Court wishes to protect a right, it finds a privacy interest under the Due Process Clause of the Fourteenth Amendment. More recently, such a privacy interest has come to include homosexuality. On the other hand, the Supreme Court defers to arguments involving morality when it wishes to bypass the Fourteenth Amendment and preserve laws, which frequently prescribe interpersonal human conduct.

As an alternative to the privacy–morality dichotomy, the First Amendment right to assemble may be a more useful Constitutional basis for deciding cases involving issues of family, since the right to assemble is linguistically more inclusive and substantively less vulnerable than privacy arguments. Part of the reason for this conclusion is that the First Amendment recognizes a specific right to assemble, whereas the Bill or Rights as a whole loosely infers the privacy right. Viewing the right to form families through the right to assemble both honors and respects notions of family, which are closer to the way that actual families form and rearrange over time.

While continuing with the exploration of the premises stressed in this text through the following chapters (i.e., The Multigenerational Family Constellation, Single-Parent Family Constellations, Lesbian and Gay Families (Gamilies), Residential and Foster Care Family Constellations, and Blended Family and Multipartner Family Constellations), readers are encouraged to reflect on the role(s) and effect(s) of language. Families affect and are affected by multiple realms of existence, and language influences our understanding of diverse family constellations as well as capabilities to be skillful when interacting and exchanging within the context of diverse families. Although it seems obvious, it cannot be overstated that families, through different degrees, will always contribute to cognitive, emotional, as well as socioeconomic or political societal dynamics. It is this author's view that dominant legal perspectives of what constitute a family will continue to change as the voices of diverse family constellations vibrate louder and clearer.

Questions for Consideration

1. Why is it important to understand the role that language plays when working with diverse family constellations?

2. What role does the legal process play in including or rejecting family forms?

3. What are the implications of some families being accepted and others rejected by social or legal definitions of family constellation?

4. How can the content in this chapter affect the role of practitioners when working with various family forms and family members?

References

Abrams, L. L. (2000). *The official guide to legal specialties: An insider's guide to every major practice area.* Chicago: BarBri Group.
Stone, G. R., Seidman, L. M., Sunstein, C., Tushnet, M. V., & Karlan, P. S. (2005). *Constitutional law.* New York: Aspen.

CHAPTER SIX

The Multigenerational Family Constellation

Dale Russell
Debra L. Welkley

> Grandparents sort of sprinkle
> stardust over the lives of little children.
>
> Alex Haley

This chapter explores concepts, principles, and assumptions related to multigenerational family constellations. It addresses potential strengths and challenges as well as ramifications concerning multigenerational families. The chapter focuses its content on two major areas: (1) the issue of elderly people living with their children and grandchildren and how they directly affect their families, and (2) the issue of grandparents finding themselves in a supportive parental role with their grandchildren. We will examine application of an eclectic approach for assessing and working with multigenerational family constellations, while considering the premises of families as multidimensional contextual non-static living entities, individuals experiencing multiple family memberships, the family as being and becoming, and the family as affecting and being affected by diverse realms of existence.

The Multigenerational Family: Being and Becoming and the Notion of Multiple Memberships

Experiences of multigenerational family constellations reveal multiple definitions and occurrences, many beyond the scope of this chapter. An observed common denominator, however, is that multigenerational families are simultaneously made up of diverse family forms (i.e., same or opposite family structures, single-family systems, blended family groups, etc.) that are related by blood, marriage, birth, legal adoption, or emotional or cognitive choices. Multigenerational families are composed of several generations (i.e., grandparents, parents, grandchildren) and often follow and are linked by ancestral heritage. In general, multigenerational family constellations can be viewed as more than one step or level in the line of descent from an ancestor, reflecting the multiplicity of individual memberships. Multigenerational families are represented by all ethnicities, sexual orientation groups, and socioeconomic statuses.

By nature of their existence, multigenerational families are multidimensional (i.e., multiple family groups unified by heritage) and reveal diverse contextual experiences (i.e., lives and backgrounds of ancestors, grandparents, parents, and grandchildren). As nonstatic living entities, multigenerational family constellations constantly reflect processes of being and becoming through the journey of time and evolution. This experience is commonly demonstrated when we explore relationships within and between three generational family constellations within the same umbrella of a multigenerational family unit (i.e., grandparents, children, and grandchildren).

The experience of being and becoming is mirrored through diverse occurrences and choices encountered by multigenerational families. These may sustain a perpetuation of similar experiences or encourage transformation of specific familial patterns. For instance, the family structure or life experiences of a set of grandparents (whether paternal or maternal) may or may not be perpetuated by the family arrangements chosen by their children or grandchildren. The union between a set of grandparents may have reflected a family constellation commonly known as nuclear (i.e., an opposite-sex family union of husband and wife with children living as a unit), while the family arrangements reflected by the children or older grandchildren may demonstrate diverse forms of family constellations (i.e., including nuclear or opposite sex, same sex, blended, foster, or single parent, to mention a few). The occurrences of being and becoming can be affected by the experience of cultural influence and cultural choice, as explained by Guadalupe and Welkley in previous chapters. In other words, through dynamics of cultural influence and cultural choice new generations may or may not continue to affiliate with political parties supported by grandparents, hold the same beliefs and values systems, celebrate the same social or religious traditions, demonstrate similar customs, or experience the same sexual orientations. To some degree, all families have experienced cultural influences perpetuated through familial interactions and exchanges. This is a reflection of being with what has been. Diverse contextual experiences often encourage family constellations to make different choices from those made by previous generations, while reflecting the component of becoming or unfolding into new ways of being, knowing, and doing.

The experience of being and becoming within multigenerational family constellations can be revealed by multigenerational pride or conflicts; for example, the parent(s) who attempts to pass on to his or her (their) children multigenerational family traditions that they consider valuable, or the children who resist to inherit generational beliefs and value systems because they believe that these beliefs conflict with their current choices and experiences. Diverse multigenerational families uniquely reflect the process of being and becoming. Thus, the experience of human diversity (the interface of human uniqueness where people can connect, and experience dissimilarities and an opportunity for growth) within the multigenerational family unit helps us recognize the distinctiveness of the experience of being and becoming within multigenerational family constellations. Understanding the diversity within the multigenerational family constellation allows us to further explore and attempt to comprehend issues of boundaries within the context of intersectionality (the space of connectiveness, interactions, and exchanges between family members). When exploring multigenerational family dynamics, the historical and current sociopolitical-economic contexts as well as cultural environmental exchanges cannot be taken for granted. These phenomena assist us in understanding unique experiences and changes that we observe within and between diverse multigenerational family constellations.

The premise of individuals experiencing multiple memberships is well mirrored within the multigenerational family constellation. Familial relations such as grandparents, parents, children, cousins, aunts, and uncles reflect multiple memberships. This is without mentioning stepparents and stepchildren, or half-siblings, -cousins, -aunts, and -uncles who often emerge through the experience of blended-family constellations. Multigenerational family constellations are constituted by the family of origin or procreation as well as by what are often considered extended family groups or diverse kinship systems, defined by Guadalupe and Welkley in chapter 2 as "people related by blood, legal agreements or marriage, adoption, or those whom one simply considered family." It is almost impossible to indicate that an individual is only a member of a single family constellation because the experience of family is often determined by a set of variables, including, but not limited to, genetics or inheritance, legal decisions, social–cultural choices, and perceptions of self and others. These elements often coexist, allowing individuals to simultaneously feel a part of multiple family constellations. Although it is perhaps easier to place individuals within single-family groups for purposes of analysis, we must be careful not to marginalize experiences that can enhance a comprehensive understanding of a person's life.

It is not a requirement, but many multigenerational family constellations live under the same roof. Although this living arrangement is not a new pattern reflected in multigenerational family constellations, the contextual and current socioeconomic and political demands are somehow distinctive to those observed in previous years. According to the U.S. Census Bureau (2000), there were 3.9 million multigenerational family households out of 104,705,000 family households in the United States. By definition, these are families where grandparents live in the same home with two or more generations of descendants. This represents almost 4 percent of all households; of these, 65 percent represent a situation where the grandparent is the homeowner and at least one of their children and grandchild reside with that grandparent.

Some current common factors that account for the number of multigenerational family constellations living in the same households include local housing shortages, recent immigrants moving in with family established in this country, growing numbers of older adults living longer, increasing the need for family caregiving, and the high cost of living and housing. As stated by the Pew Research Center (2010) there is an increased number of grandparents who take on the primary role of caring for grandchildren due to a number of factors: poverty, family violence, mental health problems, death or incarceration of a parent, serious illnesses, child abuse or neglect, or abandonment by parent. These dynamics increase the complexity of family dynamics within the context of multigenerational family constellations.

Brief Historical Perspective: Endurance and Challenges

Until the beginning of the 1900s the complete family household structure generally comprised at least three generations, represented on a continuum of individuals within the past, present, and future. Prior to World War II, low socioeconomic families who could not bear children or chose to be childless put themselves at economic risk. Also, these family constellations, unconsciously or consciously, unwillingly or willingly, broke the chain of heritage (Carlson, 2005).

In the days when agriculture was the chief source of income for most people, prior to the industrial revolution of the late 1800s, large numbers of families lived and worked on farms with very few other options for income. Most people had many offspring. Many individuals stayed in their households through adulthood and when a family member reached old age and became too frail to work, he or she often stayed in their home of origin until his or her death, while the sons and daughters took over the workload (Ruggles, Sobek, Flood, King, Schroeder, & Vick, 1997). This pattern or way of life began to change drastically during the early part of the nineteenth century, when large numbers of young adults left the farms for urban areas.

The three-generation household consisting of aging parents, their adult children, and grandchildren all living on a single farm was common prior to 1940. From 1880 to 1940 the number of three-generation homes remained fairly stable. Currently, that number has dropped significantly. Ruggles and colleagues (1997) stress the "decline of the multigenerational family [households] should be regarded as an indirect response to economic transformation, which shifted the balance of power within the family and reduced incentives for co-residence" (p. 47). Grandparents often have been associated with multigenerational, rural, extended families and with the economic transformation. The belief was that grandparents could no longer teach their children and grandchildren skills associated with making a living once they went to work in offices and factories.

The increased divorce rate and the fall in fertility also have been considered social factors changing multigenerational family ties. Some historians such as Cherlin and Furstenburg (1986) argue that the implementation of social welfare programs meant that seniors and families were less dependent on each other for both social and financial support. Grandparenthood, as it is currently perceived, a distinct stage of family life, is a post–World War II phenomenon. Cherlin and Fursten burg's argument includes the issue of longevity. According to some demographers, about 37 percent of all males and 42 percent of all females born in 1870 survived to age sixty-five, compared with 63 percent for males and 77 percent for females for those born in 1930. As of 1980, the average lifespan had increased to seventy-four years of age for white males and eighty for white females (Cherlin & Furstenburg). In 2009, the overall life expectancy rate in the United States was seventy-eight years of age (Dolgon & Baker, 2011). This contrasts with longevity for groups such as African American and other people of color who, based on health-related issues and inadequate medical care, live on average five to seven years less than their white counterparts.

Due to the aforementioned factors there are many more grandparents alive today than there were just a few decades ago. This has had a huge impact on family dynamics between grandparents, children, and grandchildren. In addition, multigenerational family interactions and exchanges are influenced by the addition of great-grandchildren. For the first time in history, many more children have the chance to spend many years growing up getting to know their grandparents or great-grandparents. For example for those born in 1900, only one in four children at birth had four grandparents alive and just one in fifty children at age fifteen had all grandparents living. By 1976, that same fifteen-year-old had a nine-in-ten chance of having two grandparents alive and one-in-six chance of having all grandparents alive (Cherlin & Furstenburg, 1986). The age at which people become grandparents has remained consistent over the past century, with the vast majority becoming grandparents from their early forties into their fifties.

ROLE OF THE GRANDPARENT

In 1950, half of American households had grandparents living in them; today those homes represent fewer than 10 percent. Kornhaber (2004) believes that a two-generational mindset of a nuclear family (parents and children) has a very limited role for grandparents. As a result, many family constellations have ended up being geographically and psychologically autonomous and independent from their family of origin. He further argues that some grandparents have opted out of all close family involvement. Some grandparents, according to Kornhaber, have removed themselves (voluntarily or nonvoluntarily) to a preferred retirement spot, have gone on to new careers or who spend time traveling after recognizing their economic ability to do so. Others have been placed in nursing homes due to their health conditions or socioeconomic demands encountered by the immediate family. Nevertheless, others live within the same household, in close proximity, or when living far away from children and grandchildren have remained accessible, thrilled, and optimistic about their role as grandparents.

Ross (2006) points out that birth rate changes have affected multigenerational family roles. In the late 1800s, women in the United States gave birth to, on average, more than four children. In many cases there were fairly young children in the home while their older siblings were marrying and leaving the home. It is argued that the role of grandparents in those times overlapped that of a parent. In 1900, about half of all women age fifty still had children under age eighteen. By 1980, this percentage had dropped to approximately one in four, or 25 percent.

Another significant change affecting interactions and dynamics within the multigenerational family constellation is that after the 1940s large numbers of families were able to afford automobiles. As more interstate highways were built and more families were able to purchase a car, the mobility of families increased as well, increasing visits to grandparents who did not live in close proximity. Technology (i.e., telephones, computers, the Internet, airplanes, etc.) has also helped to create opportunities for more frequent involvement of grandparents in the lives of their grandchildren. Furthermore, grandparents have more leisure time than ever before in the history of the United States. The average adult male can now expect to spend fifteen years of his adult life out of the labor force, much of it in retirement (Cherlin & Furstenburg, 1986). However, due to current economic challenges (in 2010) and their impact on retirement funds, there may be a trend that would decrease the number of years spent out of the labor force.

Recent survey research regarding grandparents' involvement in the lives of grandchildren found a difference between grandmothers and grandfathers. The grandmothers reported helping with homework and talked about serious subjects with their grandchildren far more often than their male counterparts reported. It has been hypothesized that grandparents are likely to play an important role for grandchildren during the process of a divorce: grandparents may represent a level of stability not experienced anywhere else in the child's life (Ferguson & Gillian, 2004).

Neugarten and Weinstein (1964) conceptualized five distinctive styles of grandparenting: formal, distant, surrogate, fun-seeking, and reservoir of family wisdom (see figure 6.1). Cherlin and Furstenburg (1986) added

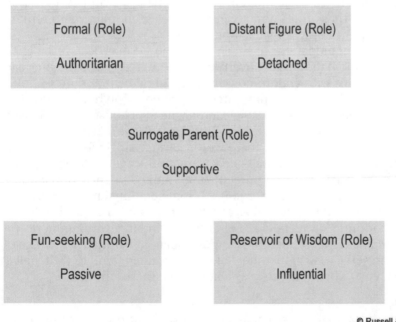

© Russell & Welkley

FIGURE 6.1 *Styles of Grandparenting:*
Combining Role and Dominant Behavioral Features

their description of grandparenting styles simply as detached, passive, supportive, authoritarian, and influential. Although it is believed that a grandparent may simultaneously take on and exhibit several roles and characteristics based on his or her own experiences and relationships within the family unit, one of these roles often seems to dominate.

The formal role of grandparent is associated with set duties and obligations such as sending gifts on birthdays to grandchildren. Grandparents may not be involved in their grandchildren's lives in a direct day-by-day function. The distant figure is someone who is not consistent and has little contact with his or her grandchildren. The surrogate parent role is one who usually by necessity has taken over the emotional, social, and economic well-being of a grandchild (children). The fun-seeking role is reflected by grandparents who enjoy spending time with their grandchildren, taking them to places, and generally entertaining the child, grandparents who usually do not take on added responsibilities such as supervising chores or homework. Finally, the reservoir of family wisdom role is demonstrated by a grandparent who can be consulted by members of the family over matters of important decision making. This role can also be demonstrated if the grandparent is assigned the role by the grandchildren's parents. Two of Neugarten and Weinstein's (1964) identified roles that seem to most dramatically affect family decision making and dynamics are the surrogate parent role and the reservoir of family wisdom. Each of these roles directly encourages grandparents to remain active within the family constellation.

The role of grandparents in single-family homes has been researched primarily through the lens of poverty and race. In 1980, African American married couples with children represented 48 percent and households headed by single females represented 49 percent of all households. The number of households with a single female head of household increased in percentage between 1980 to 1990 (Billingsley, 1990). According to the U.S. Census Bureau, in 2007 there were 9,643,157 single female-headed households with one or more children under the age of 18 living in the home, or approximately 69 percent of all female headed households (14,043,938) (Kreider & Elliott, 2009). Multigenerational households and extended families have served as an economic safety net, especially for lower-economic status persons of color. Living in a three-generation household has allowed members to participate in a mutual exchange of goods and services with members of their extended families (Mitchell & Register, 1984). Grandparents play a key role in these families.

The Multigenerational Family: Affecting and Being Affected

The concept of the nuclear heterosexual family (parents and children) living together until the child (children) leaves home to pursue higher education or a full-time job, with grandparents occupying a secondary, separated role of child rearing is a reality for a large portion of the population in the United States, a reality often based on economic realities and cultural norms. However, even in these family constellations where the observer might see this as traditional and normal, there are multigenerations that affect and are affected by the family. There may be older neighbors who live down the street who perform caregiving duties from time to time. There may be aunts or uncles who are instrumental in providing emotional or financial support to the children or the family as a whole. These are in addition to grandparent involvement, whether the grandparent resides inside the home or elsewhere.

Additionally, intergenerational types of support can come in many forms: not just grandparents or adults of an older age, parents, and children or grandchildren, but also an adult child asking his or her parents for help with a down payment on a house or to return home to live until he or she is financially ready to leave and live on his or her own. Researchers Norris and Tindale (1994) identify this as an example of the concepts of ongoing negotiation of reciprocity and attachment relations. The basic concepts are that there are many single exchanges that take place within close family relationships (often financially based). The perception is that these interactions at any given time may appear to be inequitable, but over the life cycle of a multigenerational family balance is often achieved.

A number of challenges and societal barriers exist that need to be addressed if individuals of multigenerational families are to be given a fair chance to contribute and succeed in society. For grandparents performing a parental role for grandchildren, the development of affordable legal help is needed in order to obtain guardianship or custody, and in turn to access health insurance and legally enroll children in school. Many school-related policies and procedures are geared toward two-generational families and often present obstacles for the head of the household who is not a biological parent. This can manifest itself with problems accessing school records or trying to enroll the child in school without proof of legal custody or guardianship. The same holds true for the health and mental health systems where, without parental knowledge or consent, relatives have difficulty accessing care; it is also very difficult for nonparent caregivers to include children on their private health insurance policies.

Another area of concern is housing: if a family takes on the responsibility for an older relative, the home may not be suitable (that is, might not have handicapped-accessible stairs and bathrooms). Additionally, the family may struggle with how to adequately care for their senior family member. Perhaps the biggest concern of all is the amount of stress related to the caregiving of both children and older adults. Likewise, if a grandparent(s) is living in a retirement community, there may be policies and regulations regarding children living in the community, too. This can present a challenge for the grandparents in that this is their home and their community of support yet they are in a situation where they need or want to care for grandchildren who are not able to be cared for by a parent.

Recent research has examined the implications for grandchildren being raised by grandparents. Smith and Palmieri (2007) found that custodial grandchildren of both genders are at greater risk of psychological difficulties than are children in the general population. Their results were congruent with those of many other studies showing that, among children in kinship care (living with a relative not one's parent), boys experience greater behavioral issues and less prosocial behavior compared to girls. Therefore, helpers and educators who have a heightened understanding of the issues facing intergenerational families of this type can provide environmental support to assist the development of individuals in society.

STRESSFUL SITUATIONS WITHIN THE MULTIGENERATIONAL FAMILY

Grandparent as Parent   Life, let alone family life, encounters stressors. However, there are some specific situations within the multigenerational family that are especially stressful. As has been indicated in this chapter, grandparents performing the role of primary caregiver to their grandchildren have become a not uncommon family constellation in society today. With this situation comes emotional, physical, and economic effects that may create stress for the individuals in the family as well as for the family as an entity.

Adults who take on this role may also be dealing emotionally with the issues of their child (children) who is not able to care for his or her children. The situation may be unavoidable due to the biological parent having abandoned his or her child (children) and therefore grandparents needing to step in and provide that continuity of care. Historically and currently, society emphasizes ancestral ties as being important relative to the care of offspring and maintenance of status. This may play a role in grandparents feeling a sense of obligation.

The dynamics between the grandparent and his or her child may create a strain on the relationship between the grandparent and his or her grandchild, as well as the grandchild's relationship with his or her biological parent. These emotional dimensions affect each person in the family and the individual relationships are affected by the other relationships within the family. Therefore, considering the effect of grandparent caregiving from both within the relationship and outside the relationship is important; it is also important to mention how this relationship may affect other family and community relationships.

The dynamics between grandparent and child, grandparent and grandchild, as well as parent and child not only presents emotional issues, but also physical and financial issues. Depending on the age of the grandparents there may be a higher potential for physical ailments relative to health concerns. Financial concerns occur: the grandparent may have already retired and be living on a fixed income, or the need to care for grandchildren may postpone plans for retirement in order to manage the financial needs of a family with young children.

The Sandwich Generation   According to a Pew Research Center report (Cohn, 2008), approximately half of Americans in 2005 between the age of forty and sixty were caring for one or both of their parents while also raising a child (children) under the age of eighteen. In fact, some researchers project that approximately 20 million Americans comprise what is referred to as the sandwich generation.

There are unique needs and impacts in this family unit. Balancing the emotions that arise as one realizes his or her parent(s) is becoming dependent and no longer being the independent grown-up an adult child always looked to for assistance (i.e., no longer able to easily make decisions, handle his or her health needs, possibly needing help with his or her hygiene, who is possibly deteriorating) with the constant learning process and associated emotions of parenting a young child who looks at a parent the way the parent always looked at his or her own parent is not an easy task. Time and attention demands are stretched even more when more than one child is making separate demands. The role conflict (an incompatibility between behavior expectations that are associated with one or more positions an individual holds) or role strain (an incompatibility between behavioral expectations that are a part of a particular position an individual holds) that occurs can at times become overwhelming.

Another concept that provides some light on the stress that can occur for sandwich generation adults is role discontinuity. The inconsistency between the role(s) with which an adult has become accustomed and the role(s) that is new creates a lot of unknowns. There is no preparation for becoming the caregiver for a child nor is there preparation for taking care of an aging parent. Finally, there is no preparation for doing these at the same time. There are books and classes regarding some of the physical care aspects (i.e., changing a diaper, lifting an adult from a bed to a potty chair), but nothing really prepares a person for the emotions that will accompany these physical activities. Feelings of confusion and inadequacy could be a very normal outcome to finding oneself performing these roles.

Health-care needs of an aging parent can become quite challenging for any caregiver. This would not be any different for an adult child giving care to his or her parent(s). Lifting, moving, additional cleaning, additional cooking, additional transporting, and so on can all work on one's physical agility. If not prepared or if one does not have the time to still take care of one's self, these tasks can become increasingly stressful. Additionally, they themselves may have health-care needs that the physical demands of caring for their parents and children may put at risk. If and when aging parents fall into a failing health pattern, adult children respond to the threat of attachment by assisting them in a process that reflects and is consistent with a life-span conception of reciprocity (Bond, Harvey, & Greenwood, 1991). While the individual or family, or both, recognizes the stress of the caregiving role, negative feelings that emerge may coexist with the positive dimensions of attachment built over time.

Many families choose to care for their aging parents in their home due the costs of elder care as well as cultural norms within their family. Although the costs of assisted care and nursing home facilities are quite high, the costs of caring for another person in one's home are also high. Accommodations within the home may have to be made not just of movement of one person in the house to another location to make room for the aging parents, but also other accommodations: handrails in the bathtub, a new addition on the house to provide more space, or perhaps wider doorways for a wheelchair or walker. These costs combined with the additional food, electricity, heating gas, and wear and tear on the family car and other ancillary financial needs can accumulate and cause additional strain on a family.

Children, Adolescents, and Teens   Any transition can create stress in an individual's life. Difficult transitions to a new situation can trigger emotional challenges for the child and caregiver. A few studies have attempted to measure developmental issues of children raised in a multigenerational home as compared with children raised in other types of households.

A national educational longitudinal study (Deleire & Kalil, 2002) investigated the outcomes for three cohort groups: adolescents (eighth graders) (1) living with single mothers, (2) living with single mothers in a multigenerational home, and (3) living in a home with their married parents. Outcome measures included high school graduation, college attendance, sexual activity, and self-reported substance abuse. Research findings were that teenagers living in single head of household home were less likely to graduate from high school, more likely to be involved in sexual activity, more likely to drink and smoke, and less likely to attend college. Those results did not surprise the researchers. What they were surprised by were the data from teenagers living with a single mother (never married) where at least one grandparent also resided in a multigenerational home: these teens on all four measures had developmental outcomes equal to or better than those from teenagers in married family homes.

Several other studies found similar results. Aquilino (1996) examined living arrangements of single mothers and developmental outcomes for their teenagers. This researcher found that among children born to single mothers, those prior to age fifteen who lived with their parent and at least one coresident grandparent had overall higher educational attainment than children who lived only with a single parent for their entire childhood.

Cicirelli (1983) found that attachment and accompanied feelings did in fact promote caregiving by adult children; if, on the other hand, only feelings of obligation were present it was far more likely that the adult child would not participate in the caregiving role. "Fostering attachments might well prove more productive in encouraging children to provide help to ailing parents" (p. 96).

These findings suggest that children can grow up in multigenerational homes and feel securely attached and not have any specific developmental-related hardships as a result of their home living situation. Some have suggested that whereas multigenerational homes face many obstacles, they can also serve as unique support to its members. As the typical family constellation changes, it would be wise for individuals within institutional systems to be aware of the growing trend (although not new) of a household that consists of at least three generations of family members, and be aware of barriers to their full inclusion and successful functioning in our communities.

ENHANCING MULTIGENERATIONAL FAMILY HEALTH

Fisher and Sprenkle (1978) identified several functional criteria for a healthy family: that family members are able to express themselves openly without fear of judgment, with the belief that their opinions will be taken seriously, and that family members will be able to negotiate and make changes when necessary. According to Ebert (1978), a key quality of a healthy family is that the family provides members with diverse opportunities for growth. The following have been identified as criteria that depict a healthy functioning family:

- *Nonadversarial problem solving.* The family can come to a joint decision without much friction.

- *Cooperation.* Members share daily responsibilities around the home.

- *Survival and safety needs are met.* Needs such as shelter, clothing, food, and some degree of economic security so the family is not always thinking about where their basic needs will be coming from.

- *Sharing feelings.* A nonjudgmental forum exists for members to express themselves.

- *Acceptance of individual differences.* A sense of individuality and positive self-esteem for each family member is fostered and encouraged.

- *Highly developed sense of caring.* In all matters that affect the family and family interactions, members demonstrate that they care for other members of the family.

- *Overall philosophy.* A set of implicit values common to all family members helps guide the family.

- *Sense of humor.* Members have the ability to laugh at themselves and with others in the family.

These authors have witnessed that families who possess the majority of these traits most of the time do not usually end up in therapy. Therefore, it is proposed that this could be seen as a model for which to engage as a starting point with troubled families.

An Eclectic Approach

A number of assessment strategies are available that could benefit families and individual members who come from family constructs that have been deconstructed and then reconstructed in a new configuration. Regardless of the strategies employed, it is important to establish the goal for intervention while also keeping in mind the needs of the individuals and the family unit. When implementing an eclectic approach inclusivity is important as is moving the practitioner's attention from possible stereotypes or rigid paradigms. Instead, it is important to rely on an awareness of stereotypes of the multigenerational family and knowledge of extant paradigms to explore possibilities with the family.

A starting point might be to explore the preconceived characteristics the helper associates with individuals in a multigenerational family. How one perceives the aging adult and assumptions about how family members would and should interact with their older family members could affect the work with a family. When meeting with the family, exploring this same area might be of assistance: what they do and what they believe is normal may or may not fit together. A topic of debate in society has long been whether or not family should care for aging relatives in their home or by arranging for their care through a facility. Those providing support to multigenerational families might want to explore with the family their views on this topic as well as do some self-reflection of their own. There may be an assumption that if an individual is receiving care in the latter years of his or her life at a facility, the children and grandchildren are not directly involved in their care. This may not be the situation at all and there may be a myriad of reasons as to why a facility was chosen over the family home.

An inventory of family assessment paradigms would be important when choosing what might be most helpful given the presenting issues of the multigenerational family. Importance should be placed on exploring underlying assumptions of these modalities that may need adaptation in order to best support individuals in a multigenerational family. Below is a brief overview of family focused assessment approaches. Some approaches are age specific and should only be used with the direction of a professional human services practitioner. Several are geared toward children who are dealing with family changes.

Biblio-counseling.   Biblio-counseling (Hynes & Hynes-Berry, 1986) has a child select a book that reflects his or her specific situation and challenges. The book should encourage the child's imagination and creativity, and also engage cognitive, affective, and sensory systems. Having the child think about the story and his or her feelings and reaction to the characters' dilemmas within the context of the story may lead to real-life similarities that leads to discussion of feelings as well as practical solutions to a given set of challenges.

Ecomaps.   Ecomaps are diagrams that show a family or individual within a broader societal context. They demonstrate the current resources and support systems in place that are needed to maintain specific relationships. It is essentially a diagram of the social world with the family genogram in the center and other important institutions and people depicted as how they relate to the family system. This tool can be useful in understanding how the family is affected and affected by (premise four of the model presented in chapters 1 and 3 of this text) other systems in society (i.e., school, church, the neighborhood or community at large, etc.).

Genograms.   According to Carter and McGoldrick (2005), genograms are an important assessment tool for organizing family patterns over three more generations. This should not to be used as just a one-session task, but rather a thorough examination of family dynamics over a period of time. The genogram is simply a summary graphic of detailed information gathered through interviews concerning family relationships and dynamics. It charts such things as births, marriages, divorces, and deaths over several generations in an attempt to understand cultural background as well as individual tendencies that are influenced by family patterns. A major question for the human services practitioner can be, What is this family's capacity to adapt to changes and to deal with issues that present?

Kinetic family drawing.   In kinetic family drawing (Burns & Kaufman, 1970), children draw a picture of everyone in their family doing something. After the drawing is completed a sample list of questions would be, "What is the person thinking?, What is this person feeling?, What do you like about this person?, What don't you like about this person?, How does this person get along with others?, What will happen to this person in the future?, What would you like to change about this family?" These questions, along with a set of interpreting criteria, help to assess the needs of the child.

Storytelling.   According to Lankton and Lankton (1989), two forms of stories are used: those designed to help express and resolve emotions, and those designed to change behavior. Through a creative process of making up a story, the child is guided to develop a story that involves some kind of emotion, such as sadness, confusion, love, or anger. Resolution of a conflict in some detail and any changes in feelings or behavior of the main character is a key aspect of storytelling.

The aforementioned strategies can help identify strengths and challenges experienced by the multigenerational family constellation. Although these strategies may not exactly mirror the ideal family types that were envisioned when they were constructed, that does not diminish their utility with multidimensional family contexts today. It is the practitioner's responsibility to assess the practicality and strengths of these strategies within diverse contexts prior to implementing them.

After identifying areas of strength and areas that may need added support for the multigenerational family to enhance its growth and development, many practitioners move to intervention strategies. There are a number of intervention strategies that have been applied to various multigenerational family types. Some of these are highlighted in the subsequent discussion.

A multimodal, home-based intervention.   This intervention is designed to assist the grandparent who is raising grandchildren to improve the grandchildren's physical and mental health, reduce psychological stress, and strengthen resources and social support was examined in 2001 (Deleire & Kalil, 2002). The study reported that, overall, participants demonstrated decreased psychological distress scores, increased social support scores, and improved mental health scores after receiving the home-based intervention. The study was also highlighted that participants experienced improvement in the level of public benefit received and in their legal relationships with their grandchildren.

Bowenian family therapy. This therapy is unique in that only one client needs to participate in the family counseling process. Bowen viewed family challenges in a multigenerational context, connected in various ways through successive generations. These connections involve learned behavior, emotional communications, and basic needs. Bowen believed that unresolved attachment to one's family of origin prevents one from what he termed "differentiation of self." His focus was for clients to understand and strive for the balance of two forces, individuality and togetherness. There are eight interlocking concepts to Bowen's theory of family therapy (Bowen, 1993; Gilbert, 2006; Kerr & Bowen, 1988; Kerr & Sager, 2003), which assist the practitioner in intervention with the multigenerational family.

1. Differentiation of self is being able to relate emotionally to others and at the same time being able to free oneself from one's family of origin. Differentiation of self is the ability to separate feeling and thinking from what others are feeling and coming to rational conclusions.

2. Triangles are the basic units within the family construct. The concept of a dyad is a social group consisting of two persons. In Bowen's theory, when stressed under some form of dispute, the dyad needs a third party to decrease anxiety or emotionality. Triangulation in effect freezes the system in place. The lower the adaptive functioning of the participants, the more likely the system will triangulate. The person who is most vulnerable in this system will be the family member most likely to get pulled (triangulated) into some other dyad.

3. Nuclear family emotional processes are the emotional patterns and ways of engaging each other that are passed on to each successive generation. Some reactions to this family process could include

   (a) projection of problems onto offspring,

   (b) reactive emotional distance,

   (c) overt conflict, and

   (d) emotional dysfunction in one parent.

4. Family projection processes and family emotional processes are taught and passed along from one generation to the next, often leaving them struggling with their own differentiation because it is inadequate and they have learned no other way of reacting or coping to life's demands. These processes will inevitably affect their own interactions with their children, spouse, and parents.

5. Multigenerational transmission processes are ways in which families emit and transfer their emotional processes that have been maintained for at least three generations.

6. Sibling position projects what the roles of family members are and the type of interaction expected based on birth order of siblings.

7. Emotional cutoff is the separation by either physical or emotional distance from the family of origin where the person may feel free from the influence of their family, but who, according to Bowen, is destined to repeat the same patterns he or she has rejected in attempting to build new relationships.

8. Societal emotional process is the pattern or belief about others who are defined by race, sexual orientation, class, or gender, and the potential impact of these patterns or beliefs on his or her family.

According to Bowen, optimal development occurs when members are differentiated, with low stress or anxiety, and when parents have supportive contact with their families of origin.

Minuchin.   Minuchin (1974) developed the structural family theory, which emphasizes the structural aspects of how the family is organized with respect to boundaries, alliances, and power. Conflict and subsequent adjustments are conceptualized in terms of the adaptation of family members' external and internal stressors. An important concept is the idea of family boundaries, established and maintained through intrafamilial behavior and communication. This provides another opportunity to explore how the family affects and is affected by relationships at various levels. Perception of the multigenerational family as nonstatic and as a unit that is constantly changing just as people change throughout their life spans is also enhanced through Minuchin's approach. Behavior and communication patterns define the boundaries that separate individuals within the family, providing autonomy and privacy, as well as messages of nurturing and intimacy. According to Minuchin, family disputes and dysfunction often arise from boundary disputes. The focus of this intervention is on structural changes within the family before an individual's symptoms can be reduced.

This structural family therapy approach is very dynamic and has been seen as very helpful when providing family counseling or therapy to the entire family system (Lynch & Lynch, 2000; Minuchin, 1974; Minuchin & Fishman, 1981). Specific interventions employed through a Minuchin approach include the following:

- *The family floor plan.* Explores the roles of family members and how they relate and interrelate with one another. The importance of space and one's perceived territory, levels of comfort between members, space accommodations, and rules can be discussed. This can help discern operating family triangles and subsystems.

- *Tracking.* The clinician takes careful notes concerning family stories and sequence of events. What has taken place in order for the current system to have emerged?

- *Family sculpting.* The clinician asks family members to physically arrange the family regarding a particular situation. What would the family look like? Who would be facing whom, and so on? This can help those who are nonverbal to communicate thoughts and feelings about the family.

- *Family photos.* Go through a family album together and watch for both nonverbal and verbal responses to the various photos. Practitioners can more clearly see structure, communication patterns, roles, and family relationships using this technique.

- *The empty chair.* A member of the family gets the chance to speak to someone who is not physically present and can also speak for that missing person and respond as he or she might have.

- *Family council meetings.* These are organized times at home where the family is directed to meet and share information and feelings, or to plan events. This may help provide structure for the family, facilitate better communication, and encourage participation. Contracting with teenagers for discussing rules, expectations, and privileges is a good example of how this assigned time can be useful.

- *Strategic alliances.* These involve meeting with one family member as a supportive means of helping that person change. This technique attempts to disrupt a family-wide behavioral pattern. If one part of the family system changes, it forces others in the family to behave differently.

- *Prescribing indecision.* Paradoxical methods can be used when straightforward intervention fails. A directive is given to family not to rush into a decision or to try in any way to help itself through its problems at this point.

- *Putting the client in control of the symptoms.* The practitioner attempts to place control into the hands of an individual member. Specific directives are given such as to continue the symptoms of depression or anxiety; as the client follows the paradoxical directive a sense of control over the symptoms can allow for subsequent changes to take place.

Bowenian family therapy and Minuchin's structural family therapy are family-centered approaches that attempt to incorporate many of the facets that are being addressed in this text. Naturally, training and supervision are important when a human service practitioner is attempting to use these therapeutic intervention modalities.

Illustration of the Eclectic Approach

It is not easy for the human service practitioner to embrace an eclectic approach while approaching the family as being nonstatic, deconstruct stereotypes, and understand the many dimensions by which the family is affected as well as affecting. A human service practitioner might feel this is an insurmountable task because there are so many modalities within family therapy to consider, and because he or she must now challenge those paradigms from such an inclusive perspective. However, it might be useful to illustrate the use of this approach with the aid of a vignette.

While consulting for a school social work program housed in a Title 1 grade school one of the authors had the opportunity to review and advise how to best handle this school based family challenge situation. The following case study will be viewed through the four premises that are key elements in the eclectic approach within the context of diverse family constellations, specifically multigenerational families.

Case Study: Rodrigo (age ten)

Rodrigo is a ten-year-old fifth grader at a low-income (Title 1) grade school. His teacher and principal referred him to the school human services practitioner after two incidents of aggression aimed at younger students.

Recently, he picked up and physically placed a second grade boy into a school trash can at the end of the school day. Rodrigo was given a three-day suspension for this incident. Prior to this latest occurrence, he had been suspended for five days for beating up a third grade boy for no apparent reason. The unprovoked attack happened as the two boys were walking home from school; the younger boy received a black eye and a bloody lip.

Rodrigo is Latino and lives with his mother, father, elderly grandmother, and two older male siblings ages twelve and fourteen. Both parents work outside the home; his mother works at a local restaurant and his father works in the construction industry. When not in school Rodrigo reports to just hanging out with his brothers in their neighborhood. His older brother claims to be a Norte gang member. During the first two months of school Rodrigo has been truant five days. However, prior to this academic year his attendance had been fairly good.

Rodrigo is failing two of his classes: math and language arts. According to teachers, he tends to isolate himself among peers his own age, gravitating toward older students. In a recent parent–principal conference, Rodrigo's parents remarked that they were not sure how to help their son.

The first stage in working with Rodrigo and his family would be an intrapersonal assessment, where a review of his biological, emotional, cognitive, and mental needs is evaluated. The interpersonal component of this assessment would evaluate relationships he has within the family as well as with his peers, and to look at how he sees himself as relating to others. Who influences him? Who does he want to emulate? Because he tends toward association with older peers, how much influence do his older brothers have over him? An exploration of his identity as a male approaching adolescence and as a Latino male would be important because it relates to personal goals and wants. What adults in his life does Rodrigo respect and trust? Also of interest are how he relates to adults in and outside the family and what kind of relationship and sphere of influence his grandmother may have with him.

According to Guadalupe and Welkley in this text (chapter 4), the goal of eclectic approaches is to honor the power of inclusiveness. As a result, the practitioner must identify his or her preconceived ideas relative to working with a multigenerational Latino family. Many questions come to mind when attempting to meet the challenges of these families:

- Are the family dynamics and structure the same as traditional two generational families?

- What role does the grandparent play in deciding and enforcing family rules and structure?

- Do parents defer any of their parental role to the grandparent?

- Do the children in the family respect the rules and decisions of both parents?

- In what way is respect shown to the grandmother living in the home?

All of these elements would assist the human services practitioner to understand and assess the presenting interpersonal issues.

When critically examining Rodrigo's social–cultural–political–environmental realm the practitioner should gain as much information as possible. After visiting the home, the human services practitioner observed that, when at home with his parents or grandmother, Rodrigo seems to be responsive and respectful and generally does what he is told to do by the adults in the home. The culture of this home appears to be loving and nurturing. These characteristics in the home would be strengths that support Rodrigo's development as a young male.

Upon learning that Rodrigo's oldest sibling is beginning to challenge authority both at school and at home, it becomes apparent that testing boundaries is occurring within the home. His brothers tease Rodrigo, because he is the youngest; there is a general sense that they can pick on their younger brother but they will not allow anyone else to disrespect him. Boundaries seem a bit permeable between the siblings with stronger boundaries in place regarding those outside the family. An area to explore more directly with Rodrigo is his perception of these relationships and how he feels about the messages this provides regarding his place and role within the family and the community at large.

Although he is fairly cooperative at home, Rodrigo's behavior at school has begun to worry his parents. The fighting is one example and the unwillingness to bring books home or to get excited about school activities also has the adults in his life concerned. The influence the older peers he associates with, along with the influence of his brothers, may undermine the attempts parents have made to emphasize achieving at school and getting along with others. These various influences need further exploration with Rodrigo.

At the same time, Rodrigo is at a stage of development where it is normal to test the boundaries of the various institutions with which he finds himself: family, school, and community groups. So although there may be some transitions, influences, or other issues occurring that would explain Rodrigo's change in behavior, a large part of it may be normal lifecycle development. Ascertaining the knowledge that his parents and grandmother have regarding the normalcy of some of this behavior could provide a coping mechanism not only relative to Rodrigo, but also relative to his older siblings.

Consideration of nonordinary reality for this family would have the human services practitioner attempt to understand Rodrigo's world, what motivates him, what is important to him, and how he makes decisions. Trends imply that Latino families are generally observing Catholics; whether or not they attend mass each week, the traditions and faith associated with Catholicism are very important to their approach to life and major life decisions. Exploring how this does or does not have importance for Rodrigo as well as for his family unit would be an important area of discovery. Another way to gain insight into Rodrigo's nonordinary reality is identifying what rituals and celebrations he believes are important and why. Exploring with him where he seeks guidance and support when feeling like he has none or does not know the best decision to make would also provide awareness.

As the human services practitioner applies the nonstatic living lens, consideration of how the family itself sees its constellation would be important. Stereotypically, society anticipates that Latino family constellations will very likely include an aging parent(s)—that is, a grandparent(s)—living in the home. However, at this point it is not known if the grandmother living in the home is a recent transition for the family or if this is a normal family constellation for them. Recognizing the nonstatic quality of the multigenerational family in this case might mean the human service practitioner would inquire about the grandparent(s) and what is or was their role in the family.

Rodrigo appears to have several alliances: his family of origin, his school family, and his connection with extended family members, especially his grandmother, just to name a few. Each of these entities may have expectations about his conduct at school, in the community, and at home. They all have an impact on this client. This leads to the idea of multiple memberships where it appears that Rodrigo has fragmented his family since he relates very differently to them separately. For example, from every indication, how he acts when adult family members are present is in marked contrast to his behavior when he is hanging out with his brothers or older peers. At one time the role he played for his family as youngest male was to demonstrate the good son role and convince all that he could be left alone because he was not going to get into any trouble. By performing this role, his parents could focus their time on the more problematic older siblings.

Another arena to be explored here are Rodrigo's relationships with teachers and peers at school. In what ways do his teachers and peers connect with him as family and in what ways do they connect to his family of origin?

The element of being and becoming at the early stages of self-identity; Rodrigo has had an impact on Rodrigo's family unit and vice versa. The fact that his mother works long hours and his dad is often not at home because of taking construction jobs long distances from home may indicate that many of the day-to-day caregiving duties falls to others. How many of these are performed by the grandmother, the older siblings, or neighbors, and the ways in which Rodrigo has related and currently relates to these different relationships may shed some light on Rodrigo's support system. Much of the day-to-day decision making is currently left to the elderly grandmother who has previously been capable of affecting Rodrigo's behavior; the older both she and he become and the more he is influenced by others in his environment, the more likely it is that this task may have become too large for the grandmother.

During preadolescence and adolescence youth often seek ways to feel control of their environment. It is not always easy to internalize an understanding and feeling that one's being at this stage is both affecting and being affected by what is happening all around. Rodrigo may be demonstrating the behavior that has currently come to the surface due to feeling that he is primarily affected by all that is going on around him. It would be important for Rodrigo to understand that, although he has been affected by each of these areas, he is at the same time having an impact on (or affecting) the lives and systems of those around him. Empowering him to see ways in which he has impact might help him consider his behavior differently. Another possibility might be that he may believe he has power to affect things at school and not at home, which would explain the behavioral differences in these environments. Assisting his family to acknowledge how family members' actions and words affect and are affected by Rodrigo is another mechanism by which to support this ten-year-old young man.

Summary

The trend throughout history is that multigenerational families tend to come together during difficult economic times. The current downturn in the economy with higher unemployment rates, and especially the high foreclosure rate, will most likely increase the number of multigenerational families living under one roof in the near future. Those families who cannot afford to place an elderly adult into a retirement home or those parents who cannot afford to raise their children without assistance and decide to move in with a parent for financial help are likely to become a part of this growing segment of our population: those raised in multigenerational homes. However, it is important to keep in mind that there have been more multigenerational families in society than one would expect; therefore, they have been an overlooked family constellation type or have been placed into other formulations based on their particular circumstances. Finally, we must not forget that for many the multigenerational family is not an outcome of circumstances, but a family choice regarding the formulation of family.

As related in this chapter there are advantages and disadvantages of having at least three generations of a family living together that goes beyond the obvious financial realities. As a culture we need to recognize and support all the alternatives to the accepted notions of the traditional nuclear family; in so doing we can normalize a person's reality and avoid certain types of challenges that can evolve from being seen as not coming from a normal family unit. A number of assessment and intervention strategies were briefly described but the eclectic approach as proposed throughout this text takes into account without judgment the differences between family constellations in a way that validates each person's diverse experience of how he or she relates to family. This text therefore is a helpful guide to the family practitioner.

Questions to Promote Critical Analysis

• In what ways have you encountered multigenerational families (personally or professionally)? In light of your experience, what are your preconceived ideas or assumptions about the contexts in which multigenerational families exist?

• In reference to the case study, what additional multiple family memberships might you identify?

• How would you apply the concept of being and becoming to assist Rodrigo in his growth and development?

• What assessment and intervention strategies would you employ with Rodrigo's multigenerational family and how would you adapt them to embrace an eclectic approach to practice?

References

Aquilino, W. S. (1996). The lifecourse of children born to unmarried mothers: Childhood living arrangements and young adult outcomes. *Journal of Marriage and Family, 58,* 293–310.

Billingsley, A. (1990). Understanding African American family diversity. In J. Dewart (Ed.), *The state of black America 1990* (pp. 85–108). New York: National Urban League.

Bond, J. B., Jr., Harvey, C. D., & Greenwood, L. J. (1991). Support to older parents in rural Mennonite and Non-Mennonite setting. In J. Norris & J. Tindale (Eds.), *Among generations: The cycle of adult relationships.* New York: Freeman.

Bowen, M. (1993). *Family therapy in clinical practice.* Lanham, MD: Jason Aronson.

Burns, R., & Kaufman, S. (1970). *Kinetic family drawings (K-F-D) An introduction to understand children through kinetic drawings.* New York: Brunner/Mazel.

Carlson, A. (2005). *Fractured generations*. Piscataway, NJ: Transaction.

Carter, B., & McGoldrick, M. (2005). *The expanded family life cycle: Individual, family and social perspectives* (3rd ed.). New York: Allyn & Bacon.

Cherlin, A., & Furstenburg, F., Jr. (1986). Grandparents and family crisis. *Generations, 10*(4), 26–28.

Cicirelli, V. G. (1983). Adult children's attachment and helping behavior to elderly parents: A path model. *Journal of Marriage and the Family, 45*, 815–824.

Cohn, D. (2008, June 25). *Baby boomers: The gloomiest generation*. Washington, DC: Pew Social and Demographic Trends Project, Pew Research Center.

Deleire, T., & Kalil, A. (2002). Good things come in threes: Single parent multigenerational family structure and adolescent adjustment. *Demography, 39*(2), 393–413.

Dolgon, C., & Baker, C. (2011). *Social problems: A service learning approach*. Thousand Oaks, CA: Pine Forge Press.

Ebert, B. (1978). The healthy family. *Journal of Family Therapy, 5*, 227–232.

Ferguson, N., & Gillian, D. (2004). *Grandparenting in divorced families*. Bristol, UK: University of Bristol, The Policy Press.

Fisher, B. L., & Sprenkle, D. H. (1978). Therapist's perception of healthy family functioning. *International Journal of Family Counseling, 6*, 9–18.

Gilbert, R. (2006). *The eight concepts of Bowen theory*. Falls Church, VA: Leading Systems Press.

Hynes A., & Hynes-Berry, M. (1986). *Biblio-therapy: The interactive process. A handbook*. New York: Westview Press.

Kerr, M. E., & Bowen, M. (1988). *Family evaluation*. New York: W. W. Norton.

Kerr, M. E., & Sager, R. R. (2003). *One family's story: A primer on Bowen theory*. Washington, DC: Bowen Center for the Study of the Family.

Kornhaber, A. (2004). *The grandparent solution*. San Francisco: Jossey-Bass.

Kreider, R. M., & Elliott, D. B. (2009, September). *America's families and living arrangements: 2007*. Washington, DC: U.S. Department of Commerce, U.S. Census Bureau.

Lankton, C. H., & Lankton, S. R. (1989). *Tales of enchantment: Goal-oriented metaphors for adults and children in therapy*. New York: Brunner/Mazel.

Lynch, B., & Lynch, J. E. (2000). *Principles and practices of structural family therapy*. Gouldsboro, ME: The Gestalt Journal Press.

Minuchin, S. (1974). *Families and family therapy*. Cambridge, MA: Harvard University Press.

Minuchin, S., & Fishman, H. (1981). *Techniques of family therapy*. Cambridge, MA: Harvard University Press.

Mitchell, J., & Register, J. (1984). An exploration of family interaction with the elderly by race and socioeconomic status and residence. *The Gerontologist, 24*, 48–54.

Neugarten, B. L., & Weinstein, K. K. (1964). The changing American grandparent. *Journal of Marriage and the Family, 26*, 199–204.

Norris, J. E., & Tindale, J. A. (1994). *Among generations: The cycle of adult relationships*. New York: Freeman.

Pew Research Center. (2010, March). *The return of the multi-generational family household*. Pew Social Trends Staff. Retrieved from http://pewsocialtrends .org/2010/03/18/the-return-of-the-multi-generational-family-household/.

Ross, S. (2006). *American families past and present: Social perspectives on transformation.* Piscataway, NJ: Rutgers University Press.

Ruggles, S., Sobek, M., Flood, S., King, M., Schroeder, M., & Vick, R. (1997). *Integrated public use micro-data series: Version 2.0,* Minneapolis: Historical Census Projects. Minneapolis: University of Minnesota.

Smith, G., & Palmieri, P. (2007). Risk of psychological difficulties among children raised by custodial grandparents. *Journal of Psychiatric Services, 58,* 1303–1310.

U.S. Census Bureau. (2000). *Brief: Households and families* (detailed table). Retrieved June 26, 2011, from http://www.census.gov/population/www/cen2000/briefs/phc-t17/index.html.

CHAPTER SEVEN

Single-Parent Family Constellations

Diversity, Complexity, Perception, and Practice

J. Ann Moylan

Consider the fluidity of family structure
and the role that perceptions have.

JAM

The author wishes to thank "Jenna," "Michael," "Ted," and "Brad" for allowing their stories to be told. The case study provides a clear example of the principles inherent to this chapter. Thanks also to friends and esteemed colleagues Kate Allen, Robert Heirendt, and Sue Taylor for their thoughtful contributions. Each one offered a perspective that shaped the content and the tone of this chapter.

According to U.S. Census Bureau data (2007), "The percentage of households headed by single parents showed little variation from 1994 through 2006, at about 9 percent, up from 5 percent in 1970," and "According to *Families and Living Arrangements: 2006*, there were 12.9 million one-parent families in 2006—10.4 million single-mother families and 2.5 million single-father families" (U.S. Census Bureau). But what do we actually know about these families? How much do we rely on evidence and how much do we draw from our own experience? Do we make assumptions about these families based on stereotypes, biases, and so on? As we explore the meaning of the term single-parent family, consider the following brief, spontaneous conversation between the author and a group of young teens.

> Author: I am writing a chapter on single-parent families for a book.
>
> Michael (age 13): I can tell you about single-parent families. They don't have much money to spend on you. Not like if you have two parents.
>
> Author: Hey, that's right. I could ask you about single-parent families. What else can you tell me?
>
> Michael: Not much. I'm not in a single-parent family anymore.
>
> Author: Really! Tell me about that.
>
> Michael: Well, my mother has a boyfriend.
>
> Joseph (age 12): You are still in a single-parent family if they aren't married.
>
> Michael: No, I don't think so.
>
> Jesse (age 12): Well, does her boyfriend take you shopping for stuff?
>
> Michael: Yeah.
>
> Jesse: Well, maybe you're right then.
>
> Author: What about discipline?
>
> Michael: Yeah, he does that too and I don't like it.
>
> Author: I don't think any kids like it.

Notice that for Joseph, it was marital status that mattered in determining single-parent status, while for Jesse it was a question of whether or not the boyfriend was a financial resource. My question, "What about discipline?," indicates that I associate taking an active role in discipline as relevant to parental status. The point I would like to make, however, is that it did not really matter whether Michael's family met our criteria for a single-parent or two-parent family. Michael is the one living in the family and it is his perception, and that of his mother and her partner, that matters most. (Michael later clarified his view saying that it was "kinda like half and half"—his mother's boyfriend "seemed like" a part of his family even though he did not live with them.)

Describing and Defining the Single-Parent Family

If asked what constitutes a single-parent family, one might define it as "a parent raising a child alone, without a partner." But what if the single-parent family constellation is more complex than that definition would imply? What if the term "single parent" includes a very heterogeneous group? How might we begin to understand the make-up of this diverse group?

MARITAL STATUS

A common way to describe or categorize single-parent families focuses on the parent's marital status: divorced, widowed, or single (never married). This categorical approach to describing single-parent families examines the experiences or circumstances that those in a particular category share: perhaps the anger and hurt of those who are single parents as a result of divorce, the grief and sadness of those who are single parents as a result of death of a spouse, or feelings of being judged for those having a child outside of marriage, which may include those never married, not married at the time of birth, cohabitating, same-sex partners who are not married, and so on. Imposing such a categorical structure allows researchers to explore the similarities and differences both between groups and within each group. It also enables those working with families to provide relevant information and appropriate interventions tailored to the specific situation. Parents themselves may find this system of classification useful as they seek the support of others whose experiences may be similar to their own.

A clear example of this approach can be found in *The Complete Single Mother*. Authors Engber and Klungness (1995) explore the question, "By Choice or Circumstance: How Did You Get Here?" (p. vii). The following chapter titles from their book reflect the various answers to that question and the categories in which single mothers are discussed:

- Becoming a Single Mother Through Divorce

- Becoming a Mother Outside of Marriage

- Choosing Motherhood Through Donor Insemination

- Choosing Motherhood Through Adoption

- The Widowed Mother

These are some of the most commonly used categories both in research studies and in books written for parents.

LIVING ARRANGEMENT

Bumpass and Raley (1995) contribute another way of understanding single-parent family constellations by asserting that "definitions of single-parent families must be based on living arrangements rather than on the parents' marital status" (p. 97). This way of viewing single-parent families typically yields three categories: those living alone with their children, those living with their children and a partner, and those living with their children and their parent. Bumpass and Raley explore the difference in experience between those single parents who are cohabiting and those single parents, typically women, who are living with their parents, either having moved in after a relationship ended (whether by death or divorce) or having never left their parents' home. Bumpass and Raley compare these two groups of single parents to those who do not have either a cohabiting partner or their parents participating in the day-to-day family picture. Sugarman (2007 [1998]) uses the term "cohabitants" to describe those who "are single mothers as a legal matter, even though their children are living in two-adult households" (p. 287). Sugarman notes that these cohabitants are a "complicated category, and, in turn, they complicate the data. . . . [I]n many respects these couples resemble married couples. So, many of these households are better described as two-parent, not single-parent families" (p. 290).

CUSTODY ARRANGEMENT

Yet a third way to classify single-parent families is to consider the custody arrangement. Olson, DeFrain, and Skogrand (2008) describe four types of divorced single-parent families: mothers with custody, fathers with custody, split custody, and joint custody. Split custody, which is the most rare of the four types, is an arrangement in which the children are divided between the parents, resulting in each parent having primary responsibility for one or more of the children. Joint custody may include shared physical custody, in which the child regularly spends time with each parent, or shared legal custody in which the child spends most of his or her time with one parent but both parents are involved in the child's life (Olson et al.). Looking at single-parent families in this way allows us to consider gender differences between a single mother with custody and a single father with custody. And because the family types are determined by custody arrangement, rather than marital status, this approach helps us to focus not only on what the parent is experiencing, but also on what the child (children) is experiencing.

Whereas each of these typologies or approaches expands our understanding of the single-parent family, none of these approaches (marital status, living arrangement, custody arrangement) captures what Guadalupe and Welkley mean when they describe the family as a multi-dimensional contextual nonstatic living entity. All three of these approaches imply that the status of single-parent family can be recognized, known, or understood by the family's structure or legal status. On the contrary, for the purposes of this chapter, the author uses a definition of single parent that parallels Anderson's (2004) definition of single mothers: "Anyone who considers herself a single mother is a single mother. She may be divorced, married but separated, never married, caring for a family member's child, a widow, a separated stepmother, or in some circumstances, a married woman. . . . (Some women are married or live with men who abdicate their responsibility to their children or even may be dangerous to them. Some women are married to men who for whatever reason are absent from the home for long periods, such as military duty in another location)" (p. xi).

This focus on the subjective experience or perception is critical to our consideration of single parenting. In addition to restating Anderson's (2004) description to include fathers, this chapter acknowledges that (a) parents can and do move from one constellation to another, experiencing a fluidity of statuses and experiences in an ever-changing social, cultural, political, economic context; and (b) parents may be experiencing more than one constellation at any point in time, or, as Guadalupe and Welkley state in chapter 1, "[W]e are often simultaneously a part of multiple family constellations."

In this chapter the reader will expand his or her understanding of single-parent families by using another lens. Additional categories are offered based on individual and family perception rather than on marital status, household composition, or custody arrangements. It is imperative to acknowledge that the categories proposed in this chapter are not intended as a way to contain any family unit. Families may perceive that they fit more than one category at any point in time, or that they alternate between these categories from one point in time to another, or from one circumstance to another, reflecting what Guadalupe and Welkley refer to in earlier chapters: Family constellations are constantly in a process of being and becoming (chapter 1).

This chapter reviews the traditional concepts, principles, and assumptions associated with single-parent families. It explores what we know about single-parent families within the context of the United States society with a focus on diversity, and challenges the reader to consider nonstereotypical practice skills within an eclectic professional approach, using case examples to individualize practice at the intrapersonal (micro), interpersonal (mezzo), environmental (macro), and nonordinary reality (magna) levels. Of particular significance, this author will be departing from the traditional categorizations often used to describe single-parent families for several reasons: (1) in order to allow for a more in-depth consideration of the diversity within the many single-parent experiences, (2) as a pathway to moving beyond our stereotypes of those families, and (3) as a framework for providing family-centered practice.

One note is in order before beginning this new look at single-parent families. Although we have seen a recent increase in the number of single-father households, and a corresponding increase in research on these families, we still have a body of literature that is predominantly focused on the single mother rather than on the single father. This can be explained to some degree by the demographics of the single-parent population—23 percent of all children live in a household headed by a single mother whereas 5 percent of children live in a household headed by a single father (U.S. Census Bureau, 2005). But when we view the number of single mothers and single fathers (rather than looking at the children per se), we find that single fathers now account for almost 25 percent of all single parents, up from only 10 percent of all single parents in 1970 and 18 percent of all single parents in 2003 (U.S. Census Bureau, 2007). What we know about children and the parents with whom they live will be significantly improved by the 2007 changes to U.S. Census Bureau's Current Population Survey (CPS). Beginning in 2007, the CPS added questions that identified unmarried partners in the household (other than the head of household) and questions that identified the number and type of parents in the household (U.S. Census Bureau, 2008). Unfortunately, this does not negate the fact that to date more research is available on single mothers than on single fathers.

In this chapter the author has included findings from some of the most recent studies on the differences between single-mother families and single-father families, and presents a model for understanding single-parent families without regard to the gender of the parent. This should not be taken to mean that the gender of the parent is unimportant, but rather that the parent's relationship or lack of relationship with another adult is an important—critically important—factor that has so far been overlooked by most models for representing single-parent families and their experiences.

Traditional Conceptions, Principles, and Assumptions

It is not the same thing to be a single parent today as it was even thirty years ago. The shift in demographics, social mores, public attention and public acceptance, have all served to

1. reduce some, though certainly not all, of the stigma associated with being a single parent;

2. increase some supports available to single parents (books, articles, on-line support groups, community-based support groups, etc.); and

3. in some circles, heighten the criticism of single parents based on interpretations of research on the outcomes for children living in single-parent households.

DEMOGRAPHIC CONSIDERATIONS

In recent decades, the percentage of children living with both parents has dropped, but the percentage living with a single parent has increased (see figure 7.1). In 2005, 67 percent of children lived with two parents, 23 percent lived with only their mother, and 5 percent lived with only their father. Another adult was present in the household for about two out of every five children living with a single mother and three out of every five children living with a single father. No parents were in the household for 5 percent of all children. (U.S. Census Bureau, 2005, p. 1)

Considering these data in historical perspective, we note the following trends: In the United States today, based again on 2005 census data, 28 percent of children are living with a single parent. That figure has increased gradually from 12 percent in 1970, 19 percent in 1980, 25 percent in 1990, and 27 percent in 2000 (U.S. Census Bureau, 2005; see figure 7.2).

But a historical perspective does not tell the whole tale. Once race or ethnicity is taken into consideration, we can see how disproportionately single-parent families are distributed in the population (see figure 7.3). "In 2005, about half of black children lived with a single mother. Sixteen percent of non Hispanic white children and 10 percent of Asian children

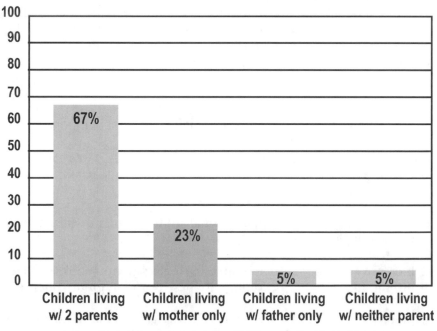

FIGURE 7.1 *Living Arrangements for Children in the United States—*
Source: *U.S. Census Bureau (2005).*

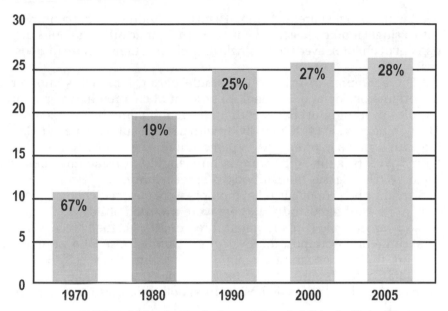

FIGURE 7.2 *Children Living in Single-Parent Households in the United States—*
Source: *U.S. Census Bureau (2005).*

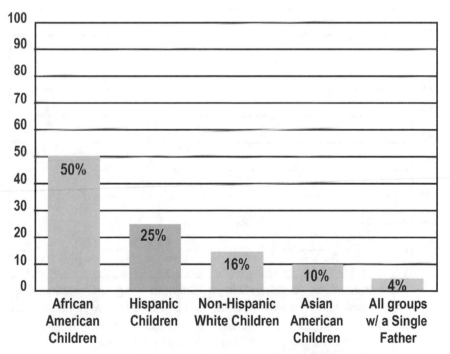

FIGURE 7.3 *Children in Single-Parent Households in the*
*United States by Race or Ethnicity—*Source: *U.S. Census Bureau (2005).*

lived with a single parent. Among Hispanic children, 25 percent lived with a single mother. Regardless of race or Hispanic origin, about 4 or 5 percent of children lived with a single father" (U.S. Census Bureau, 2005, p. 2).

"The economic distribution of single parent families is another important consideration. In 2004, 14 percent of children in two-parent families lived in households with an annual income below $30,000. Thirty-nine percent of children living with a single father, 62 percent living with a single mother, and 59 percent living without either parent (grandparents, aunts, etc.) were in households with incomes below $30,000" (U.S. Census Bureau, 2005, p. 2; see figure 7.4).

Sixty-four percent of custodial mothers were awarded child support, and 40 percent of custodial fathers were awarded child support. Of those awarded child support, about three-quarters actually received at least some of the support that was due: "Among those who were due support, the average [annual] amount received in 2003 was $3,600 for custodial mothers and $2,800 for custodial fathers" (U.S. Census Bureau, 2005, p. 5). These figures are total dollars received per year, not per child!

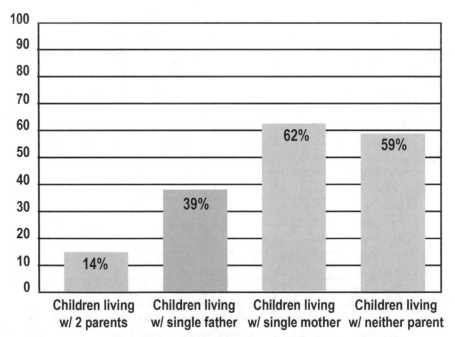

FIGURE 7.4 *Percentage of Children Living in Families With Income Below $30,000*—Source: *U.S. Census Bureau (2005).*

Finally, in sheer numbers, here is what we are talking about: "In 2004, an estimated 14.0 million parents had custody of 21.6 million children whose other parent lived somewhere else, according to the April 2004 supplement to the CPS [Current Population Survey]. Of all custodial parents, 83 percent were mothers. Among all children under age 21 living in families, 27 percent had a parent living somewhere else" (U.S. Census Bureau, 2005, p. 5). The number of children whose parent(s) lived somewhere else is a tremendously high number and a high percentage of our population, and these children and families deserve our attention as a profession and as a nation. As we take a look at some of the research that has been done on the impact of living in a single-parent family, bear in mind that much of the data presented are correlational data, indicating simply that certain factors can be found more prevalently among single-parent families, and does not provide evidence of a causal nature. Also, coming into the twenty-first century, we have a larger body of knowledge based on a modern or scientific model—one that seeks to determine or promote universalities of experience, averages, or norms, often basing these on white, middle-class families and the so-called traditional nuclear family than on a postmodern model—one that places greater emphasis on individual experiences, alternative family forms, and other ways of knowing. This presents a challenge to those who seek not to describe families in general terms, but rather to understand real, individual, unique families with all their particular circumstances, histories, cultures, strengths, challenges, goals, values, and so on. How do we come to understand single-parent families with whom we work so as to best partner with them as they move along their life path?

RISKS AND CHALLENGES

Much research over the past several decades has painted a rather bleak picture of the risks and challenges associated with the single-parent household. Davidson and Moore (1996) state that "Society portrays single-parent families as a root cause of many social problems, including substance abuse, juvenile delinquency, unmarried motherhood, and school failure" (p. 700). Hanson and Sporakowski point out, "As a group, single-parent families have a higher rate of poverty, greater geographical mobility, and a lower level of education for the head of household" (as cited in Davidson & Moore, p. 700). Because single-parent families as a group differ in income, mobility, and educational level from two-parent families, it can be difficult to determine if some of the reported social problems are due to a single-parent family structure or if the differences are reflective of the coexisting risks.

Weinraub, Horvath, and Gringlas state, "Because the child's experience depends on the specific conditions in his or her family, it is difficult to generalize about the effects of being reared in a single-parent family. Many studies suggest that children in single-parent families are at greater risk for developing emotional and academic problems" (as cited in Brooks, 2008, p. 462). Brooks continues, "This should not be surprising, as it is more difficult for one parent to provide as much nurturance, monitoring, and supervision as two parents, who have the additional benefits of greater resources and support from each other" (p. 462). It is these resources, including social and emotional supports, that should be the focus of our work with many single-parent families.

Single-Mother Families   Elaborating on the importance of social support for single mothers, Simons, Beaman, Conger, and Chao state there are greater levels of stress associated with female-headed families because of internalized negative self-images, ideas about the future, and limited social support. Emotional and psychological stress as well as inadequate parenting practices are connected with lack of support (as cited in Davidson & Moore, 1996). Furthermore, Webster-Stratton states, "Compared to married mothers, single-parent mothers report significantly more child-behavior problems and personal stress" (as cited in Davidson & Moore, p. 701). Additionally, Thomson, Hanson, and McLanahan believe that "children usually receive less attention in single-mother families because the single parent [mother] exercises weaker control and makes fewer demands than do married parents" (as cited in Davidson & Moore, p. 702). This latter statement has been a point of contention for some practitioners who believe that statements such as this unfairly lay blame at the feet of the single mother, while absolving the absent father who exercises even weaker controls and makes even fewer demands on the child than the mother, who is present and active in the child's life, does. Nevertheless, these are some of the factors that have been found to contribute to the added stress in single-mother households.

A discussion of the importance of resources and support for single mothers would not be complete without considering the impact of added financial stressors for the single mother. Women continue to have less earning capacity than men. "Women working full-time, year-round earn about 30 percent less than their male counterparts" (U.S. Census Bureau, 2008, as cited in Newman, 2009). Having custody of children can make it even more difficult for single mothers to make ends meet. Though divorce is not the only route to becoming a single mother, as Peterson states, "[D]ivorced women (and their children) experience, on average, a 27 percent decrease in their standard of living" (as cited in Newman).

Single-Father Families   Single fathers have their own set of risks and challenges. In their review of research studies that compare single moms and single dads, Biblarz and Stacey (2010) cite the following factors as placing single fathers at a disadvantage when compared to single mothers: "Single-father households tended to be newer and inhabited by children who had switched custody arrangements. . . . Single fathers more often received custody of boys, older children, and those with behavioral problems. . . . Single-father families often formed when mothers lacked interest in parenting, lost custody because of neglect or abuse, or when their children actively sought to live with their father . . . because of conflicts with mothers, stepfathers, or their mothers' partners" (p. 15). DeGarmo, Patras, and Sopagna find that "divorced single fathers, in particular, are often not prepared for the greater parenting responsibility" (as cited in Coles, 2009, p. 1313). The challenges of parenting can be even greater for single black custodial fathers. Coles, in a study of single African American custodial fathers, finds that "parenting stress is exacerbated by the cultural expectation that Black fathers are 'normally' absent and by the clustering of stresses that Black men are more likely to encounter . . . [such as]. . . higher rates of under- or over-employment and poverty, residence in neighborhoods with concentrated poverty, complex paternity, and various losses such as health, divorce, and widowhood" (pp. 1311–1312).

However bleak a picture the literature paints, it is also recognized that much of the difficulty afforded single parents (in most cases, single mothers) is tied to socioeconomic status; and the additional stress single parents face can be alleviated, at least in part, by supportive kin networks (Davidson & Moore, 1996). Brooks (2008) echoes these sentiments in noting that the "evidence from many studies [indicates that] when children (1) have stable living arrangements through legal adoption, living in a three-generation family, or living with a stable single parent and (2) experience positive parenting, they have greater social and cognitive competence. As we can see, the same qualities that predict effective functioning in children in two-parent households predict positive outcomes for children of never-married mothers" (p. 464).

Undoubtedly there are difficulties and challenges faced by single parents, and research has supported a greater likelihood of less than optimal outcomes for children raised in single-parent households. But this information is of limited usefulness when working with any particular family. Unless we know specifics about the family's economic situation, network of social supports, employment patterns, mobility patterns, child-care arrangements, and so on, it does us little good to know about the aggregate data. Also, these challenges and difficulties are only part of the picture. Here we consider research exploring the benefits associated with single parenting.

BENEFITS AND PROTECTIVE FACTORS

Olson and colleagues (2008) offer a balanced look at the single-parent family experience. They note that single mothers with sole custody often face problems associated with limited finances, loneliness, and ongoing battles with a former spouse; and single fathers with custody experienced sorrow over the loss of the complete family, loneliness, and difficulties with balancing work and family. But they temper this by noting the strengths often associated with the single mothers who have sole custody—"specific joys, such as the freedom to make decisions about their own lives and the lives of their children" (Olson et al., p. 454); and benefits experienced by the single fathers with custody, such as having greater control over parenting, and having closer bonds with their children. "For many fathers, single parenthood means getting closer to their children. One father proudly related how he had become closer to his children after adjusting his priorities in life by putting the children before his job and the housework" (p. 456).

Edin (2005) also discusses the value that single parents, mothers in particular, place on control. "When we ask mothers what they like best about being a single mother, many tell us that they enjoy being in control. . . . Having and caring for a child often reveals in unmarried mothers competencies they did not know that they possessed" (p. 504).

The Coles (2009) study of single black custodial fathers found that, "for more than half of these fathers, parenting represented a desirable strategy to compensate for the wounds of fathering in their own childhood and as a means of improving their own life trajectories and hopefully that of their children. Moreover, they garner public rewards for doing something that appears rare. For those reasons, they may not have perceived their stress to be severe, or at least the meaning that parenting held for them outweighed the stress" (p. 1334).

Although there is great value in having a balanced view of the single-parent experience, it would be naive to leave the discussion at this point. What this author notices in the current body of literature is both a dichotomy of views and an apparent swing of the pendulum, so to speak. It is easy to see two camps, one more deficit based, focused on the harm to women and children as a result of parenting without a father, and the other more strengths based, focused on acknowledging that there is not one right way to "do family," and looking at the strengths within the single-parent family. Is one right and one wrong? Because we pathologized single-parent families for so long, it is essential that we now acknowledge that many single-parent families have formed strong functioning units, which is why the pendulum has swung in that direction. Yet recognition of the strengths in many single-parent families should not prohibit us from acknowledging that in many, though certainly not all, single-parent families, the absence of the other parent is a source of pain that continues for years, and often follows the children into adulthood. If we are committed to appreciating, in a postmodern sense, the individual experience, then even anecdotal evidence is worthy of consideration. In other words, we know from life experience that some children in single-parent families long for the missing parent. We know that there are children who feel that they have been abandoned by their mother or their father, and these children often struggle with associated emotional and relational issues.

We must also be aware, as Hanson (1986) poses, that there are differences between what can be referred to as a clinical population and the general population; looking at one population over the other will skew our perspective. If we study single-parent families who are in counseling, for example, we know this is not a randomly assigned group. We may find them to be a more troubled population, a population more open to seeking help, a population more in touch with feelings, or a population that values and seeks wholeness.

Although it is certainly true that some single-parent families are struggling and hurting, other single-parent families are doing quite well. In seeking to avoid stereotypes and preconceptions about single-parent families, we must also be careful not to undervalue the importance of either mothers or fathers in the lives of their children, and not to be misled into believing, as we focus on family strengths, that children do not feel a real sense of loss when their mother or their father is absent from their lives. In most cases, a mother cannot be replaced by just any other mother figure, nor can just any other father figure replace a father. Children who have known their parents, and many who have never known their parents, may long for the relationship that was or the relationship that was never to be. As important as a strengths-based perspective is, we must not let our commitment to a perspective blind us to real sources of pain that exist within some of the single-parent family constellations we will be discussing.

Perceptions of the Single-Parent Family Constellation

The language we use to describe families is often a reflection of ingrained societal perceptions, prejudices, and stereotypes. For example, historically we have referred to the single-parent family after divorce as a broken home and to children born to unmarried mothers as illegitimate. These attitudes can promote a self-perception by those within single-parent families as victims, or somehow lesser parents than those parenting with partners. Partly in response to this notion of the single parent as victim, we now see a growing group of unwed mothers who identify with the label single mothers by choice (SMBC) (Mattes, 1997). They did not become pregnant unexpectedly, but rather "chose" to parent without a partner. Orenstein's (2000) research with this group found that, whereas these SMBC did see single parenting as a choice, it was not always their first choice. According to Orenstein, the unmarried heterosexual mothers had as their first choice "The Dream," which she describes as "a loving husband who would be a committed father, whose career, while not too demanding, paid well enough to allow [her] the option, once they had their two children, to quit her job" (p. 143). Orenstein is referring for the most part here to women in their thirties or older who decided to become parents through artificial insemination, often through use of a sperm bank. "While still statistically small in number, women aged thirty-five and older are actually the fastest growing group of unwed mothers: At a time when the teenage birth rate is dropping, their rates of childbirth have more than doubled: from 2.4 percent in 1980 to 5.8 percent in 1995" (p. 145).

To make this point about language a bit more clear, ask yourself if you would consider any of the following scenarios to describe a single parent. Although not typically counted among single parents, could an individual experience single parenting even in an ongoing coupled relationship?

Work separation or deployment.   Tobias is on his second tour of duty in Iraq. His wife Trista is living on base with their three children. In the seven years that they have been married, Tobias has lived in the home with his family for a total of three years. The military community provides some financial and emotional supports for Trista, Tobias, and the children, yet Trista often feels lonely and isolated.

Incarceration of partner.   Gerald is married to Paula and they have two children, ages five and nine. Paula has been incarcerated for the past three years. The family is struggling to get by on Gerald's limited income. Gerald can be overwhelmed with the responsibilities associated with work and parenting and a lack of social support. Because women's federal prisons are less abundant than men's prisons, the closest, where Paula is housed, is five hundred miles away from her family. Gerald finds it next to impossible to get the children to the prison to visit their mother, and is ambivalent about whether doing so would be a good idea even if he could get there.

Incapacitation or withdrawal of partner from parenting role.   Mary and Christine are newly married same-sex partners who together are raising their three children. Christine has a long history of substance abuse, which makes it very difficult for her to be a dependable parent for the children. This leaves Mary to be responsible for almost all of the day-to-day care, as well as the financial and emotional support of the children and Christine.

Each of these scenarios involves individuals who would not typically be considered single parents because there is a second parent to whom the parent is legally married or emotionally committed, yet each case involves a parent who is experiencing some of the same challenges—loneliness, isolation, financial problems, work- and role-overload—that are associated with single parenting. These issues are not the exclusive domain of single parents by any means; however, the individual may consider himself or herself to be a single parent. Let's acknowledge here that a family that identifies itself as a single-parent family, regardless of whether it meets a legal definition or fitting an existing stereotype, is in fact a single-parent family. In accepting this self-definition, we embrace a constructivist approach, one that recognizes that the individuals and the family have active roles in creating and defining their own reality. These scenarios also depict what Guadalupe and Welkley describe as a process of being and becoming—constructing, deconstructing, and reconstructing the family identity and experiences. Our work with families will depend on how well we are able to understand that families are not holding still while we seek to understand them, just as they are not standing still as they seek to better understand themselves. Nor are families to be understood without close and careful consideration of the rich context in which they live. A contextual perspective reminds us to consider all aspects of the environment in which the family lives—physical, sociocultural, economic, historic, and so on.

Being and Becoming:
Fluidity in the Single-Parent Family Constellation

To better understand the concept of fluidity in a single-parent family constellation, consider the following fictitious case of Jonathan and Maria.

Jonathan was born into a family with a mother and a father who were married and living together. When he was four years old, his father died and, as a result, he and his mother, Maria, moved in with her parents, who were his grandparents. Also living in the grandparents' home was Jonathan's uncle Joe. Both grandparents and Uncle Joe took on an active role in supporting Maria and Jonathan. Uncle Joe was involved in coaching Jonathan's soccer team, helping with homework, and staying with Jonathan so that Maria could go out with her friends on occasion. *[At this point, would Jonathan feel that he was living in a single-parent household? Would Maria feel that she is operating as a single parent?]*

After three years, when Jonathan was seven, he and his mother moved into an apartment of their own. Maria managed to balance work and family by both drawing on and contributing to a network of close friends who supported one another by sharing meals and child care. *[Now would Jonathan feel that he was living in a single-parent household? Would Maria feel that she is operating as a single parent?]*

After two years, Maria's boyfriend, Paul, moved in with Maria and Jonathan. Paul provided financial and emotional support to the family and developed a close relationship with Jonathan. *[Would Jonathan feel that he is living in a single-parent household? Would Maria feel that she is operating as a single parent?]*

The next year, when Jonathan was ten, Maria and Paul married and Paul legally adopted Jonathan. Four years later, Paul and Maria divorced. *[If Paul continues to coparent with Maria will she perceive that she is a single parent?]*

These questions force us to consider the fluidity of family structure and the role that perceptions have—not only the perceptions of the parent, but also the perceptions of the child(ren). The example above highlights what Guadalupe and Welkley previously describe as the family "constructing, deconstructing, and reconstructing" its identity and experiences. It provides a way of understanding, in the case of the single-parent family constellation, what is meant by considering the family as a multidimensional contextual nonstatic living entity, with the emphasis in this case on nonstatic.

Representation of Diverse Single-Parent Family Constellations

Employing a constructivist approach, this author proposes seven single-parent family constellations that are based on the following two principles: (1) the family exists as a multidimensional contextual nonstatic living entity, and (2) the family constructs its own reality. Critical to remember, so as not to view this approach as an attempt to put families in boxes, are these three key points:

1. Family constellations are constantly in a process of being and becoming. At the very time that a family is gaining an understanding of who the family is and how it operates, the family is changing and evolving. Someone is being born and someone is dying, everyone is growing older, someone is moving away or moving back home, someone is getting married or divorced, relationships are becoming closer or more distant, and so on.

2. Individuals can be simultaneously a part of multiple family constellations. When asked, "Who is in your family?" many of us would think first of those with whom we live, or the family that raised us when we were children, or perhaps of our children or our parents, though we may no longer live with them. But when given an opportunity to expand on this question, most of us would not hesitate to acknowledge that we belong to many families. We live our lives as members of many family constellations. One can be married and raising children while still being in a family relationship with parents, siblings, cousins, aunts and uncles, grandparents, and so on. In addition, we find that we are part of a family we have created among our friends, neighbors and others in our community with whom we may have established a relationship close enough to function as, and we con sider to be, family, or fictive kin.

3. While the descriptions offered below are from the parents' perspective, the child's perspective is equally important and a complete picture of the family experience would take both, as well the perceptions of others in the family, into consideration.

AUTONOMOUS OR ISOLATED SINGLE-PARENT FAMILY

The key to understanding the Autonomous or Isolated Single-Parent Family constellation (represented in figure 7.5 with three variations of boundaries) is in recognizing that while the family is still influenced by, and has an influence on, its social environment, the members perceive that they are going it alone, that the parent-child relationship more or less singly defines the family. The parent and child may experience this constellation as autonomous; as isolated; as simultaneously autonomous and isolated; or somewhere on a continuum between autonomous and isolated. Note that the lines which contain or surround this family may be thick, thin, or broken, indicating that the family may perceive its boundaries anywhere on a continuum from thick and rigid (thick line); to firm but flexible (thin line); to open, permeable, or loosely defined (dotted line). Caution must be taken, however, not to associate the family's placement on this continuum with being good or bad. For example, one family may perceive that their boundaries are very thick and rigid and this is what protects them from abuse from those outside the parent–child dyad and strengthens their family bonds. In other words, the thick walls or rigid family boundaries make them a strong unit, an autonomous unit, able to make it on their own. But another family may perceive that their walls, equally thick, and their

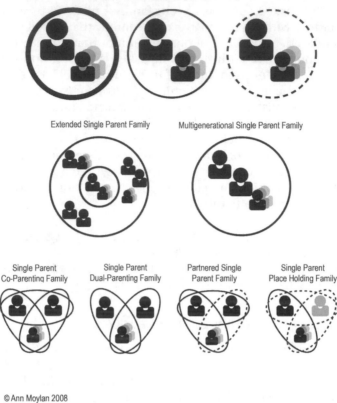

© Ann Moylan 2008

FIGURE 7.5 *Single-Parent Family Constellations*

boundaries, equally rigid, are due to having been rejected or abandoned by others. In this case, the separation or isolation they experience is not of their own making, and the single parent or child may perceive that this is not a positive or healthy aspect of the family's being, but rather a barrier to their well-being. Similarly, there may be positive, negative, or neutral perceptions, experiences, or associations with the other boundary types.

EXTENDED SINGLE-PARENT FAMILY

Members in the extended single-parent family perceive that they function within the context of a larger family unit. The larger family unit may be supportive of the nucleus, may be nonsupportive, or may vary in its support from one member to another, from one point in time to another, or from one situation or circumstance to another. Likewise, the single parent and child nucleus may be supportive of the extended family, nonsupportive, or variably supportive and nonsupportive. Nevertheless, the members of the nucleus view themselves as part of a larger family. The larger family unit may be made up of biological kin, nonbiological kin, friends, or other supports such as child-care providers, neighbors, a religious community, a subculture, and so on.

Although one might initially assume that the extended single-parent family constellation is stronger than the isolated or autonomous single-parent family, that is not necessarily the case. Keep two points in mind: (1) whereas these extensions of the family may be supportive, they may also be a source of criticism, conflict, competing needs, and so on; and (2) the constellations are not mutually exclusive. A family may view its experience as a combination of any of these constellations. Members could be experiencing their family as a predominantly autonomous unit, while recognizing that they function within the context of a larger family unit. For simplicity, we have not offered all the combinations possible, so bear in mind that families may experience the extended single-parent family constellation with thick, thin, or more open boundaries surrounding that parent–child nucleus. In other words, the parent and child view themselves as part of a larger family, but to what degree do they offer and are they offered what Guadalupe and Welklcy refer to as "exchanges" and "interactions"?

MULTIGENERATIONAL SINGLE-PARENT FAMILY

The defining feature of the multigenerational single-parent family is the presence of a family member (may be fictive kin) from a third generation—a biological or honorary grandparent(s), great aunt or great uncle, great-grandparent, and so on. This third generation need not be residing in the household with the parent and child, as we are not basing these classifications on household. And this multigenerational single-parent family may perceive itself as simultaneously an autonomous or isolated family or an extended single-parent family in that even the addition of a third generation does not necessarily change the family's perception of its relative autonomy or isolation or integration within a larger unit.

There are many circumstances in which one may find a multigenerational single-parent family. A single parent may be living in the home of parents, grandparents, aunt, uncle, and so on, as a way to share resources; as a way to receive assistance with parenting; as a way to share emotional support after a loss, such as the loss that results from separation, divorce, or death of a partner, and so on; or as a way to provide support to aging parents, grandparents, and so on. In other cases, a grandparent may be the primary caregiver for the grandchild due to the limited functioning or limited presence of the parent (e.g., due to addiction, work or school schedule, location, or in some cases due to the parent's young age or lack of preparation for parenting), or as a result of cultural norms in which the grandparent typically performs the primary parenting functions for the grandchildren.

Understanding the specific circumstances of the multigenerational single-parent family is critical when working with individuals or multiple family members who are experiencing, whether in the short or long term, this family constellation. Understanding the motivations, assumptions, challenges, and strengths that the family attributes to this arrangement will help the human service provider work effectively in partnership with the family. The human service provider must check his or her own assumptions and biases regarding this type of family arrangement. To assume that this constellation is necessarily a source of strength or a reflection of weakness is to limit one's ability to understand the experience from the perspective of the family and the individuals within the family.

SINGLE PARENT AS COPARENT

A single parent who identifies as a coparent views his or her role as taking place within the context of another parenting relationship. The other parent may be the child's biological parent, a stepparent, a grandparent, a foster parent, or, in the case of sperm or egg donation, donor coparents, and so on. The relationship between the two parents may be supportive, but may also be contrary, antagonistic, or a combination of these, depending on circumstances, point in time, and so on. The key to understanding this family constellation is that the parent views the parental role, like it or not, as being shared with another. The single parent perceives that he or she is parenting in a context in which there is some level of communication, negotiation, or collaboration with another parent.

SINGLE PARENT AS DUAL PARENT

In some circumstances, a single parent will be parenting more or less autonomously from a second parent, though the second parent may be an actively involved parent. For example, a child may move from one home to the other with very little or no interaction between the parents of the two households. Perhaps one parent has the child (children) for the nine months of the school year and the other parent has the child (children) in the summer. If there is little communication between the parents, they may be functioning in dual or parallel roles. Even married parents in a two-parent intact family may experience this type of constellation if the communication between the two parents has been compromised to such a degree that the parents are functioning more or less independently—that is, as single parents. It is not a divorce or separation that defines this experience, but rather the lack of communication and cooperation between the two parents, and the perception of going it alone, without support of another.

Parents can view their family constellation as anywhere on a continuum between coparenting and dual parenting; fluctuating between the two depending on time, issue, or other circumstances; or moving, gradually or quickly, in one direction or the other as the other parent gets increasingly distant or increasingly close. As a human service provider, it is not for us to decide if the shoe fits, so to speak. The significance of recognizing the single parent as a dual parent constellation is in understanding how this arrangement is experienced by the parent, the child (children), and the second, or in some cases third or fourth, parent (such as when a former spouse cohabits or remarries a new partner). When the parents are not in close communication regarding parenting decisions, one may see an increase in the children feeling that they are caught in the middle, that their loyalties to one parent or the other are being challenged, or that they are in fact being asked to choose between one parent and the other. On the other hand, such as in some cases where parents are not in close geographic proximity, the independence in parenting may result in less conflict between the parents and a more harmonious experience for the child (children). It is only through paying close attention to the parent's or parents', child's or children's experiences that one may come to understand the individual and family nuances of this constellation.

PARTNERED SINGLE-PARENT FAMILY

In the previous two constellations, the single-parent coparenting family and the single-parent dual-parenting family, both parents maintained an active role in parenting the child (children). The difference between the two was in the degree of collaboration between the parents: the coparenting model indicating that the two parents were engaged at least to some extent in communicating about parenting decisions, and the dual-parenting model indicating that the two parents were functioning more or less independently in their parenting of the child (children). What distinguishes the partnered single-parent family, then, is not the degree of one parent's engagement with the other, but rather the degree to which the single parent's partner is engaged with the child(ren).

This type of single-parenting family can be seen in some stepparent families or cohabitating families, where the parent's partner does not have a close relationship with the child(ren), or perhaps has simply not yet taken on an active parenting role, leaving the primary parent (biological, adoptive, foster, etc. parent) to perceive that he or she is in fact a single parent, even though in a partnered relationship. In some cases, it is to the child's and the family's distinct advantage that what we refer to here as the primary parent is maintaining his or her role as a single parent. The parent may be intentionally preserving his or her role, family traditions and rituals, and so on, in the face of a new partner relationship as a way of providing stability and consistency for the child. The primary parent may be benefiting from the partner's support (financial, emotional, etc.) and may find that his or her parenting is stronger because of this support. In other cases, this constellation may leave the primary parent feeling that he or she has more than his or her share of the load, and could lead to resentment or feelings of sadness that the other parent does not have a close relationship with the child. In either case, the family may function in this manner for the short or long term, depending on many factors, such as the age of the child (children), the specific relationship established between the parent's partner and the child, the duration of the relationship between the parent and the partner, and so on.

SINGLE-PARENT PLACEHOLDER FAMILY

The term "placeholder" is used to denote that even when one parent is absent—either physically (perhaps due to work, marital separation, incarceration, etc.), or psychologically (perhaps due to preoccupation with an ongoing project or issue, addiction, or significant mental illness), the parent who is present with the child (children) may experience parenting in such a way as to hold the place of the absent parent. This single-parent family constellation is related to Boss' (2002) description of family boundary ambiguity and the two types of ambiguous loss: physical absence with psychological presence, and physical presence with psychological absence. According to Boss, "An ambiguous event is more difficult to deal with than a clear-cut event" (p. 53). And furthermore, "When there is ambiguity regarding a family member's presence or absence in the family system, the situation is called "ambiguous loss." How the family interprets or perceives this situation of ambiguous loss is called "boundary ambiguity," and it is a risk factor or barrier to the management of stress" (p. 95).

    A key to understanding and working with the placeholder family is an awareness that the single parent may feel some ambivalence about whether or not to hold a place for the other parent. If the absence is due to abandonment, addiction, abuse, incarceration, and so on, the remaining parent may not wish to hold a place for the other, yet even in these circumstances, the psychological presence of the absent parent may have an impact on parenting choices, behaviors, and attitudes. Cases in which the parent does wish to hold the place of the other include those where the intent is to make the absent parent's reentry into the family easier following a separation, and cases where place-holding is seen as a way of preserving the memory of the absent parent, as in the case of one who is deceased and whose memory is cherished.

An important clarification noted by Boss (2002) cautions us not to assume that cases of divorce will necessarily result in ambiguous loss. "Because divorce and remarriage are common, they may not be considered by many as loss in the classical sense, despite the ambiguity. For example, children in divorced families may think of their father not as 'lost' but simply as living in another house or apartment to which they have access. Many families with more elastic family boundaries may not view boundary ambiguity as a problem because family relationship and process boundaries are not necessarily the same as household boundaries" (p. 98). Although a parent may consider that he or she is functioning as a single parent, the child may or may not sense the same extent of reduced involvement of the second parent, and consequently the child may not feel that he or she is being raised by a single parent, but rather by two parents who simply do not reside together.

Boss' (2002) focus on "how the family interprets or perceives this situation" is key to understanding each of the single-parent family constellations presented in this chapter. It is also important to remember that the models presented in this chapter are offered in the spirit of expanding other conceptualizations, not as a way of limiting what may in fact be infinite possibilities for perceiving and describing the experiences of single-parent family constellations. When we remember that an individual has membership in multiple family constellations at any one time, the number of possibilities is truly endless. In the words of Guadalupe and Welkley in chapter 3 of this book, "It can be detrimental to expect a family to change and conform to fit into a model. . . . [T]he family is a unique and individual experience that needs to be honored, recognized, and endorsed if the overall intention is to promote family wellness and optimal health. It is for today's human service practitioners to keep an open mind about the diverse possibilities of what may constitute a family and to allow family constellations to identify and describe family dynamics in their own terms." Essentially, do we allow family constellations to characterize or identify what family means to them?

Implications for Nonstereotypical Practice Skills

Recognizing the many variations within single-parent family constellations helps sensitize us to the diversity in experiences and situations that these families may face, the challenges they may confront, and the many strengths that they likely have developed in managing family life. This recognition of diversity within the single-parent family constellation—or, more accurately, recognition that there are multiple constellations within what has traditionally been referred to as "the" single-parent family constellation—positions us to advocate for the consideration of ways that move beyond traditional or stereotypical perspectives that uphold the idea of a one model fits all, as Guadalupe and Welkley refer to in chapter 2. This last section, therefore, will provide a framework and some considerations for practice. As we begin this section, the reader is reminded to consider the last two premises posited by Guadalupe and Welkley:

- The family affects and is affected by intrapersonal (micro domains), interpersonal (mezzo domains), environmental (macro domains), as well as nonordinary reality (magna domains).

- An eclectic asset-based approach is likely to enhance our practice within the context of diverse family constellations.

Self-Awareness, Knowledge, and Skills

As stated by Guadalupe and Lum (2005), "Professional competence often requires a balance between learned skills and cultivated values of respect regarding human diversity or uniqueness, a degree of professional self-awareness and evaluation, confrontation of discriminative cognitive patterns and actions promoted in the name of professionalism, as well as a level of trust in the wisdom of uncertainty" (p. 16). According to Lupe Alle-Corliss and Randy Alle-Corliss (1999), "Effective practice requires a balance among the three key elements of self-awareness, knowledge, and skill development. The absence of any one of these will impact some aspect of practice negatively and could possibly have an adverse effect on clinical treatment" (p. 1).

Self-awareness.   Because those of us who work with families must use ourselves in the helping process, our effectiveness as helpers will be limited or enhanced by our capacity to be introspective, self-aware, and motivated to grow and develop. We must study our own thoughts, feelings, biases, and behaviors. When working with others, the issues they face may trigger our own issues, so we are obligated to have spent the requisite time and made the necessary investment in ourselves that will allow us to focus on the other. Another place where self-awareness is of critical importance is in working with clients who are from backgrounds that are different from our own. It is likely that each of us harbors some biases, prejudices, and stereotypes about those from other social classes, races, ethnicities, religions, ages, genders, sexual orientations, professions, nationalities, and so on. Learning more about our own values and assumptions is a critical first step toward developing nonstereotypical practice skills.

Burger (2008) summarizes the literature as pointing to several characteristics of effective helpers: empathy, genuineness, objective or subjective balance, self-awareness, acceptance, desire to help, and patience. In this case, self-awareness is seen as one among several important characteristics. What do you think? Are there characteristics you would add to or subtract from the list? Is it possible to come up with a list that has meaning across different cultures and settings?

Speaking to the personal challenges in serving an increasingly diverse population, Garcia (1994) states the need for another quality—personal commitment.

> We need not be fooled by any liberal or conservative rhetoric. We have not achieved educational equality for our culturally diverse population. If we are to make any substantive progress, we will need further resolve. It is often said that with universal prenatal care, Head Start, school choice, and the like, we have solved or soon will solve the problem of at-risk, linguistically and culturally diverse populations. Please do not misunderstand: these contributions may be important, but our own past suggests that we should remain doubtful about any miracle cures. No new interventions, reorganizations, or resources will satisfactorily address this problem unless the individuals who implement these initiatives are deeply committed to the enterprise. The change that is necessary must be fueled by the type of social energy that sent us forward in the past with vigorous and consistent resolve. As in the New Frontier and War on Poverty eras, we must grasp the importance of this challenge. (pp. 264–265)

Knowledge.   Just as families are dynamic, involved in an ongoing process of being and becoming, so are our knowledges, our understandings, our assumptions of the known and the unknown. "Poststructuralism posits that knowledge and meaning are unstable and culture bound" (Marsten & Howard, 2006, p. 97). Knowledge therefore is neither singular nor static. Rather, it is always being constructed, deconstructed, and reconstructed, depending on many factors, including personal experiences; social, political, economic, cultural, and environmental contexts; scientific data; theory; intuition; and possible understandings of nonordinary realities.

Cultures, families, and individuals differ with regard to how highly they value the different ways of knowing. For example, some cultures, families, and individuals are more open to the realms of the nonordinary than are others, and your openness to this potential source of knowledge may lead you in new directions, directions that are more compatible with the families with whom you are working. On the other hand, you may find that you are more open to the realm of the nonordinary realities than are those with whom you work. It may also be that people are simply reluctant to share their experiences about that which cannot be proven or is experienced differently by different people. If they do share these experiences, you may hear them preface their experience with comments such as, "This is kind of 'woo-woo,' but . . ." Our interest in and affirmation of these other ways of knowing is essential to understanding the experience from the family's perspective. Lupe Alle-Corliss and Randy Alle-Corliss (1999) remind us to "[b]e very alert to generalizing or stereotyping based on your experience. Remember that the most effective way to get accurate information about your clients and their issues is to ask them. . . . Important knowledge about a person's cultural values, family structure, religious practices, child-rearing customs, experience of oppression and racism, and level of acculturation can be obtained by direct ethnographic client interviewing and by informal observation of clients in their environment" (p. 3).

Another strategy for learning about the family is to allow and encourage the family members to tell their story their way. Different from a structured interview, the narrative approach supports family members in telling their story. This is likely the best way to help the client(s) see that you view him or her or them as the expert, and you are the learner. The reader is reminded that

a. knowledge and understanding are created, not discovered, which is consistent with a constructivist perspective. (Refer back to chapter 1, table 1.1, for assumptions and general principles of the constructivist orientation.)

b. people need to be understood within the context of their environment, which is consistent with an ecological orientation. (Refer back to chapter 1, table 1.2, for assumptions and general principles of the ecological orientation.)

Skill development.   Clearly, self-awareness and knowledge are lifelong endeavors. The same is true of skill development. As human service practitioners, we must always be alert to the goodness of fit between our practice and the individuals with whom we work. We may become comfortable with certain types of interventions or supports, those that have perhaps served us well in the past, yet these may be inappropriate for the family or individuals with whom we are currently engaged.

Burger (2008) discusses nine "basic helping skills" that are necessary for human service professionals: listening, communicating, giving feedback, observing, confronting, clarifying, problem solving, interviewing, and report writing. How would this list match up with your own if you were to list what you believe to be essential helping skills? Would such a list be relevant across cultures and settings and circumstances? If we cannot come up with a list, how do we support professionals in learning the "skills of the trade" so to speak? Is the very act of listing things culturally bound, culturally valued, and culturally relevant? What are other ways of understanding that which is essential?

Family–Professional Partnership, Family Support, and Family-Centered Practices

In previous chapters, Guadalupe and Welkley discuss the importance of family-centered practices. Here, we explore the meaning of three overlapping constructs: family support, family-centered practices, and family–professional partnerships. In doing so, note that many principles and skills are identified as being consistent with one or more of these concepts, and the concepts can be discussed as being subsumed, one within the other.

Roberts, Rule, and Innocenti (1998) discuss what they refer to as the five principles of care that are necessary if we are to see effective family–professional partnerships. "These principles include a community base of services, cultural competence, service coordination, family-centered care, and a seamless system of care" (p. 1). So in this conceptualization, family-centered care is seen as an essential part of the family–professional partnership. Dunst (2002) indicates, "Family centeredness characterizes beliefs and practices that treat families with dignity and respect; individualized, flexible, and responsive practices; information sharing so that families can make informed decisions; family choice regarding any number of aspects of program practices and intervention options; parent-professional collaboration and partnerships as a context for family-program relations; and the provision and mobilization of resources and supports necessary for families to care for and rear their children in ways that produce optimal child, parent, and family outcomes" (p. 139). Dunst and Trivette (as cited in Dunst) describe family-centered practices as having both relational and participatory components. The relational components include the skills and attitudes we discussed in the previous section, such as listening skills, empathy, and attitudes toward families. The participatory components include those practices "(a) that are individualized, flexible, and responsive to family concerns and priorities, and (b) that provide families with opportunities to be actively involved in decisions and choices, family-professional collaboration, and family actions to achieve desired goals and outcomes. The simultaneous use of *both* sets of practices by professionals is what distinguishes the family-centered approach from other approaches to working with families" (pp. 139–140).

Finally, table 7.1 provides both the principles and premises of family support as outlined by Family Support America (1996). We will use these concepts of family support, family-centered practice, and family–professional partnership as we consider how to work with the family in our case example. As you read through the principles and premises,

Table 7.1   Family Support

Principles of Family Support

1. Staff and families work together in relationships based on equality and respect.
2. Staff enhances families' capacity to support the growth and development of all family members—adults, youth, and children.
3. Families are resources to their own members, to other families, to programs, and to communities.
4. Programs affirm and strengthen families' cultural, racial, and linguistic identities and enhance their ability to function in a multicultural society.
5. Programs are embedded in their communities and contribute to the community-building process.
6. Programs advocate with families for services and systems that are fair, responsive, and accountable to the families served.
7. Practitioners work with families to mobilize formal and informal resources to support family development.
8. Programs are flexible and continually responsive to emerging family and community issues.
9. Principles of family support are modeled in all program activities, including planning, governance, and administration.

Premises of Family Support

1. Primary responsibility for the development and well-being of children lies within the family, and all segments of society must support families as they rear their children.
2. Assuring the well-being of all families is the cornerstone of a healthy society, and requires universal access to support programs and services.
3. Children and families exist as part of an ecological system.
4. Child-rearing patterns are influenced by parents' understanding of child development and of their children's unique characteristics, personal sense of competence, and cultural and community traditions and mores.
5. Enabling families to build on their own strengths and capacities promotes the healthy development of children.
6. The developmental processes that make up parenthood and family life create needs that are unique at each stage in the life span.
7. Families are empowered when they have access to information and other resources and take action to improve the well-being of children, families, and communities.

Source: Family Support America (1996).

note that the emphasis is on the partnership between the practitioner and the family. Note also the emphasis on family strengths and on the contextual dimensions within which the family functions. As an exercise, ask yourself if these principles and practices will work across all families. Would they need to be adjusted in cases where the family does not enhance the well-being of its members? Or would the principles and premises hold, but the implementation be subject to modification from family to family, or from one organization to another?

Case Study: Jenna (age thirty) and Michael (age thirteen)

STRENGTHS

- *Up until her pregnancy, Jenna was an excellent student, and even with her pregnancy she completed high school at age seventeen. For the majority of her son Michael's life, Jenna's work has provided the primary source of income for the family and has been the primary caregiver. Over the years, she has made decisions that have demonstrated her strength and agency. She moved Michael and herself away from Michael's father, who was addicted to drugs. "I kicked him out. He was sucking me dry." She moved to another state, closer to her father and stepmother, and now lives in a community where she has good steady work and the schools are some of the best in the state. Jenna has good relationships with Michael, her current partner Ted, and several close friends. She is a very intelligent, attractive, personable woman, caring friend, and devoted mother. She manages her money well and takes care of herself as well as Michael.*

- *Michael is a bright and attractive young man at age thirteen. He helps out with chores around the house, is on the school track team, takes music lessons, and has several close friends. He has maintained a level of relationship with his father, while also accepting Ted as a potential father figure, at times calling him "Dad." He demonstrates his independence in traveling across country to attend summer camp in another state, and to visit friends and family several states away.*

CHALLENGES

- *As a seventh grader, Michael was doing poorly in school, failing to complete his homework, and hiding this from Jenna. At one point she learned that he had more than thirteen homework assignments missing in one subject alone. Jenna met with teachers and school practitioners who recommended some assessments for Michael. Michael was diagnosed as having Attention Deficit Hyperactivity Disorder (ADHD).*

- *Michael had a trip planned to visit his paternal grandparents. A week before he was to go stay with them, his father was released from prison and moved in with the grandparents. Jenna was torn as to whether or not to allow the trip. Michael's father had in the past stolen from family members, including Jenna and Michael, had been struggling with crack addiction for years, and had been in and out of prison on several occasions. On the other hand, Jenna wanted Michael, then twelve, to have a relationship with his father and an opportunity to know him without her filters.*

- *Jenna was struggling with where her relationship with Ted was going. Ted, who lived in an apartment in another town, about ninety minutes away, wanted Jenna and Michael to move into a house with him. He was willing to move to the town where Jenna and Michael lived, but the duplex Jenna and Michael lived in was too small to accommodate the three of them. Moving in with Ted would involve Jenna giving up the duplex she had rented for several years and could afford on her own. Affordable housing was very hard to come by in this town, and losing her duplex might mean that later, if things did not work out with Ted, she would be faced with the decision to move out of town or take in a roommate, neither of which seemed an acceptable alternative to Jenna.*

While Jenna was actually dealing with all of these issues at the same time, for sake of discussion, we will consider them one at a time.

THE SCHOOL ISSUE: JENNA AND MICHAEL

From the perspective of a practitioner, whether attached to the school or not, one of the most important considerations is how to get to know Jenna and Michael. In assessing the situation, the practitioner will need to be open to knowing the individuals and the family as whole entities, and moving beyond a narrow focus on school performance, but without being intrusive with regard to other aspects of their lives. Rather than starting from a position of knowing or assuming to know the problem and having some solutions already in mind, the practitioner can simply extend an invitation, one that may begin with a question such as, "What brings you here today?" or in the case where that was obvious at the time the appointment was made, "How can I help you today?" What we want to do is make room for Jenna and Michael to tell their story. If we rush to questioning Jenna—"How do you supervise Michael's homework?" or Michael—"Describe the space where you do your homework," we may shift the conversation in a direction that is not helpful to the parent or child. Questions such as these may be taken to imply that Jenna must not be supervising his homework properly or providing an appropriate workspace within the home environment. Both could put the parent on the defensive and undermine our goal of getting to know the family and its members' circumstances.

From a strengths perspective, it is important that we attune our focus to looking at what Jenna and Michael have done with their lives so far. This provides a window to their strengths, their values, and their challenges. Being a good listener as Jenna shares parts of her story (experiences, perceptions, questions, challenges, desires) may bring to light some surprises. For example, Jenna has shown great determination to make it on her own, has found the resources that allow her to provide a stable home in a supportive community, and does not typically think of herself as a single parent, but rather as a parent. Consider what she had to say about being a single parent and how this gives us some insight into the intrapersonal domain, or micro level of practice.

> I hear people talk about single moms and they feel sorry for them, they feel like they are always struggling. There is a stereotype of the single mom and it is "poor single mom." I don't feel like people should look at me that way. I don't do anything different from a nonsingle mom—I just do it without a dad in the house. Other than moving, I don't think my parenting would be very different if I were single or not single. People are where they are because of choices they make. I'm here because I choose to be here. I don't feel sorry for me, so I don't think others should feel sorry for me.

Sometimes, in an attempt to let someone know that we empathize with their situation, that we understand their experience, we may instead show sympathy, or even pity—"It must be difficult trying to do everything on your own." (Of course, it is the tone that can convey so much, and we miss that in written forms of language.) A more appropriate and potentially effective direction of response would be to reflect back to Jenna the strength she has just exhibited in this description, one in which she does not describe herself as a victim but rather as an agent, one able to produce an effect or result. Recognize, and help her recognize, the strengths she has just conveyed.

During the ensuing conversation, Jenna may share that during this time of dealing with Michael's school difficulties, she had one particularly rough day when she remembers being on her drive into work and feeling overwhelmed, "tired of doing it all myself. No one there to back you up, to say, 'this is your mother and she knows what she is talking about!'" Then and only then, might it be appropriate to say, "It must be difficult trying to do everything on your own." Now the statement is offered in response to her identification of a struggle, not based on any preexisting assumptions about single parents. This is a very important distinction and cannot be overemphasized here. While still acknowledging her strengths, this may be the time to help her focus on defining the challenges she faces, and then moving to a consideration of the possibilities.

All that is being said about working with Jenna is also true for working with Michael. Staying away from stereotypes is critical. "He is a preteen, therefore . . ." or "He is a boy, therefore . . . ," or "He lives in a home without a father, therefore. . . ." Instead, the focus should be on how Michael views himself, his school experience, his family experience, his peer relationships, and so on. What challenges does he identify? What possibilities does he see for himself?

This is not to say that our understanding of development, of gender differences, or of single-parent family constellations will be of no use. In fact, it may help the practitioner and Jenna to think about evidence-based knowledge as they seek to understand Michael's perceptions, strengths, and challenges. An eclectic approach is clearly open to these considerations. But—and here is the key—the body of knowledge per se tells us little about Michael. It can only provide us with a lens through which we may begin to understand his reality. What is equally important is what Guadalupe and Welkley refer to in this text as "knowledge emerging from the realms of nonordinary realities." What does Michael intuit about his being and his becoming? What might he know about himself and what might we learn about him, beyond that which can be grounded in science? What might the practitioner learn if he or she is willing and able to trust his or her own intuition? What might Jenna know if she is able to trust her intuition?

As we move to a discussion of the relationship between Jenna and Michael (or any other relationships), we are acknowledging the next level, the mezzo domain. The same considerations that guided practice at the micro level apply here: identifying the strengths that exist within the relationship, being open to hearing about any challenges Jenna and Michael face, and then moving toward possibilities. These three steps allow us to keep our practice strengths based, family focused, and non-stereotypical. At this level, the practitioner may support Jenna and Michael in identifying aspects of their relationship that are mutually rewarding, aspects of their relationship that are causing difficulties for one or the other or both of them, and possibilities for improving those challenging aspects of the relationship. In this case, it is likely that Michael's hiding the fact that he was not completing his homework was as troubling or perhaps more troubling to Jenna than the fact that the homework was not completed. If the practitioner were simply to offer some tried and true suggestions on how to better manage time, better keep track of homework, remember to turn homework in, and so on, he or she could be missing the underlying issues of trust and deception that allowed Jenna to be in the dark about the missing assignments.

In the macro domain one of the contexts for our consideration would be the school itself. How does the school environment exacerbate or alleviate any of the issues faced by Jenna and Michael? In the same way, one has to ask in what way do Michael and Jenna exacerbate or alleviate the issues faced within the school environment? How does the school change the family and how does the family change the school? Specific questions for consideration might include, but are certainly not limited to, the following:

1. In what way does the school's assignment of homework affect Michael's self-concept, feelings of competence, development of skills and knowledge, and so on?

2. In what way does the school's assignment of homework affect Jenna's feelings about herself as a parent? as a single parent? as an intelligent individual?

3. In what way does the school's assignment of homework affect the relationship between Jenna and Michael? their ability to work together? their communication patterns?

4. In what ways does Michael's self-concept, confidence, knowledge, skills, and so on affect the school environment, himself, his teachers, and his peers?

5. In what ways does or might Jenna affect the school environment? For instance, by participating on campus or on field trips? by involvement in the PTA? by speaking with the teachers individually? by requesting a list of homework assignments? by requesting less homework for her son? by sending to school a child who is ready to learn?

6. In what ways does the relationship between Jenna and Michael affect the school environment, such as Michael's completion of his homework, Michael's relationship with his teachers, Michael's conduct on campus, and so on?

THE VISITATION ISSUE: JENNA, MICHAEL, AND BRAD

One consideration for a human service provider at the macro level is the question of what we are doing within our prison systems to support the ongoing relationships, or in some cases to establish relationships, between incarcerated parents and their children. In our eclectic practice, whereas we might use our knowledge of developmental theory in the first issue presented above, here we might also draw on attachment theory (understanding the psychological connectedness between people [Bowlby, 1979]) to explore our understanding of interpersonal issues, the mezzo domain. Attachment is a lifelong process and affects our relationships at every age. Even in cases in which the parent is incarcerated without the possibility of parole and will not be coming home again, might there still be a role for the parent to play in the life of the child? Might the child still long for a relationship with the parent?

When shown the diagram (figure 7.5) of the single-parent family constellations, Jenna immediately pointed to the placeholder single-parent family constellation and identified with that experience. She and Brad were never married and there is no formal or legal custody arrangement, no formal child support arrangement, and no visitation schedule. While she believes it is important for Michael to continue a relationship with his biological father, she wants to allow Michael to set his own parameters and handle the relationship on his own terms. She does not look to Brad to meet any of her needs, but she is able to allow him a place in the family, so to speak, so that Michael can continue to develop his own understanding of his biological father's role in his life.

Perhaps we should be asking:

- How do we as a society secure and support the best relationship possible between the imprisoned parent and the child?

- How might this relationship help with the healing of our prisoners?

- How might it enrich their lives?

- Might it even serve as their reason for living?

- Might this enriched relationship help in the healing of the children or partners left behind?

Knowing that Jenna sees value in the continuation of the relationship between Brad and Michael, a human service provider could help her and Michael explore ways to strengthen this relationship. Perhaps Michael could communicate with Brad in a way that informs his father of his interests and accomplishments, giving Brad an opportunity to express his pride in his son. Perhaps Michael could express to his father some of the things he has felt during the years that they have been apart. Perhaps Jenna could call on Brad from time to time to be the one to say, "This is your mother and she knows what she is talking about!," thereby serving in a parental role, even from afar. Even if none of these actions is explored, a sensitive practitioner would acknowledge for Jenna the strength and maturity she demonstrates by seeing the value in this relationship for Michael. "Michael is so lucky to have you as his mom. What great examples of decision making you are showing him."

THE HOUSING ISSUE: JENNA, TED, AND MICHAEL

In working with this family, it is insignificant that affordable housing is so limited in the community in which Jenna and Michael live, a macro-level consideration. Jenna's indecision about moving her relationship with Ted to the next level, living together, is complicated by the fact that she may in the process lose her ability to afford adequate and acceptable housing for herself and her son should the relationship with Ted come to an end. As we begin to consider the interpersonal relationships somewhat apart from the housing issue, we are moving more into the mezzo domain. This provides a good example of how the domains are intricately connected, how practice includes movement between the domains, and how one issue relates to another.

Jenna and Ted have been dating for five years now, ever since Michael was seven years old. Ted is a consistent and positive presence in their lives. Jenna and Ted, like many couples today, see cohabitation as a natural progression in a committed relationship and a way to move closer while keeping the change manageable for Michael. A practitioner working with this family would be interested to know how each person views this family. Jenna may see this as a partnered single-parent family, one in which Ted is not fully in the role of a second parent at this time. But how do Michael and Ted view the family? (See the first pages of this chapter for Michael's answer.)

NONORDINARY REALITY OR MAGNA DOMAIN

Here we consider the nonordinary reality or magna domain and how awareness of this domain could inform practice with this family. First, ask yourself this question: Because neither Jenna nor Michael, Brad nor Ted, have discussed spirituality or religion in their lives, would it be appropriate for the human service provider to ignore this last domain in this case?

Certainly, a consideration of the magna domain is a larger part of our work with some families than it is with others. We do not want to impose a spiritual understanding on a family in terms other than its own. With that said, in this case we might at least be aware that Jenna does not see herself as a spiritual seeker at this point in her life. Nor does she report that she has been harmed in life by religious or spiritual dogma, practices, attitudes, and so on.

What we might also notice is that in one sense of the term, she is a person of faith. Her life as she lives it and as she describes it gives testimony to her faith in life, faith in herself, faith in her power to affect change, faith in her ability to heal, faith in her ability to love and be loved, faith in her ability to provide for her son, faith in her ability to parent. She in fact takes a leap of faith when she allows Michael to visit his grandparents in the presence of his father. She may also, at some point, decide to take a leap of faith regarding the decision to move into a new place with Ted and Michael. While one could question, and perhaps disagree with either decision, Jenna demonstrates a reliance not only on her ability to think this through, but also on her ability to go with what feels like the best or right thing to do. This is not what we typically mean when we consider a person's faith, but this may be the most relevant connotation of the term in this particular case.

In much the same way, a practitioner must often depend on what Guadalupe and Welkley call "practice wisdom" earlier in this text—a way of knowing that emerges from our being open to "the great unknown." Bein (2008) describes this in his book, *The Zen of Helping*: "As helping practitioners, we project the reality that we are on a sacred journey with our clients. We are profoundly fortunate to experience a connection with people in spite of the truth that we rarely *know* what we are doing" (pp. 1–2). Bein goes on to explore twelve spiritual principles of helping. Although it is beyond the scope of this chapter to explore these in detail, a few will suffice to introduce the reader to this way of viewing families, the helping professions, and life in general.

- The main ground of helping and professional practice is uncertainty and not knowing. Although theory and knowledge of the other may be helpful, it often interferes with our direct perception and engagement with clients.

- As we increasingly trust the present moment, our responses emerge from deep wisdom rather than fight-or-flight reactions or superficial attempts at grasping for certainty.

- We are intimately connected with our clients and communities. We tune into our essential nonseparateness in a manner that is spiritual. This nonseparateness means that my client's narrative is my own and were it not for some circumstances or biological or social condition, I could easily be in the client's chair, and she could be in mine. We fully embrace that we, as practitioners, are no better than our clients. (pp. 2–3)

Summary

An increasing number of children experience life in a single-parent family, for part of or all of their childhood. It is imperative that we commit ourselves to a better understanding of these families. This chapter set out to open up a new way of viewing single-parent family constellations. Moving beyond marital status, household, and custody arrangements, we focused on the single-parent family as perceived by the single parent and by the child (children) in the single-parent family. This awareness led to a consideration of seven single-parent family constellations: autonomous or isolated single-parent family, extended single-parent family, multigenerational single-parent family, single-parent coparenting family, single-parent dual-parenting family, partnered single-parent family and single-parent placeholding family.

By broadening our way of viewing these single-parent family constellations, we are able to understand the single-parent family as a multidimensional contextual nonstatic living entity. In light of this context, we understand that families and the individuals within them are continually in a process of both being and becoming. We acknowledge that individuals experience family within multiple family memberships and that they affect and are affected by the many environmental contexts in which they live.

We consider the role that self-awareness, knowledge, skills, and openness have in our practice with families. Moving beyond stereotypical practice, we finetune our listening skills, respond reflectively, and strive to be ever open to the great unknown within the human spirit.

Questions for Continued Consideration

When working with a single-parent family, it is critical to check one's assumptions at the door. The following questions may help to remind us of exactly what that means.

1. What experiences do we have with single-parent families?

2. What feelings are associated with those experiences?

3. What do we assume to be true in single-parent families?

4. Are we open to noticing and seeking out individual and family strengths as well as challenges?

5. Do we see the individual as a resource, not only for their own well-being, but also as a resource for others in the family and the community?

6. Do we also see the family as a resource?

7. Are we able to bear in mind the many ways in which the family is an agent of change?

8. Do we make room for the family to solve its own problems?

9. How do we monitor our own practice with families to ensure that we are not operating from a position of stereotypical assumptions?

10. How does our self-awareness, our knowledge, and our skills as a whole inform our practice?

11. Are we open to the great unknown as a force in our lives and in the lives of others?

12. Are we prepared to consider all domains in our practice with families: micro, mezzo, and macro?

13. Are we open to hearing the family's stories as told in their terms—the family's narrative?

References

Alle-Corliss, L. I., & Alle-Corliss, R. (1999). *Advanced practice in human service agencies: Issues, trends, and treatment perspectives*. Belmont, CA: Wadsworth.

Anderson, J. (2004). *The single mother's book* (2nd ed.). Atlanta, GA: Peachtree.

Bein, A. (2008). *The Zen of helping: Spiritual principles for mindful and open-hearted practice*. Hoboken, NJ: John Wiley & Sons.

Biblarz, T. J., & Stacey, J. (2010). How does the gender of parents matter? *Journal of Marriage and Family*, 72(1), 3–22.

Boss, P. (2002). *Family stress management: A contextual approach* (2nd ed.). Thousand Oaks, CA: Sage.

Bowlby, J. (1979). *The making and breaking of affectional bonds*. London: Tavistock.

Brooks, J. (2008). *The process of parenting* (7th ed.). Boston: McGraw-Hill.

Bumpass, L. L., & Raley, R. K. (1995). Redefining single-parent families: Cohabitation and changing family reality. *Demography*, 32(1), 97–109.

Burger, W. R. (2008). *Human services in contemporary America* (7th ed.). Belmont, CA: Thomson Brooks/Cole.

Coles, R. (2009). Just doing what they gotta do. *Journal of Family Issues*, 30(10), 1311–1338.

Davidson, J. K, Sr., & Moore, N. B. (1996). *Marriage and family: Change and continuity*. Boston: Allyn & Bacon.

Dunst, C. (2002, Fall). Family-centered practices: Birth through high school. [Electronic version.] *Journal of Special Education*, 36(3), 139–147. Retrieved September 5, 2008, from Academic Search Premier database.

Edin, K. (2005). Few good men: Why poor mothers stay single. In A. S. Skolnick & J. H. Skolnick (Eds.), *Family in transition* (13th ed.) (pp. 496–506). Boston: Allyn & Bacon.

Engber, A., & Klungness, L. (1995). *The complete single mother*. Cincinnati, OH: Adams Media Corporation.

Family Support America. (1996). Making the case for family support. Chicago, IL: Family Support America. Retrieved July 17, 2006, from www.familysupport america.org.

Garcia, E. E. (1994). Addressing the challenges of diversity. In S. L. Kagan & B. Weissbourd (Eds.), *Putting families first: America's family support movement and the challenge of change* (pp. 243–275). San Francisco: Jossey-Bass.

Guadalupe, K., & Lum, D. (2005). *Multidimensional contextual practice: Diversity and transcendence.* Belmont, CA: Thomson Brooks/Cole.

Hanson, S. M. H. (1986). Healthy single parent families. *Family Relations, 35*(1), 125–132.

Marsten, D., & Howard, G. (2006). Shared influence: A narrative approach to teaching narrative therapy. [Electronic version.] *Journal of Systemic Therapies, 25*(4), 97–110.

Mattes, J. (1997). *Single mothers by choice: The classic guidebook for single women who are considering or have chosen motherhood.* New York: Three Rivers Press.

Newman, D. M. (2009). *Families: A sociological perspective.* New York: McGraw-Hill.

Olson, D. H., DeFrain, J., & Skogrand, L. (2008). *Marriages and families: Intimacy, diversity, and strength* (6th ed.). New York: McGraw-Hill.

Orenstein, P. (2000). *FLUX: Woman on sex, work, love, kids and life in a half-changed world.* New York: Anchor Books.

Roberts, R. N., Rule, S., & Innocenti, M. S. (1998). *Strengthening the family-professional partnership in services for young children.* Baltimore: Paul H. Brookes.

Sugarman, S. D. Single-parent families. (2007). In S. J. Ferguson (Ed.), *Shifting the center: Understanding contemporary families* (3rd ed.) (pp. 287–299). New York: McGraw-Hill. Chapter originally published in 1998.

U.S. Census Bureau. (2005). The living arrangements of children in 2005. Population Profile of the United States: Dynamic Version online. Retrieved July 30, 2008, from http://www.census.gov/population/www/pop-profile/files/dynamic/LivArrChildren.pdf.

U.S. Census Bureau. (2007). Single-parent households showed little variation since 1994, Census Bureau reports. Retrieved February 15, 2010, from http://www.census.gov/Press-Release/www/releases/archives/families_households/009842.html.

U.S. Census Bureau. (2008). Improvements to demographic household data in the current population survey: 2007. Housing and household economic statistics division working paper. Retrieved February 15, 2010, from http://www.census.gov/population/www/documentation/twps08/twps08.pdf.

Resources for Parents and Practitioners

Ahrons, C. (2004). *We're still family: What grown children have to say about their parents' divorce.* New York: Harper-Collins.

Alle-Corliss, L., & Alle-Corliss, R. (1999). *Advanced practice in human service agencies: Issues, trends, and treatment perspectives.* Belmont, CA: Wadsworth.

Anderson, J. (2004). *The single mother's book: A practical guide to managing your children, career, home, finances, and everything else* (2nd ed.). Atlanta, GA: Peachtree.

Bein, A. (2008). *The Zen of helping: Spiritual principles for mindful and open-hearted practice*. Hoboken, NJ: John Wiley & Sons.

Berends, P. B. (1987). *Whole child, whole parent* (rev. ed.). New York: Harper & Row.

Berg, I. K. (1994). *Family-based services: A solution-focused approach*. New York: W. W. Norton.

Boss, P. (2002). *Family stress management: A contextual approach* (2nd ed.). Thousand Oaks, CA: Sage.

Brooks, J. (2008). *The process of parenting* (7th ed.). New York: McGraw-Hill.

Burger, W. R. (2008). *Human services in contemporary America* (7th ed.). Belmont, CA: Thomson Brooks/Cole.

Carlson-Paige, N. (2008). *Taking back childhood: Helping your kids thrive in a fast-paced, media-saturated, violence-filled world*. New York: Penguin Group.

Coontz, S. (Ed.). (2008). *American families: A multicultural reader* (2nd ed.). New York: Taylor & Francis.

Das, L. S. (1997). *Awakening the Buddha within: Tibetan wisdom for the Western world*. New York: Broadway Books.

Diss, R. E., & Buckley, P. K. (2005). *Developing family and community involvement skills through case studies and field experiences*. Upper Saddle River, NJ. Pearson Merrill Prentice Hall.

Dolan, P., Canavan, J., & Pinkerton, J. (2006). *Family support as reflective practice*. London: Jessica Kingsley.

Drexler, P. (2005). *Raising boys without men: How maverick moms are creating the next generation of exceptional men*. New York: Holtzbrinck.

Edin, K., & Kefalas, M. (2005). *Promises I can keep: Why poor women put motherhood before marriage*. Berkeley: University of California Press.

Elias, M. J., Tobias, S. E., & Friedlander, B. S. (1999). *Emotionally intelligent parenting*. New York: Three Rivers Press.

Engber, A., & Klungness, L. (1995). *The complete single mother: Reassuring answers to your most challenging concerns*. Holbrook, MA: Adams.

Erickson, M. F., & Kurz-Riemer, K. (1999). *Infants, toddlers, and families: A framework for support and intervention*. New York: The Guilford Press.

Ferguson, S. J. (2007). *Shifting the center: Understanding contemporary families* (3rd ed.). Boston: McGraw Hill.

Greene, R. R. (Ed.). (2008). *Human behavior theory and social work practice* (3rd ed.). New Brunswick, NJ: Transaction.

Hulbert, A. (2004). *Raising America: Experts, parents and a century of advice about children*. New York: Random House.

Hutter, M. (2004). *The family experience: A reader in cultural diversity*. Boston: Pearson Education.

Kagan, S. L., & Weissbourd, B. (Eds.) (1994). *Putting families first: America's family support movement and the challenge of change*. San Francisco: Jossey-Bass.

Karen, R. (1994). *Becoming attached: First relationships and how they shape our capacity to love*. New York: Oxford University Press

Kennedy, M. (2005). *Without a net: Middle class and homeless (with kids) in America*. New York: Penguin.

Koplow, L. (Ed.) (1996). *Unsmiling faces: How preschools can heal.* New York: Teachers College Press.

Landy, S., & Menna, R. (2006). *Early intervention with multi-risk families: An integrative approach.* Baltimore: Paul H. Brookes.

Lareau, A. (2003). *Unequal childhoods: Class, race, and family life.* Berkeley: University of California Press.

Locke, D. C. (1998). *Increasing multicultural understanding: A comprehensive model* (2nd ed.). In Paul Pedersen (Series Ed.), *Multicultural aspects of counseling series.* Thousand Oaks, CA: Sage.

Lopez, R. A. (2002). Las comadres as a parenting support system. In N. V. Denokraitis, *Contemporary ethnic families in the United States: Characteristics, variations, and dynamics.* Upper Saddle River, NJ: Prentice Hall.

Lynch, E. W., & Hanson, M. J. (2004). *Developing cross-cultural competence: A guide for working with children and their families* (3rd ed.). Baltimore: Paul H. Brookes.

McKnight, J. (1995). *The careless society: Community and its counterfeits.* New York: Basic Books/Perseus Books Group.

Nelson, J., Erwin, C., & Delzer, C. (1999). *Positive discipline for single parents: Nurturing cooperation, respect, and joy in your single-parent family* (2nd ed.). New York: Three Rivers Press.

Olson, D. H., DeFrain, J., & Skogrand, L. (2008). *Marriages and families: Intimacy, diversity, and strengths* (6th ed.). New York: McGraw-Hill.

Ornstein, P. (2000). FLUX: *Women on sex, work, love, kids, and life in a half-changed world.* New York: Random House.

Roberts, R. N, Rule, S., & Innocenti, M. S. (1998). *Strengthening the family-professional partnership in services for young children.* Baltimore: Paul H. Brookes.

Schorr, L. B. (1997). *Common purpose: Strengthening families and neighborhoods to rebuild America.* New York: Random House.

Sidel, R. (2006). *Unsung heroines: Single mothers and the American dream.* Berkeley: The University of California Press.

Siegel, D. J., & Hartzell. M. (2003). *Parenting from the inside out: How a deeper self-understanding can help you raise children who thrive.* New York: Penguin Putnam.

Skolnick, A. S., & Skolnick, J. H. (2009). *Family in transition* (15th ed.). Boston: Pearson Education.

Stacey, J. (1991). *Brave new families: Stories of domestic upheaval in late twentieth century America.* New York: Harper-Collins.

Stacey, J. (1996). *In the name of the family: Rethinking family values in the postmodern age.* Boston: Beacon Press.

Sugarman, S. D. (2007). Single-parent families. In S. Ferguson (Ed.), *Shifting the center: Understanding contemporary families* (3rd ed.) (pp. 287–299). New York: McGraw-Hill.

Thayer, E. S., & Zimmerman, J. (2001). *The co-parenting survival guide: Letting go of conflict after a difficult divorce.* Oakland, CA: New Harbinger.

CHAPTER EIGHT

Lesbian and Gay Families (Gamilies)

Jan Osborn

Is life not a hundred times too short
for us to stifle ourselves.

Friedrich Nietzsche

Lesbian and gay families experience the same joys and challenges that heterosexual families do. (Multiple family constellations exist within the lesbian, gay, bisexual, transgender, intersex community. However, this chapter focuses on issues related to gay or lesbian family forms.) However, there also exist challenges that are specific to the lesbian and gay communities. Many of these challenges are the direct result of the interface lesbian and gay individuals have with the larger society. Although societal beliefs (constructions) are forever shifting and in some segments of the dominant heterosexual culture are becoming more positive, the ever-present negative constructions of lesbians and gays continue to afford these individuals and families challenges to overcome. The constructions of the dominant culture have led to laws prohibiting the legal sanction of lesbian and gay families. Although these laws present tremendous adversity, strong and committed lesbian and gay families blossom in the face of it.

In order for practitioners to be competent to assist lesbian and gay families, an understanding of societal constructions within a historical context is necessary. Thus, an explanation of the historical and current societal constructions will be offered, as will the results of research that strongly counters these beliefs. An explanation of how one comes to a lesbian or gay identity (narrative) will also be discussed. Some of the laws that affect the formation of families will be covered, as will a description of the varying family constellations that lesbians and gays create despite these laws. Oppression and its impact will be discussed, as will working with lesbians and gays in therapeutic or helping settings. The continual deconstructing and constructing of individual and family beliefs in their process of being and becoming will also be explored.

Social Construction That Informs Lesbian and Gay Narratives

It is impossible to comprehend the complexities of lesbian and gay families without looking at the societal constructions that influence them. Dominant constructions of models of normalcy typically do not include the lesbian and gay community. It is difficult to understand the constructions of the present without placing them in a historical context. The concept of a lesbian or gay identity began to take shape toward the end of the nineteenth century. The biomedical view represented homosexuality as a medical condition, stigmatized it, and set it apart from the rest of society as a symptom of degenerate lifestyles. The first Diagnostic and Statistical Manual (DSM) of the American Psychiatric Association published in 1952 contained homosexuality as a form of mental illness. People could be hospitalized with no concurrent diagnosis. Inclusion of this diagnosis in the DSM was not based on empirical data but rather on the constructions of psychiatrists, which reflected the constructions of the dominant culture (Herek, 2000). In 1957, a study conducted by Evelyn Hooker was published in the *Journal of Projective Techniques* that concluded homosexuality did not constitute a clinical entity and was not inherently associated with pathology.

In the 1960s, the civil rights movements for minority groups laid the foundation for activism on the part of the lesbian and gay community. This made the lesbian and gay community somewhat more accessible and allowed for some to become more comfortable with their lesbian and gay identities. In 1973, the board of directors of the American Psychiatric Association removed homosexuality from the DSM. This was accomplished after numerous empirical studies for men and women had supported Hooker's original conclusion in 1957 as well as the changing societal norms and the development of politically active lesbian and gay communities. This declassification has been supported by the American Psychological Association and many other professional and academic groups (Herek, 2000). As a result, the therapy literature on homosexuality has shifted from a focus on pathology to an emphasis on the formation of positive narratives for those in the lesbian and gay community. A pathological view is still held by many in the dominant culture, including practitioners; therefore, the identity development of lesbian and gay people is still negatively affected. Constructions have shifted in some contexts from those that supported regular police raids of lesbian and gay establishments, involuntary confinement of lesbian and gay persons to locked psychiatric wards who had no other psychiatric diagnosis than homosexuality, and loss of child custody when lesbian and gay orientations were disclosed, to the legalization of lesbian and gay marriage, and adoption of children by same-gender couples in some states. Even with these shifts, however, lesbian and gay families face difficulties and strife that are directly related to dominant constructions leading to oppression. Consider the politically correct description of lesbian and gay families as alternative. Although this is meant to be supportive and judgment neutral, it is clear that lesbian and gay families are an alternative to what is normal rather than what Guadalupe and Welkley refer to as one of a multiple ways of being (see chapter 1).

Constructions: Choice vs. Biology

One construction that greatly affects how lesbians and gays are viewed, as well as how they view themselves, is the debate over whether sexual orientation is a life choice or is biologically driven. The answer to the question of choice is far less impactful than what one does with the information. Choice implies free will; therefore the religious right views homosexuality as a sin. The opposite view is that love is beautiful and all have the right to love whomever they choose. Biological causation has similar opposing views. The conservative view is that lesbians and gays are sick or damaged from birth. On the other hand, the discoveries in the field of biology and sexual orientation are a welcome relief to some in the lesbian and gay community. If religious, then one can view oneself as expressing God's gift, rather than being persuaded into believing that one is a sinner. Osborn and Filiatreaux (2007) found that all the lesbians they interviewed believed that their sexual orientation was biologically driven. One woman who had been ex-communicated from her church, which included leaving her college because it was church based, and who had become suicidal during her coming out process, stated, "I had everything, why would I 'choose' to give all that up?"

Briefly let's explore various areas through which research has been conducted regarding homosexuality:

- *Genome Research:* Causal studies of sexual orientation have focused on biological causes including genetics, anatomy, neuroendocrine, and environmental, including focuses on psychodynamic and social learning theories.

- *Genetics:* Hamer, Hu, Magnuson, Hu, and Pattatucci (1993) published a National Institute of Health study that found that gay men are passed homosexuality from their mothers via the X chromosome. Later studies by Rice and Ebers (1999) did not support this, and no further studies have been done;

- *Anatomical:* Three major studies were conducted in the early 1990s, all focusing on the hypothalamus. Swaab and Hofman (1990) compared homosexual male brains to heterosexual male brains post mortem. A structural difference in a small portion of the hypothalamus, the auprachiasmatic nucleus, was found. In gay men it was twice the size of heterosexual men. LeVay (1991) studied cell groups in the hypothalamus and found that two of the groups were larger in gay men.

- *Hormonal and Neuroendocrine:* Ruse (1984), after reviewing the hormonal research, stated that there were conflicting results and in general there was little evidence of the difference in adult hormones. However, sexual orientation is thought to be primarily determined by the degree to which the nervous system is exposed to testosterone, estradiol, and other sex hormones while neuro-organization is taking place in utero (Ellis & Ames, 1987). Prenatal levels of androgen on the neural structures during fetal development determines sexual orientation. If highly exposed to androgen, the fetus will be masculinized or attracted to females. A Stanford study examined hormonal levels of both male and female rats. Female rats with increased levels of androgen showed higher levels of aggression and sexual behavior with other female rats. Male rats that were deficient in androgen levels were submissive and willing to receive sexual behaviors from other male rats. Congenital adrenal hyperplasia (CAH) is a genetic disorder that causes a fetus to secrete large amounts of androgens from the adrenal glands, enough so that newborn girls with the condition often have virtualized genitalia. Several studies have shown that girls with the condition have high rates of masculine behavior including preference for so-called masculine toys, increased rough-and-tumble play activity, and other tomboyish behavior. Additionally, they have an increased rate of homosexual feelings (Ehrhardt et al., 1985; Money, 1986).

• *Environment Studies:* Studies have been done with twins with the idea that if homosexuality is genetically, rather than environmentally, based, then identical twins will have higher rates of homosexuality than fraternal twins and fraternal twins will have higher rates than adoptive twins (twins who are individually adopted by two separate families). Bailey and Pillard (1991) found that identical twins had rates of homosexuality of 52 percent (29 out of 56), fraternal twins had rates of 22 percent (12 out of 54), and adoptive twins had rates of 11 percent (6 out 57). This was exactly as predicted and supports genetic causality.

Dominant Constructions of Lesbian and Gay Parenting

Social constructions within the United States have formulated and perpetuated a dominant belief that most gay men cannot be trusted with children and that children should be raised by straight women. This is based on some of the following dominant social orientations: homosexuality is an illness or disorder, lesbians are less maternal than heterosexual women, and gay men are too involved in sexual relationships to parent effectively. Those constructing the negative views of lesbians and gays have characteristics in common. Men tend to be more homonegative than women. A man's hostility toward lesbians and gays is associated with the extent to which he perceives that his friends are in agreement with a person's negative attitudes. Interpersonal contact with gays is related to attitudes that are more positive toward homosexuality. This reflects negative views being based on ignorance and fear, which are dispelled in the reality of knowing someone who is lesbian or gay. Higher levels of religiosity and traditional ideologies of family and gender often mediate disapproval of homosexuality. Believing that homosexuality is a choice is associated with a more negative view. Thus, those who are the most likely to be negative are highly traditional men who believe that homosexuality is a choice, who know few if any gay or lesbian people personally, and who are surrounded by others who share their view. Sherman (1995) found that 60 percent of Americans disapprove of legally sanctioning gay couples' rights to adopt children and 42 percent oppose openly gay or lesbians teaching in schools (Lacayo, 1998).

The social constructions that lesbians and gays were inferior—and even dangerous—parents led to research looking to prove or disprove how negatively affected children would be by having lesbian or gay parents. There was a solid belief that children were being damaged by lesbian and gay parents based solely on their parent's orientation, though there was no evidence to support this. With each study came more and more evidence to the contrary. Not only were the negative constructions not supported, but also lesbian and gay parents were actually shown to be as nurturing or even more nurturing parents than heterosexuals. For example, lesbian and gay parents typically adopt a child-centered approach to rearing their children, and lesbian and gay partners generally are highly committed to maintaining family integrity (Lynch & Murray, 2000).

Positive Outcomes of Lesbian and Gay Parenting

GAY FATHERS

When compared to heterosexual fathers, gay fathers report being firmer in setting appropriate standards for their children and using more reasoning strategies when responding to the needs of their children (Tasker, 2005). Additionally, gay fathers, relative to heterosexual fathers, do not differ in their intimacy or involvement with their children and show higher levels of warmth and responsiveness combined with control and limit setting in their parenting patterns (Lambert, 2005). After studying twenty gay male families including those with children who were not from previous heterosexual unions, Mallon (2004) stated that he came to an enduring impression of the gay dads interviewed, one of deep commitment to parenting their children regardless of the many obstacles faced in a society that sees heterosexuals as the primary parental resource. Studies also have shown that gay fathers have much higher levels of self-esteem than gay men who are not fathers, and that gay coparents are more likely than heterosexual men to share household responsibilities, including child care (Frommer, 1996; McPherson, 1993).

LESBIAN MOTHERS

Studies have shown that lesbian mothers demonstrate greater awareness of the necessary skills for effective parenting than heterosexual parents do. Vanfraussen, Ponjaert-Kristoffersen, and Brewaeys (2002) found that lesbian mothers also tend to express greater warmth, spend more time interacting with their children, and have interactions with their children that are higher in quality. In addition, these mothers prove to be very skillful in their ability to discover critical issues in child-care situations and to effect appropriate solutions. Bos, van Balen, and van Den Boom (2004) studied one hundred lesbian couples with children and 100 heterosexual couples with children and found them to be the same in all regards except that lesbians are less likely to have conformity as a child-rearing goal, because these parents are less attuned to traditional parenting styles. Lesbian couples share parenting duties more equally (Hand, 1991; Osterweil, 1991; Patterson, 1995) as do gay men (McPherson, 1993). Due to the societal construction that heterosexual women are highly effective parents, lesbian mothers felt that they needed to defend their positions as mothers. Additionally, lesbian mothers generally stress to their children factors such as tolerance for diversity (Eldridge & Barrett, 2003; Lambert, 2005). On a personal level, lesbian mothers have demonstrated higher levels of functioning and well being than heterosexual mothers, and are happier in their couple relationships. Green, Mandel, Hotvedt, Gray, and Smith (1986) compared fifty lesbian mothers and forty heterosexual mothers and found that lesbians were more confident and seek leadership roles more often than heterosexual mothers do. This finding may be related to gender roles in heterosexual relationships.

CHILDREN

Children are affected by both the dominant societal constructions and their parents' reactions to them. A review of studies from 1978 to 2000 conducted by Anderssen, Amlie, and Ytterøy (2001) found that in twenty-three studies children raised by lesbian mothers or gay fathers did not systematically differ from other children on any outcomes. Only three studies included gay men, and all others looked at lesbians. Although children were essentially the same across the studies, some significant differences were found, which confirm that the dominant constructions of lesbians and gays as inadequate parents are fear based and inaccurate. For example, boys of lesbians have more feminine characteristics, and *do not have fewer male characteristics*. This is a very important finding because it counters the dominant construction that boys need men in their lives to avoid being too feminized. The only difference found on the California psychological inventory was that the children of divorced, single, heterosexual mothers had more problems with self-esteem than did children of lesbian mothers. Children of lesbian mothers were found to be more open to diversity and to have broader definitions of gender roles. This reflects the findings of Eldridge and Barrett (2003) and Lambert (2005), that lesbian mothers stress the acceptance of diversity to their children. Children of lesbians report feeling closer to their mothers than do children of heterosexual mothers (Steckel, 1987). Children of heterosexual parents saw themselves as more aggressive than did children of lesbians, and they were seen by both parents and teachers as being more bossy, domineering, and negativistic. Children of lesbian parents saw themselves as more lovable and were seen by parents and teachers as more affectionate, more responsive and more protective toward younger children.

MacCallum and Golombok (2004) found that children of lesbians had more interaction with their mothers and perceived her as more dependable and available than did children from homes with fathers. Children in the planned lesbian families had secure attachment patterns, and there was greater involvement of nonbiological mothers in child care compared with that of most fathers in heterosexual two-parent families (Tasker & Golombok, 1998). More children of heterosexual mothers had psychiatric symptoms than did children of lesbian mothers. Contrary to the dominant belief that children of lesbians do not have enough contact with men, lesbian mothers were found to be more concerned with making sure that their children had contact with men than were heterosexual mothers. Additionally, children from a previous heterosexual union with lesbian moms had more contact with their fathers than did children of heterosexual mothers. Surprisingly, even sexual orientation rates were the same for children of gay and lesbian parents and children of heterosexual parents.

Only one longitudinal study (Tasker & Golombok, 1998, a follow-up of Golombok, Spencer, & Rutter in 1983), compared children of lesbian mothers to children of heterosexual mothers. They found no differences in emotional functioning or rates of sexual preference. There also were no differences found on levels of stigma, although the children of lesbians were more teased about their sexuality. Children of lesbians had more of a willingness to challenge traditional sex-role stereotypes, and an ability to fashion creative, nurturing, healthy relationships in the face of a sometimes oppressive society (Lambert, 2005).

Identity Development Models

It may be the case that before one can become part of a lesbian or gay family one may have to identify oneself as having a lesbian or gay narrative. This process is different for each person. Some lesbians and gays state that they always knew that they were lesbian or gay, while others come to acceptance late in life. The process of coming to a lesbian or gay identity is greatly affected by societal constructions, demands, and dynamics of interactions. People of differing ages have different histories in relation to the societal constructions they experienced, which greatly affects the development of their identity.

CASS MODEL

The Cass (1979) model has become the classic outline for the study of lesbian or gay identity formation and has set the groundwork for future lesbian and gay identity models. The model assumes that sexual identity is not fluid, but rather fixed from birth, and does not vary throughout one's life span (Morris, 1997). Cass believed that the incongruence that each stage creates interpersonally motivates movement through the stages of the model. Interface with the dominant constructions of society and sometimes one's family may make it impossible for movement through the stages to occur. Below is a description of the stages that Cass proposed:

- Stage 1, identity confusion, is characterized by the first conscious awareness that lesbian and gay identity has meaning to one's own narrative. Conflict internally and isolation is typical of this stage.

- Stage 2, identity comparison, entails a beginning integration of a lesbian and gay narrative. The main task is to handle the social alienation that results as one becomes increasingly aware of the differences between one's own narrative and that of others.

- Stage 3, identity tolerance, brings with it an increased sense of alienation resulting in a movement toward connection with others with similar narratives. The critical factor in this stage is the emotional quality of the contact with other lesbian and gay people (Cox & Gallois, 1996).

- Stage 4, identity acceptance, incorporates increased contact with others with lesbian and gay narratives and a resulting sense of feeling normal (Sophie, 1986). The lesbian and gay subcultures become increasingly more important in one's life at this stage.

- Stage 5, identity pride, entails a nearly complete acceptance of one's lesbian or gay narrative as well as an increased identity with the lesbian and gay community. One becomes aware and owns being a part of a minority group, and often is ostracized by the dominant heterosexual culture. Group identity and activism may be very strong at this stage.

- Stage 6, identity synthesis, is reached when the individual is able to integrate his or her homosexual narrative with other important narratives. The lesbian or gay part of one's narrative is no longer seen as one's sole narrative, but rather as a very important narrative among many.

TROIDEN'S MODEL

Eleven years after the development of the Cass model, Troiden (1988) introduced an identity model based on social constructionism. The social constructionist argument challenges the basic assumption of essentialism and, in addition, invites the examination of the historical and social context in which any social behavior occurs in order to fully understand behavior. The belief is that no two individuals can have the exact same identity or arrive at their identity in the exact same way, regardless of similar experiences. Troiden's model is a social constructionist theory of human sexuality that is influenced by genetic predispositions and by social environment and historical contexts. It is based on the idea that sexuality is fluid in nature and not fixed at any point in development. Because the model is based on social constructionism, it focuses on the relationship between self-perception, social settings, sexuality, and romantic context, the interaction of which produces the narrative of sexual identity. Troiden hypothesized that lesbian or gay identity existed on three levels: self-concept, imagined perception by others, and actual presentation to the outside world. When the three are in agreement, a lesbian or gay narrative is most fully embraced by the individual. Troiden postulated that an individual goes through four stages in the formation of a lesbian or gay narrative.

- Stage 1, sensitization stage. The individual has homosexual feelings or experiences without understanding the implications for her or his own narrative. During this time he or she feels marginalized and different from peers. Teasing and negative labeling for traits or behavior contribute to the internalization of a negative self-narrative.

- Stage 2, identity confusion, may bring conflicts between a person's former narrative and the newly emerging lesbian or gay narrative, which is not accepted by the dominant culture. Coping mechanisms for dealing with this possible confusion that are stressed at this stage include denial (I am not gay), avoidance (awareness of lesbian or gay narrative but choosing isolation), repair (conversion therapy), or acceptance.

- Stage 3, identity assumption, brings a reduction in social isolation and an increase in contact with other lesbian or gay people. The primary task at this stage is learning to manage the social stigma of embracing a minority narrative. People cope with this stress through capitalization (unconditional surrender to a negative view of homosexuality), ministralization (adopting exaggerated homosexual mannerisms or behavior), passing (selectively concealing one's sexual orientation), and group alignment (immersion into the lesbian and gay community to the exclusion of heterosexual contexts).

- Stage 4, commitment, is an integration of a lesbian or gay narrative to the extent that it becomes a way of being. Once Stage 4 is reached, there are increased levels of self-satisfaction and happiness. A lesbian or gay narrative may become one of many narratives. There can be a decrease of earlier coping mechanisms. Interfacing with the dominant heterosexual community may lead a person to hide her lesbian or his gay narrative. One may also consider the lesbian or gay narrative inconsequential. A third adaptation is to take on the lesbian or gay identity as a dominant narrative.

It is important to consider context as an important aspect of the development of a lesbian and gay narrative. The social constructions that offer a lack of acceptance of lesbians and gays in our culture have a negative effect on the development of a lesbian or gay identity. Understanding some of the issues people face during narrative development helps a person to understand the effect on creating a new family.

Family Constellations of Lesbian and Gay Families (Gamilies)

Similar to heterosexual families, lesbian and gay families reflect much diversity. Nevertheless, it is helpful to think about two general types of lesbian or gay family constellations with children: families in which children are part of a previous heterosexual union, and families in which children were brought into an established lesbian or gay family via insemination, adoption, or surrogacy.

LEGAL ISSUES

It is impossible to understand the adversity that lesbian and gay families face when forming without looking at the ways in which laws, which vary from state to state as stressed in chapter 5, affect what is legally possible for them. There are two main areas of law that affect gamilies (gay or lesbian family constellations). The first is that of the legality of marriage or some sort of legal union. The debate over gay and lesbian marriage rages in many parts of the United States. A clear distinction is being made between the legal and the religious aspects. Currently six states, one federal district, and one Native American tribe grant same-sex marriages. These include Connecticut, the Coquille Indian Tribe in Oregon, Iowa, Massachusetts, New Hampshire, New York, Vermont, and Washington, DC. California allowed same-sex marriages between June 16, 2008, and November 4, 2008. Presently all same-sex civil unions in California are given the legal rights of marriage within the state; however, only those obtained during the short period in 2008 are given the designation of marriage. Maryland, New York, and Rhode Island recognize same-sex marriages, but do not perform them. Several other states allow marriage-like civil unions for lesbian and gay residents. The rights of these unions vary from state to state. These states include California, Colorado, Hawaii, Maine, Maryland, Nevada, New Jersey, Oregon, Washington, Wisconsin. The backlash to this civil rights effort is the explicit ban on same-sex unions in twenty-nine states and the Cherokee Nation.

No laws in support of gamilies with children existed until 1993 when a precedent case took place in Vermont. Laws vary greatly from state to state on the issue of lesbian and gay parents' ability to adopt. The most conservative states include Arkansas, which does not allow any non-married couple to adopt (and which prohibits lesbian and gay marriage) and Florida, which prohibited any gay or lesbian person from adopting until September 2010. States that allow single gay or lesbian parent adoption, joint adoption by a lesbian or gay couple, and second-parent adoption include California, Colorado, the District of Columbia, Illinois, Massachusetts, New Jersey, and New York. The majority of states allow single lesbian or gay parent adoption, do not clearly prohibit joint adoption, and either allow second-parent adoption in some states, or are unclear on second-parent adoption. Those who allow second-parent adoption in some areas include Alabama, Alaska, Arizona, Delaware, Hawaii, Iowa, Kansas, Kentucky, Louisiana, Maryland, Minnesota, Montana, and Nevada. Maine allows single-parent adoption. Mississippi and Michigan allow single parent, disallow joint and are unclear on second parent. Missouri is unclear in all three areas. Nebraska allows single-parent adoption, is not clear on joint, and disallows second-parent. Of particular interest is New Hampshire: although it is one of only five states that allow same-sex marriage, it does not support joint adoption and its position on second-parent adoption is unclear. Second-parent adoption allows for both parents to obtain custody of the couple's children. This does not mean, however, that a couple can adopt at the same time. Rather, one parent must have custody either biologically or through adoption, and allow the other to adopt. If the couple separates before the second parent, who may in fact be in a primary role, is able to adopt, that parent may be left with no rights at all.

Even with all of these constraints, the nonbiological parent is still in a far better place legally than those who are not able to adopt at all. Without laws to protect them, some of these parents may lose all rights to their children after years of parenting. The more liberal social constructions of people in cities such as Chicago, Austin, and Madison helped these laws to become enacted. Societal constructions are shifting enough to provide gamilies with rights in some areas, but these changes are in no way universal. This nonuniversality creates a tremendous strain, because parents with no legal rights often feel marginalized and are not protected legally. Additionally, the liberal change in constructions has brought with it a conservative backlash. For example, Oklahoma and Utah expressly prohibit known gays and lesbians from adopting. In addition, some states still have sodomy laws that make sexual activity between consenting adults of the same gender illegal. These laws unfortunately do not simply remain on the books, but are actively enforced in some jurisdictions. California has laws that allow for minors of certain ages to have intercourse without it being reportable to the department of child protective services, whereas oral and anal sex is reportable. Thus, families face differing issues based on where they live.

FAMILIES OF CREATION

The types of lesbian and gay families are as varied as are the issues they face. In many respects, the motivational factors organizing lesbians and gay men to become parents are no different from those cited by heterosexuals, that is: a desire to nurture children through active parenting and a wish to have children because, like heterosexuals, lesbians and gay men enjoy children and want children to have a valued place in their lives (Bigner & Jacobsen, 1989). However, because of the ways in which the fear-based societal constructions leading to homophobia and heterosexism affect the lives of lesbians and gay men, their decision to parent must be seen within the current societal context. For instance, gay men and lesbians living in the 1950s, when their sexual behavior and identity was considered illegal and immoral, had only one acceptable route to parenthood: heterosexual marriage. Thus, they were forced to choose between having an appropriate life partner and having children. Though the societal climate has changed somewhat, many are still forced to make this choice. Those who do maneuver around the societal climate and choose a same-sex partner are many times faced with parenting without legal sanction of their unions or their coparenting. They are also faced with the complexities of bringing children into their families without the ability to create the life of a child together biologically.

LESBIAN INSEMINATION GAMILIES

Even within the same type of family, the issues faced can be quite varied. In the case of lesbian insemination, once the couple decides to have children, they must decide who will have the first child and how this will occur. Some partners clearly do not want to be pregnant while others are very invested in being biological mothers. Thus, this issue needs to be resolved in a way that clearly heterosexual couples do not need to think about. When the partner who is deeply invested in being pregnant suffers the deep pain of infertility, the other partner may get pregnant, or in some cases may even donate eggs to her partner, allowing her to experience pregnancy. Once the decision has been made as to who will become pregnant, couples must decide between donors known to them or anonymous donors.

Lesbians seeking insemination face different issues based on whether they use a donor known to them or an anonymous donor from a sperm bank. Lesbians who choose to use a known donor may be faced with issues of paternity and custody, even if a contract was drawn up before the birth of the child indicating the parental status of the donor. They also are faced with explaining the relationship with the donor to the child. On the positive side, some couples choose to use a family member of the nonbiological mother, affording the child with genetics from the families of both his or her mothers. Again, the relationship will need to be explained: a man may be the child's uncle socially and father biologically.

On the other hand, women using unknown donors are faced with the cost of purchasing sperm, having limited information about a donor, explaining to a child the difference between father and donor, and facing the concerns that arise if a child wishes to meet the donor. Some banks have now opened up the opportunity for children to contact their donors, if the donor consents to this. There are also organizations that allow women (or adult children) to locate biological half-siblings created by the use of the same donor. This reality greatly broadens the definition of family.

The issues associated with second-parent adoption and marginalization also comes into play here. A second-parent adoption includes the financial and emotional strain of hiring a social service agency to provide a home study in order to approve both parents as fit parents. In some states, a biological or adoptive parent who is heterosexual may allow his or her partner to adopt without such a study (due to the uninvolvement of a social service agency). Thus, there is the potential of a heterosexual parent allowing a convicted sex offender or active addict to adopt his or her child. However, a lesbian (gay) parent must prove her (his) own worthiness as well as that of his (her) wife (husband), no matter what law-abiding citizens they are based solely on their sexual orientation. If the donor is known, and is claiming paternity, the second parent, who may actually be a primary parent, will not be able to adopt until the biological father's or donor's rights are terminated. Once the child is born, the biological parent must pay to put advertisements in local newspapers announcing that the child will be adopted if no one claims paternity!

ADOPTION GAMILIES

The primary way for gay men to create families is through adoption. Lesbians sometimes choose this option as well. There are issues facing the lesbian and gay community when they are involved in the adoption process. Oppression is an enormous factor for lesbian and gay people who want to become adoptive parents. Lesbians and gays are made to stand up to scrutiny that heterosexual parents are not. As noted earlier, in some states, such as Utah, known lesbians and gays may not adopt at all. In more states than not, one parent may adopt, but the other parent cannot, leaving that parent without the legal rights of parenthood, while still assuming equal parenting responsibilities. When adopting from some countries internationally, only one parent may adopt, and not even then if she (he) is thought to be lesbian (gay). Thus, many couples choose to leave the nonadopting parent home on the occasion of becoming parents, for fear of being found out. Gay men face the most discrimination due to the misperception that gay men are pedophiles (when the majority of pedophiles are, in fact, heterosexual men), and that women are better parents.

When same-sex couples adopt, the decision of who will be the adoptive parent or the first adoptive parent must be made. This process requires a tremendous amount of trust between partners. Again, the second parent is not legally protected until his or her adoption process is finalized. For those living in states without the ability to adopt as a second parent, this finalization never comes.

SURROGACY GAMILIES

Another option open to some gay men in states like California is surrogacy. In these cases the surrogate (known or unknown until the contract for surrogacy) is inseminated with the sperm of one or both of the partners. The partners pay a fee for this service in addition to all medical care costs. If lesbians use this option, then it may entail egg donation and sperm donation. The intended parents are protected legally in this case. Due to the expense and lack of states that offer surrogacy protection, this option is not open to many, unless it is done by known surrogates with private contracts. The legal issues facing gay parents in states that do not sanction surrogacy are enormous, as the surrogate could decide not to give custody as agreed.

COPARENTING GAMILIES

Some lesbians and gays choose to coparent together. This may be an arrangement of a nonpartnered lesbian and gay man, or among couples, or a combination. This arrangement affords the child with both male and female parents. The child may be biologically connected to two of the parents, as one of the lesbians may use the sperm of one of the gay men to become pregnant.

Communication regarding expectations of parenting responsibilities is essential. Issues as to where the adults and children will reside must also be addressed. If couples are involved, then only two parents will have legal custody, thus all the issues of being a parent with no rights apply. This is an example of the larger society not recognizing alternative families, as in these family constellations there may well be more than two parents.

POLYAMOROUS GAMILIES

Some lesbian and gay families challenge the dominant construction of monogamy. Individuals can have very different constructions of what it means to be polyamorous (defined as "the philosophy and practice of loving or relating intimately to more than one other person at a time with honesty and integrity"; Unitarian Universalists for Polyamory Awareness [UUPA], 2010), thus it is crucial that all members of the poly family understand each other's definitions and resulting expectations. Some families have primary couple relationships with other secondary partners, while others have multiple relationships. These are double minorities and thus face the resulting oppression.

Polyamorous family constellations raise many issues for consideration, including parenting, child rearing, interpersonal communication within the family, as well as how these family constellations and the individuals within them are perceived by other groups and individuals in society (i.e., the school, the church, the community). Some people may argue that this type of family constellation can be detrimental to a child's development, but others may propose that children are raised by a community, which may be reflected by this type of family constellation. Therefore, practitioners working with these gamilies need to gain an understanding of polygamilies in general and the family they are treating specifically.

PREVIOUS UNION GAMILIES

Some lesbian and gay families were not always so, as parents may have come to their lesbian or gay identities after having children within heterosexual marriages. These families face unique issues such as lesbian and gay parents coming to terms with their lesbian or gay narratives and the reactions of children, spouses, friends, and families of origin to it; divorce, and all the issues that divorcing families face; and coming together as a stepfamily and all the issues therein. Sometimes lesbian and gay people begin to realize their changing narratives because they fall in love with someone of the same gender. Thus, there is sometimes an emotional or physical affair and the shame that can accompany it.

A major difference between families who began as lesbian and gay minority families and those who come to it after living within the dominant majority culture is giving up the majority status while simultaneously dealing with the reactions of others. Spouses may be very supportive or at least not hostile, often for the sake of the children. They may, however, be hostile, speak badly of the lesbian (gay) parent and her (his) sexual orientation to the children, and try to take custody based on their spouse's or ex-spouse's homosexual orientation. Many times a major factor in how children adapt to the new sexual orientation of the lesbian or gay parent and to the divorce may be related to the reaction of the heterosexual parent. Therefore, children whose heterosexual parent reacts badly may have a hard time adjusting to the change. Young children, particularly with a lesbian or gay parent who is comfortable with the orientation, and children who have supportive heterosexual coparents adjust quite easily. The most difficult adjustment is for adolescents who were not raised with the belief that homosexuality is a positive orientation. Lesbian and gay families who have children from previous heterosexual unions may also face disapproval and even cut-off relationships with families of origin and families-in-law. Thus, at a time that may be confusing for all, the support may be lessened. These gamilies also face all of the issues that many stepfamilies face.

STEPGAMILIES

Prior to the coming together of the stepfamily there has been divorce or the separating of the family and possibly resultant custody issues. Therefore, there are issues that many stepgamilies face, including loyalties to biological parents, attitudes toward stepparents, custody arrangements, coparenting, attitudes of the other biological parent and stepparent, communication between parents, and the place children have in parental conflicts.

Even with all of this in common, not all stepfamilies are created equal. In addition to the issues facing stepfamilies, there are added differences in stepgamilies. Furthermore, stepgamilies face different issues, depending on whether the lesbian or gay family was previously a heterosexual family or whether it was lesbian or gay all along.

One of the issues facing previous union gamilies is when to tell children of the parent's lesbian or gay orientation. Adolescents seem to have the most difficulty with this information. This may be due to many factors, such as the fact that they are dealing with their own sexuality and self-image. How adults in the child's life react to the changed narrative also greatly influences the child's adjustment. How supportive the ex-spouse is can make the difference in the child accepting the new narrative, as well as their overall functioning. Huggins (1989) found a tendency for children whose fathers were rejecting of their mother's lesbianism to report lower levels of self-esteem than those whose fathers were neutral or positive. Similarly, if the lesbian (gay) parent is uncomfortable or shameful about her (his) orientation, children will find the adjustment more difficult. Lesbian and gay parents new to the narrative are sometimes afraid to share this narrative with their children. Older children may find this difficult, because they often already know on some level, but are given the message that there is a prohibition to talking about it. The family may also be torn apart by negative attitudes toward homosexuality. Children may be cut off from key family members and not have an understanding as to why this has happened.

Family Constellations Within the Context of Dominant Culture

There is no schema prescribed by society for lesbian and gay families as there seems to be for heterosexual families, such as institutionalized structures approving of their status as a family (Hequembourg, 2004; Lynch & Murray 2000). Therefore lesbian and gay individuals face adversity and potential discrimination when attempting to form families (Lynch & Murray). Living a minority narrative within a dominant culture is challenging for any minority group. Oppression by the dominant culture is one of the most difficult challenges that minority groups face. In light of this reality, minority groups often find solace and belonging within the safety of that group. Most minority group members find among this safe haven family members such as parents and siblings. This is often not the case for lesbians and gays. Family members may even be some of the strongest sources of oppression. Lesbian and gay youth are sometimes forced to live on the street, losing the safety of family upon disclosing lesbian and gay narratives.

In addition to being outcasts, even from families at times, there are laws in the United States and other countries that actually prevent lesbian and gay people from enjoying rights given to all others of the society. In chapter 2 of this text, Guadalupe and Welkley speak of the inability in our past of minority slaves to marry. Most now see this as an outrage. There is little public outrage for the lack of marriage rights for lesbians and gays. Children are taught that they have the right to grow up and marry regardless of ethnic status, and all adult heterosexuals enjoy the right to marry. Lesbians and gays overall do not share this basic human right.

The lack of civil rights for lesbians and gays affects greatly the children in these family constellations. The fact that lesbians and gays cannot legally marry sends the message that they are less than, thus so is their family. One man spoke about the difficulty of explaining to his child why it was illegal for her daddies to marry. The child equated illegal with bad, breaking the rules, and jail, and was therefore fearful that her daddies would go to jail. Lesbian and gay families face loss of children, loss of disabled partners to families of origin who are not supportive of their children's union, loss of jobs, harassment in the workplace, and even murder, based on their lesbian and gay narratives.

The oppression against lesbian and gay families is then sometimes used as an argument against sanctioning lesbian and gay families. The fact that children may be discriminated against for having lesbian and gay parents can be used by adoption agencies to not allow adoptions. Thus, the dominant majority may discriminate against the minority and then use that very oppression, as a reason to oppress further, never taking responsibility for the oppression that is induced. There is also the construction that children of lesbians and gays may be isolated and not exposed to the dominant heterosexual culture. Minority groups, on the contrary, are very aware of the dominant culture as a means of survival. It would be impossible for a child to attend school and not be exposed to the dominant heterosexual culture of the majority of his or her teachers and parents of his or her peers. In light of this oppression, lesbian and gay parents, like parents of other minority cultures, are faced with the task of assisting their children to deal with the oppression that faces them. In addition to this, they sometimes face the struggle of dealing with the anger of their children who are being discriminated against for their parent's minority status, when they may not have minority status themselves.

It is beyond the scope of this chapter to cover all the horrible and tragic stories of oppression gamilies face; however the following is an example. It is tragic, but it is not surprising.

In 1996, a woman lost custody of her child of whom she had custody since her divorce some time before, until her ex-husband, who had been convicted of murdering his first wife, used her lesbianism as a reason to obtain custody. While her case was being appealed for this outrageous injustice she mysteriously died. Choosing a known murderer over a lesbian or gay is not by any means the only example of courts choosing less-fit parents over lesbian and gay parents based solely on sexual orientation.

Oppression breeds many things, one of which is resiliency. To meet the challenges of oppression, many lesbian and gay family constellations have created ways of being a family and exhibit a unique strength and flexibility that assists all the members of their family in the transitions to family life (Lynch & Murray, 2000; Oswald, 2002). Strategies used by lesbian and gay families to affect their environments have included intentionality and redefinition (Oswald). Intentionality includes behavioral strategies that sustain and legitimize relationships through the conscious formation, ritualization, and legalization of relationships considered as family. Furthermore, external supports are created and the visibility of homosexuality inside and outside of their familial network is recognized and managed. Redefinition comprises semantic strategies that create symbolic and linguistic mechanisms to affirm gay and lesbian familial networks. These strategies may include the development of an inclusive and politicized view of the family, the use of familial names to reinforce relational ties (e.g. referring to friends as brother or sister), and the incorporation of lesbian and gay relationships with significant life dimensions (Oswald). Furthermore, research demonstrates that, in response to oppression, lesbian individuals often develop a strong sense of self, flexibility, and inclusiveness within the family and maintain equity in their relationships when they become parents, leading to increased satisfaction in both parents and children (Fredriksen-Goldsen & Erera, 2003). Lesbian and gay families often cope with oppression by developing mutually balanced and interdependent family relationships (Connolly, 2005).

Family Practice: An Eclectic Approach

The uniqueness of living as a lesbian or gay in the dominant heterosexual culture has been addressed throughout this chapter. Gaining such an understanding is important when working with any nondominant culture. Equally important are the fundamental beliefs of the practitioner. Knowledge is helpless in the face of deep-seated prejudice. Saunders (2000) suggests that the most relevant determinant of outcomes in working with lesbian and gay couples is the practitioner's fundamentally held beliefs as to how he or she understands gayness itself. For instance, is a helping professional able to affirm a lesbian or gay identity as having equal value to that of a heterosexual identity? In other words, does he or she take seriously the specific cultural contexts that shape beliefs, values, and behaviors—not only those of their clients, but also of themselves (Tasker & McCann, 1999)? This is not to suggest that the practitioner needs to be lesbian or gay, rather that the practitioner has the ability to empathize with and accept the client. To this end, all practitioners must develop a knowledge base that incorporates examination of heterosexism and that unearths the roots of fear and prejudice with regard to sexuality in general (Davies, 1996).

Most human service practitioners have the intention of creating safety for clients, but it is not always the case. For example, Platzer (2003) found that same-gender couples that are parenting children complain that their specific family patterns and situations are from time to time not properly recognized or valued by the human service practitioner. They experience practitioners using inappropriate models of parenting based on heterosexual couples with rigid and segregated gender roles.

Clinical Issues

To create and maintain a warm, intimate, and loving home in the face of societal stigma can engender stress of varying degrees. Thus, the issues brought to the helping process include many of the usual problems that any family might encounter, although they are sometimes complicated with an overlap of the kind of tensions unique to gamilies. There are also many different levels of interface that need to be considered.

As we reflect on these different dimensions, it is critical to remember, as Guadalupe and Welkley emphasize in this text (chapters 1 through 4), families are multidimensional contextual nonstatic living entities. As observed throughout this discussion of gamilies, there is not one gamily type, but there are many arrangements that are affected by their context of time, place, individuals, politics, the law, and so on. These constellations have been changing and will continue to change based on individual membership and social constructions and demands.

Intrapersonal. The interface between the intrapersonal and other levels is recursive, with each level affecting the other levels. The development of one's individual narrative is tremendously affected by the interpersonal and societal dimensions (Morgan, 2000). Thus, it is imperative for the practitioner to understand the intersection and interdependence of these realms of experience.

- How does the lesbian (gay) person think about the lesbian or gay aspect of her (his) narrative?

- Are they struggling to accept it or are they "out and proud"?

- How important a role do they feel sexual orientation plays in their lives?

- How much support do they have from their families of origin, the lesbian and gay community, the spiritual community, and so on?

- Are they experiencing isolation or lack of connection from the lesbian and gay community and from their families and larger heterosexual culture?

- Do they identify strongly with a particular type of lesbian or gay, such as butch, femme, or drag queen?

- What types of oppression have they experienced?

- How are they coping with oppression?

- Are these healthy ways of coping, such as joining lesbian and gay groups, or are they more self-destructive, stemming from oppression-induced shame, such as drug and alcohol use?

Internalized oppression can greatly affect the development of one's narrative. The fear-based negativity can seep into the narrative of the lesbian or gay person. The reaction to oppression causes some to be stronger, while it causes others to feel beaten and victimized.

Spirituality is another important issue.

- How has the client made sense of his or her spirituality and gay (lesbian) identity?

- Who knows about the individual's lesbian or gay narrative?

- Is the person out in all settings, or are there settings in which the client feels forced or in which the client chooses to be private or closeted?

- What does the client believe will be the consequence of being open?

- Will (Have) they lose (lost) family, jobs, children?

Depending on where a client lives, these consequences can vary greatly. A lesbian or gay person in a liberal, diverse city has a different experience of oppression from the experience of a person living in a conservative small town, for example.

Interpersonal. Each individual narrative interfaces with the individual narratives of others (Morgan, 2000). Thus, whether working with an individual or with many family members, it becomes important to understand each narrative and how these interface with one another. When working with a couple, it is important to understand how each thinks about the above questions and how these interface. For example, if one person is very out and another is very in, how do they deal with this difference? Or, if one person's family is very supportive and the other person's is not, how do they cope? A couple may not understand why they are having difficulties until they notice the differences and how they can support each other and develop a positive couple narrative.

In working with families of origin such as parents, these issues also become important. Many assumptions may have been made about the others' narrative and the practitioner can help families talk openly and learn to hear from other members what is genuinely true for them. In the case of a gay or lesbian who came to this narrative after having children, there is the added issue of discussing beliefs with the children. Because lesbian and gay gamilies are forever confronted with choosing when to come out and how far to come out, so are their children. Adults and children may be in differing places around these choices. Some parents may expect their children to defend lesbian and gay rights, and the child may want to hide the fact that their parents are gay or lesbian or at least be private about it. Conversely, children may openly discuss the make-up of their family to the discomfort of their parents. As mentioned earlier, family constellations that once enjoyed heterosexual privilege have different struggles interfacing than do those of original lesbian and gay gamilies.

Multiple memberships. Some lesbians and gays take tremendous solace in being members of the lesbian and gay community. As one progresses through the stages of identity development, there is more focus on other aspects of one's life. This is not to say that a lesbian or gay identity becomes less important, but rather that it is not as paramount. Heterosexuality is the dominant orientation of our culture, thus lesbian and gay people are still members of the straight society. Lesbians and gays are also members of their families of origin, though these relationships are sometimes strained due to the latter's lack of acceptance. Lesbians and gays may also be a part of a spiritual community. This is often the result of an intense process of reexamining one's beliefs from childhood. One must reckon these beliefs with one's beliefs about his or her sexual orientation and develop a place of faith that fits with one's present circumstances. Lesbian and gays also are a part of communities that most people are a part of such as their workplace, neighborhood, and families.

Being and becoming: Construction, deconstruction, and reconstruction.
The process of individual and family narrative construction, deconstruction, and reconstruction is a life-long process. For example, a client who was raised in a family with very conservative and negative constructions of lesbians and gays may initially deny a lesbian or gay construction of self altogether. Once deconstructing one's heterosexual narrative and tentatively accepting a lesbian or gay narrative, one may see this as a negative narrative and experience self-loathing. Upon further deconstruction, one may be able to construct a positive lesbian or gay narrative.

Families go through a similar process. The family may have to deconstruct its views of homosexuality and its spiritual views in relation to it, as the alternative may be to disown the lesbian or gay member. Families with a lesbian or gay couple also go through processes of deconstruction and reconstruction. Many beliefs will need to be reexamined when a couple or family comes together. Issues around what it means to be a man or woman, lesbian or gay, monogamous or polygamous, parents or a couple without children, will all need to be examined and reconstructed as a couple. It is the practitioner's role to assist in this process of construction, deconstruction, and reconstruction.

Individuals and families are in a constant state of change. Sometimes these changes are imperceptible whereas others are major shifts. The process of becoming is very important to the lesbian and gay community. Individual narratives of coming to a lesbian or gay identity, the historical and current societal reactions to lesbians and gays, families' changing reactions over time all affect the individual's being and becoming and that of the families of which they are a part. Counseling or other supportive services can be a very valuable part of this process while assisting families with these changes.

Practitioners need to understand that as individuals and family constellations, within the gay and lesbian community, encounter the process of being and becoming, they are also affecting and being affected by intrapersonal, interpersonal, and environmental realms of existence. For instance, their actions reflect resilience within the context of vulnerability while affecting as well as being affected by current, and changing, federal and state laws regarding same-sex parenting and marriage.

Goals of the helping process.   The therapeutic work of assisting families to shift old constructions, cocreate new ones, and experience themselves differently is a process that evolves over time. Because this process is cocreated between practitioner and families, each case is unique. The general progression of this process, however, occurs in phases (Osborn, 2000).

- The development of a therapeutic relationship with the practitioner and among relevant family members.

- Clear, nonreactive communication among family members. This includes the development of a free flow of emotional energy, access to all feelings, and the ability to tolerate feelings without defending against them. Each person is able to be clear and honest about his or her own views, meanings, feelings, vulnerabilities, and defenses.

- The ability to coconstruct new more expansive realities that incorporate parts of the realities of each family member. This new frame is likely to have some fragments of the old realities and some pieces that are entirely new. Before this is possible, each family member must have the ability to share their inner awareness with one another and to tolerate any reactive response from others to that sharing. This will allow them to experience being together in a new way.

- Successful termination of the helping process that addresses feelings and concerns related to ending professional supportive services. Unsuccessful or incomplete terminations leave unresolved issues for both the clients and the practitioner.

Summary

Lesbian and gay gamilies cannot be understood without examining the constructions of the larger society in which they are situated. Although lesbian and gay gamily constellations experience the same joys and struggles that heterosexual family forms do, there are unique challenges facing lesbian and gay families due to their interface with the negative constructions held by the larger society and the resultant oppression of those constructions.

Some of the constructions held are that lesbian and gay life is an immoral choice, whereas many lesbians and gays believe that their orientation is genetically based and that the only choice is to acknowledge their genetics. Another strongly held construction is that lesbian and gay parents are doing harm to their children. On the contrary, the research on lesbian and gay parents and children finds that children of lesbian and gay parents feel closer to their parents, are more open to diversity, and are kinder and less aggressive than children of heterosexual parents. Children of lesbian and gay parents are often, not surprisingly, more stigmatized than are other children.

Living a minority narrative within a dominant culture is one of the most challenging issues for all types of gamilies to address, sometimes without the support of families as oppression may come from there as well. Lack of rights such as marriage and the ability to adopt children together sends the message to children that their families are less than other types of families. Gamilies, to deal with oppression, have a unique strength, resiliency, and flexibility. Even with all of the negative views of their lifestyle, lesbian and gay gamilies continue to form and flourish. Lesbians and gays have had to be innovative to fulfill their desire to have children—thus, there are many types of families, each with its unique strengths and struggles. Family constellations include lesbian insemination gamilies, adoptive gamilies, surrogate gamilies, coparenting gamilies, polyamorous gamilies, previous union gamilies, and stepgamilies. The legal issues these gamilies face when attempting to legitimize the relationships of all partners and parents and their children varies from state to state.

Practitioners must have an understanding of how individual and family narratives are affected by the constructions of the larger society and the resulting oppression faced by these gamilies. Individual narratives are then brought together into family perspectives. Practitioners working with lesbian and gay gamilies must be open to understanding narratives of oppression and triumph that affect the entire family constellation, deconstruction of negative constructions, and assisting in reconstructing narratives of strength, resiliency, and hope.

Questions for Reflection

1. What has been your perspective regarding gay and lesbian family constellations? Do you respect and embrace their existence? Do you support or reject the notion that gay and lesbian familial relationships are multidimensional contextual nonstatic living entities with unique strengths, challenges, and needs? Explain.

2. In your experiences, to what degree have gay and lesbian family constellations been recognized and honored within the context of the United States' dominant culture? Provide concrete examples.

3. To what degree have you observed gay and lesbian family constellations engaging in a constant space of being and becoming? Explain.

4. In your experiences, how has the notion of diverse realms of existence affecting and being affected by the family been reflected within experiences related to gay and lesbian family constellations?

5. What would you consider important for the construction of an eclectic approach aimed at supporting and working with gay and lesbian family constellations? Illustrate a template.

References

Anderssen, N. Amlie, C., & Ytterøy, E. A. (2002). Outcomes for children with lesbian or gay parents. A review of studies from 1978 to 2000. *Scandinavian Journal of Psychology*, *43*(4), 335–351.

Bailey, J. M., & Pillard, R. C. (1991, December). A genetic study of male sexual orientation. *General Psychiatry*, *48*(12), 1089–1096.

Bigner, J. J., & Jacobsen, R. B. (1989). The value of children to gay and heterosexual fathers. In F. W. Bozett (Ed.), *Homosexuality and the family* (pp. 163–172). New York: Harrington Press.

Bos, H. M. W., van Balen, F., & van Den Boom, D. C. (2004). Experience of parenthood, couple relationship, social support, and child rearing goals in planned lesbian mother families. *Journal of Child Psychology and Psychiatry*, *45*, 755–764.

Cass, V. C. (1979). Homosexual identity formation: A theoretical model. *Journal of Homosexuality*, *4*(3), 219–235.

Connolly, C. M. (2005) A qualitative exploration of resilience in long-term lesbian couples. *The Family Journal: Counseling and Therapy for Couples and Families*, *13*, 266–280.

Cox, S., & Gallois, C. (1996). Gay and lesbian identity development: A social identity perspective. *Journal of Homosexuality*, *30*(4), 1–30.

Davies, D. (1996). Towards a model of gay affirmative therapy. In D. Davies & C. Neal (Eds.), *Pink therapy: A guide for counselors and therapists working with lesbian, gay and bisexual clients*. Buckingham, UK: Open University Press.

Ehrhardt, A., Meyer-Bahlburg, H. F. L., Rosen, L. R., Feldman, J. F., Veridiano, N. P, Zimmerman, I., & McEwen, B. S. (1985, February). Sexual orientation after prenatal exposure to exogenous estrogen. *Archives of Sexual Behavior*, *14*(1), 57–77.

Eldridge, N. S., & Barrett, S. E. (2003). Biracial lesbian-led adoptive families. In L. B. Silverstein & T. J. Goodrich (Eds.), *Feminist family therapy: Empowerment in social context* (pp. 307–318). Washington, DC : American Psychological Association.

Ellis, L., & Ames, M. A. (1987, March). Neurohormonal functioning and sexual orientation: A theory of homosexuality-heterosexuality. *Psychological Bulletin*, *101*(2), 233–258.

Fredriksen-Goldsen, K. L., & Erera, P. L. (2003). Lesbian-headed stepfamilies. *Journal of Human Behavior in the Social Environment*, *8*, 171–187.

Frommer, M. S. (1996). The right fit: A gay mans quest for fatherhood. *In The Family*, *2*(1), 12–16.

Golombok, S., Spencer, A., & Rutter, M. (1983, October). Children in lesbian and single-parent households: Psychosexual and psychiatric appraisal. *Journal of Child Psychology and Psychiatry and Allied Disciplines*, *24*(4), 551–572.

Green, R., Mandel, J. B., Hotvedt, M. E., Gray, J., & Smith, L. (1986). Lesbian mothers and their children: A comparison with solo parent heterosexual mothers and their children. *Archives of Sexual Behavior*, *15*(2), 167–184.

Hamer, D. H., Hu, S., Magnuson, B. L., Hu, N., & Pattatucci, A. M. L. (1993, July 16). A linkage between DNA markers on the X chromosome and male sexual orientation. *Science*, *261*, 321–327.

Hand, S. I. (1991). The lesbian parenting couple. Unpublished doctoral dissertation, Professional School of Psychology, San Francisco.

Herek, G. M. (2000, February). The psychology of sexual prejudice. *Current Directions in Psychological Science*, *9*(1), 19–22.

Hequembourg, A. (2004). Unscripted motherhood: Lesbian mothers negotiating incompletely institutionalized family relationships. *Journal of Social and Personal Relationships*, *21*, 739–762.

Hooker, E. (1957). The adjustment of the male overt homosexual. *Journal of Projective Techniques*, *21*, 18–31.

Huggins, S. (1989). A comparative study of self-esteem of adolescent children of divorced lesbian mothers and divorced heterosexual mothers. *Journal of Homosexuality*, *18*(1–2), 123–135.

Lacayo, R. (1998, Oct 26). The new gay struggle. *Time*, *152*, 32–37.

Lambert, S. (2005). Gay and lesbian families: What we know and where to go from here. *Family Journal*, *13*, 43–51.

LeVay, S. (1991, August 30). A difference in hypothalamic structure between heterosexual and homosexual men. *Science*, *253*(5023), 1034–1037.

Lynch, J. M., & Murray, K. (2000). For the love of the children: The coming out process for lesbian and gay parents and stepparents. *Journal of Homosexuality*, *39*, 1–24.

MacCallum, F., & Golombok, S. (2004, November). Children raised in fatherless families from infancy: A follow-up of children of lesbian and single heterosexual mothers at early adolescence. *Journal of Child Psychology and Psychiatry*, *45*(8), 1407–1419.

Mallon, G. P. (2004). *Gay men choosing parenthood*. New York: Columbia University Press.

McPherson, D. (1993). Gay parenting couples: Parenting arrangements, arrangement satisfaction and relationship satisfaction. Unpublished doctoral dissertation, Pacific Graduate School of Psychology, Palo Alto, CA.

Money, J. (1986). Homosexual genesis, outcome studies and a nature/nurture paradigm shift. *American Journal of Social Psychiatry*, *6*, 95–98.

Morgan, A. (2000). *What is narrative therapy? An easy read introduction*. Adelaide, Australia: Dulwich Centre.

Morris, J. F. (1997). Lesbian coming out as multidimensional process. *Journal of Homosexuality*, *33*(2), 1–22.

Osborn, J. L. (2000). The quart bottle: A social constructionist/experiential case study. *Journal of Family Psychotherapy*, *11*(1), 21–45.

Osborn, J. L., & Filiatreaux, L. R. (2007, October). Genome and the lesbian, gay, bisexual community. American Association for Marriage and Family Therapy Annual Conference. Austin, TX.

Osterweil, D. A. (1991). Correlates of relationship satisfaction in lesbian couples who are parenting their first child together. Unpublished doctoral dissertation, California School of Professional Psychology, Alhambra, CA.

Oswald, R. F. (2002). Resilience within the family networks of lesbians and gay men: Intentionality and redefinition. *Journal of Marriage and the Family*, *64*(2), 374–383.

Patterson, C. J. (1995). Families of the lesbian baby boom: Parents' division of labor and children's adjustment. *Developmental Psychology*, *31*, 115–123.

Platzer, H. (2003). Lesbian, gay and bisexual identity work in mental health: an evidence-based guide for people who work with families. Unpublished report. Pace Center, London.

Rice, G., & Ebers, G. (1999, April 23). Male homosexuality: Absence of linkage to microsatellite markers At Xq28. *Science*, *284*(5414), 665–667.

Ruse, M. (1984, Winter). Nature/nurture: Reflections on approaches to the study of homosexuality. *Journal of Homosexuality*, *10*(3/4), 141–151.

Saunders, G. L. (2000). Men together: Working with gay couples in contemporary times. In P. Papp (Ed.), *Couples on the fault line: New directions for therapists* (pp. 222–256). New York: Guildford Press.

Sherman, N. (1995, Summer). The moral perspective and the psychoanalytic quest. *Journal of the American Academy of Psychoanalysis and Dynamic Psychiatry, 23*(2), 223–241.

Sophie, J. (1986) A critical examination of stage theories of lesbian identity development. *Journal of Homosexuality, 12*(2), 39–51.

Steckel, A. (1987). Psychosocial development of children of lesbian mothers. In F. W. Bozett (Ed.), *Gay and lesbian parents* (pp. 75–85). New York: Prager.

Swaab, D. F., & Hofman, M. A. (1990, December). An enlarged suprachiasmatic nucleus in homosexual men. *Brain Research, 537*(1–2), 141–48.

Tasker, F. (2005, June). Lesbian mothers, gay fathers, and their children: A review. *Journal of Developmental and Behavioral Pediatrics, 26*(3), 224–240.

Tasker, F., & Golombok, S. (1998). *Growing up in a lesbian family: Effects on child development.* New York: Guilford.

Tasker, F., & McCann, D. (1999). Affirming patterns of adolescent sexual identity: The challenge. *Journal of Family Therapy, 21*(1), 30–54.

Troiden, R. R. (1988, March). Homosexual identity development. *Journal of Adolescent Health Care, 9*(2), 105–113.

Unitarian Universalists for Polyamory Awareness (UUPA). (2010). Retrieved February 12, 2011, from http://www.uupa.org/.

Vanfraussen, K., Ponjaert-Kristoffersen, L., & Brewaeys, A. (2002). What does it mean for youngsters to grow up in a lesbian family created by means of donor insemination? *Journal of Reproductive and Infant Psychology, 20,* 237–252.

CHAPTER NINE

Foster Care
Family Constellations

Debra L. Welkley

I'd forever know what feelin' special really was . . .
When somebody did everything in they power
to make someone feel special
                        Regina Louise—*Somebody's Someone*

Whether discussing children in foster care, foster care, foster families, or residential care for children, society tends to see children in foster care as children without a family. Yet this is far from reality. Of the just under five hundred thousand children in foster care in the United States, almost half (46 percent) live in nonrelative foster family homes (Adoption and Foster Care Analysis and Reporting System [AFCARS], 2010). Approximately 24 percent are in a relative foster family home, which indicates that the caregiver is either related or a close family friend to the child in care. Additionally, 51 percent of children in foster care have the case goal to reunify with their parent(s) or principal caretaker(s), and 20 percent of the children in foster care have the case goal of adoption. These statistics are indicators that children in foster care are a part of two or more family constellations, and are not without a family.

Depending on the point of reference, foster families may be viewed through the lens of foster parents, children in foster care, child-care workers, biological families of children moved in to foster care, as well as the state, county, or court, depending on whichever political entity has the economic and social responsibility of the child in care. These are only some of the vantage points through which a foster family can be viewed. The point is that, depending on the lens and needs of that entity, a foster family can be viewed and explained in very different ways. Additionally, although there may be a common definition for foster family the norms, regulations, standards, and goal plans differ from state to state and even from county to county. Therefore, it is beneficial for practitioners working with individuals and families in foster care to consider the foster family from a multidimensional perspective that reflects on the nonstatic nature of foster families, the multiple memberships of these families, how they are a family while they also are becoming a family, and how the unit and its members are both affecting and being affected.

Generally, the definition of a foster family is as follows: a family where children under the age of eighteen have been removed from their family of origin and placed with a certified parent(s); responsibility for the child ultimately rests with the designated governmental authority (i.e., the court, the state, the county). Children are removed from their families of origin for a myriad of reasons but primarily due to neglect or physical or emotional abuse. Additionally, it should be noted that whereas children under the age of eighteen may be removed and placed in foster care in many states the child could remain in the foster care system beyond the age of eighteen if he or she has not yet graduated from high school and that policy is within the state's regulations.

One of the common misconceptions of children in foster care is that they are in care due to their own behavioral or emotional issues. In fact, only 11 percent of children in foster care are in care due to the child's "commitment of status or delinquent offenses" (CASAnet Resources, 1997, para. 1). There are a myriad of reasons for children being removed from their home of origin. These include but are not limited to, parental drug or alcohol abuse, physical abuse, neglect, inadequate housing, sexual abuse, incarceration of the biological parent, and abandonment by or death of a parent. However due to the mitigating circumstances of a child removed from his or her home and placement in care, "children in foster care are three to six times more likely than children not in care to have emotional, behavioral and developmental problems including conduct disorders, depression, difficulties in school, and impaired social relationships" (CASAnet Resources, para. 3).

Another common belief is that children in care are all up for adoption. This is also not the case. When a child enters care a permanency plan is created. The permanency plan has the intent to create stability for the child so that he or she may maximize his or her development (i.e., educationally, socially, etc.) in a safe and conducive environment.

According to the AFCARS Report (AFCARS, 2010), 49 percent of the children in 2009 in foster care had the case goal to reunify with their parent(s) or caretaker(s) and 25 percent had the case goal of adoption. Additionally, only 4 percent were placed in a preadoptive home. However this does not mean that a portion of those who hoped to be reunified with their families did not at a later point move into the adoption percentage. The multiple family memberships of these children in a foster family and family of origin as well as the dynamics of the various family constellations of which they are a part have an impact on their individual development.

Although regulations and policies may differ from state to state regarding how an individual can become a foster parent, one criterion that holds constant is that adults over the age of eighteen who are interested in foster parenting must become certified. The expectations and standards for that certification are different throughout the nation. Many times this entails a certain number of hours of training focused on understanding children in foster care, on common issues experienced by children in foster care (i.e., attachment issues or reactive attachment disorder), expectations of foster parents, standards that will be enforced regarding the foster parent's home, and state regulations regarding the care of the child placed in care. In some states, the state or county issues the certification, in others agencies are contracted by the state to perform this function, and in other states there is a combination of foster care agencies and county agencies certifying homes. If a parent is interested in adopting or possibly adopting a child who is in foster care, there is another procedure to go through in order to qualify as an adoptive parent. Some aspects of the process are similar, and again the policies differ from state to state. Another constant regardless of the state, as well as whether the potential foster parent is interested in fostering only or adoption also, is that a criminal record check and a Child Abuse Index Clearance is garnered prior to any children being placed in a home.

The process of becoming a foster parent or adoptive parent can take anywhere from two months to a year. This depends again on regulations, as well as on the timeliness of parents' completion of the various steps and training requirements. If a child is placed and adoption is the case goal, the final adoption of the child may take close to two years from the time of placement. Parental rights of the biological parent(s) must be terminated in order for the adoption to become a reality. Just the way in which foster families or adoptive families are formed reflects their unique constellation.

Potential adoptive parents tend to primarily be interested in adopting infants and toddlers. However, the average age of children in foster care is ten. Although, as of 2009, 11 percent of children in foster care had been in foster care for five or more years, the average length of time a child remains in care is anywhere from 1.28 (median) to 2.23 (mean) years (AFCARS, 2010). Approximately 66 percent of children who enter foster care are reunited with their birth parents or caregivers of origin within two years (American Academy of Child and Adolescent Psychiatry, 2006). African American children comprise approximately 25 percent of the foster care population (AFCARS, 2010) and statistics indicate that they remain in care longer than children of other backgrounds (American Academy of Child and Adolescent Psychiatry). The AFCARS report further states that 20 percent of children in foster care are Latino, 1 percent are Asian, and 44 percent are white non-Hispanic. When comparing the number of children in foster care across states in the United States, the number of children in care in the state of California accounts for the highest percentage of all states, with 18 percent of all children in foster care being from California. The second-largest percentage is from New York state with 6.6 percent.

This information provides a landscape for the more intimate foster family constellations that need to be considered when understanding the multidimensionality of the foster family. A foster family may have one or more foster parents and can have one to six children in foster care in the home in addition to other children who are not children in foster care. It is important to note that as of 2010 in some states (i.e., California) there is the allowance of up to six children that can reside in the home regardless of the origin of the child. The other children that may be in the home who are not children in foster care may be adopted, biological, or kin to the foster parent. The adult in the home, who is held responsible by the certifying entity, is identified as the foster parent; however there may be other adults in the home who assist with daily caregiving duties of the child. The length of time for which a child remains in the foster home can be one night to multiple years, which reflects the family constellation in a constant process of being and becoming.

Other foster family constellations may be group home or residential care facilities for children in placement. These arrangements are larger and generally do not have one or two adults who live at the facility but rather adults who work at the facility to provide care to the youth. A group home is generally smaller than a residential institution. The youth live at the group home or residential institution, while adults provide supervision and care for their daily needs, rotating in and out throughout the day and night.

Foster Families and Multidimensionality

The dynamic nature of foster placements interrelates with the nonstatic multidimensionality of foster families. It is not uncommon for children in foster care to move from one home to another due to incompatibility between the child and foster family (parent[s] or other children), changes in the family structure (i.e., birth of child, death in the family), behavioral, emotional, or physical needs that the foster parent(s) is unable to provide for the child in foster care, among other reasons. At times the child's biological family interferes with the stability of a foster placement with hostile telephone calls, physical appearances at the foster home, or giving misinformation to the child about the case plan or foster home. In addition to these issues, the child may be dealing with issues of abandonment or attachment (Ainsworth & Bowlby, 1991; Ainsworth, Blehar, Waters, & Wall, 1978; Bowlby, 1979, 1988).

Many of the various family constellations already discussed in this text also are dimensions of a foster family. For instance, the caregivers or parents may be homosexual, or reside together but not identify themselves as married although there is a commitment or agreement to be a family. The foster family in many ways is a blended family, whether it is made up of two married adults, each with his or her own children from previous marriages or arrangements, or not. There is a blending of a child (children) placed in foster care and a caregiver(s) or parent(s) who, prior to this family arrangement, were accustomed to family norms, structures, comforts, and understandings that may have been both similar and different from that which they are now a part.

Foster parents commit to providing a safe environment to children in need of care. As they become certified, they become aware of paperwork they must maintain relative to the child in foster care, such as keeping track of allowances and clothing money, medication logs (even for over-the-counter medication), as well as expectations of the physicality of their home that may entail keeping all medication (even vitamins) locked up, all detergents and cleaners locked up, only two children sleeping in a bedroom, to name a few. These stipulations can minimize the home-like atmosphere. Foster parents are also encouraged to engage with children in foster care as they would children who were their own. Add to the various regulations aspect of their role as foster parent, the reality of a case plan that intends to reunify the child with his or her biological parent and one can see how this expectation can be difficult to carry out. When you know that the child you are caring for may not be staying as a part of your family unit, how do you incorporate him or her into the family as you would a child you anticipate will be with you throughout their developmental years? What expectations can you place on the child who has a very different idea of politeness, family norms (i.e., eating meals together at a table), schedule (i.e., when to go to bed), and sibling interactions when he or she knows he or she will not be with you very long and will, hopefully, be returning to his or her family of origin? Add to these dilemmas the emotions the child is dealing with as she or he attempts to learn these new expectations and the sense of loyalty she or he may have to those patterns of behavior that were created by her or his biological parent(s). It is no wonder that many behavioral and emotional issues present when children are in foster care, not to mention those that are due to the reasons for placement in the first place.

A very tenuous tightrope is created as political organizations place demands and requirements on social services departments who manage the economic and service components for foster families. Although the court system imposes court orders, time lines, and visitation requirements, foster parents are still expected to incorporate the child into their home life. Consider as part of this picture the child's attorney, the biological parent's attorney, and the attorney representing Child Protective Services (CPS), who are all attempting to state what they believe is best for the child. (In many states the entity that is held responsible for following up on cases of possible child abuse and neglect and subsequently to provide services that may include foster care family placement is referred to as CPS, but this is not a national term. In some states that entity is referred to as the Department of Child and Family Services [DCFS], in others Child and Family Services [CFS]; for continuity in this chapter the term "CPS" will be used.) A difficulty that presents is that, from a political and economic standpoint, every seven to ten years we see the pendulum regarding policies and monies invested in social services swing back and forth on a continuum. Decisions regarding policies and budgetary allocations for social services are in part affected by whether we have a Democratic or Republican Congress, president, governor, and so on due to their general perspectives on these types of issues. When there is a Republican Congress there is generally a trend to put less money into these services, which in turn affects the child in foster care, foster family, and biological family of children in placement.

Whereas these entities operate at a national level relative to policies and legislation and then at a regional or local level regarding the bureaucratic implementation of the laws put in place, foster parents are charged with the daily emotional and physical care of the child placed in their home. They are to not make the child feel different because she or he is a child in foster care, yet the child knows she or he is no longer in her or his home and around what she or he understands to be normal. Therefore, the child is continually affected by the various dimensions as many different people want to spend time to talk or observe her or him, as her or his parent comes to visit (or does not show for the visit she or he was prepared for), as her or his foster parents provide thrift store clothing that does not fit quite right since the foster parent is unsure how long the child will be in their home, as they go to school and the school clerk will not assign her or him to a class because there are not any immunization records or school transcripts to accompany the child, and on and on. This is not to imply that all foster homes or children in care have these exact experiences. Rather, this list is provided to give some insight to some of the possibilities.

At times the system seems to promote the notion that if foster parents would just treat children in foster care as their own, then there would be a better environment for the child. In some ways, treating a child in foster care as if he or she were one's own (biological or adopted) child can exacerbate issues the child is dealing with, as it can become another situation that does not get addressed. The child may begin to pretend the things that occurred leading to placement outside the family of origin did not occur. At times the child may feel he or she cannot talk about his or her family of origin because he or she then feels it is disrespectful or will hurt the foster parent who is now taking care of him or her. At the same time, the child may feel he or she cannot talk to his or her biological parent about what may be good, enjoyable, and supportive in the foster home because it might hurt the parent's feelings. Children in foster care very easily fall into the role of attempting to make things easier and better for the adults around them due to these messages that may be given to them but also the messages that may be given to their foster parents.

As mentioned earlier in this book, understanding the family as a complex multidimensional contextual entity is central to the model proposed and to seeing the family through a lens that is different from the traditional lens. Therefore, attention needs to be given to the many different facets of the family, and foster families are no exception. Foster parents come from a variety of different backgrounds and their family structures, prior to participating as a foster parent, are just as diverse. Single parents, married couples, unmarried couples, same-sex couples, and extended family structures are all possible family forms of foster parents who become certified. People of many different religious backgrounds, faiths, and spiritual practices become foster parents. These dimensions as well as various gender and sexual orientations, socioeconomic status, occupation, culture of the foster parent's family of origin culture, and age of foster parents intersect with the individual's view of self and her or his role as a foster parent. These facets will have an impact on values and meanings that are placed on different behaviors, things, and ideas. For instance, a foster parent who is unmarried but cofoster parenting with a significant other of the opposite sex, who comes from a family where the parents were married, sees herself as a very religious person, is from an Asian and African American background, and makes approximately $20,000 a year in California will see family, the role of parent, and the parent–child relationship through a different lens from someone who is married, identifies herself as spiritual but not religious, comes from a single-parent home, is Caucasian, and whose household income is $120,000 living in Alabama. Not only are their life experiences different based on the obvious differences, but also geographical location will most likely influence their worldview, view of children, and view of necessities for growth.

Children who are placed in care also have these various dimensions since they too come from many different races or ethnicities, religious backgrounds and practices, family structures, and gender and sexual orientations. This interface, with those of the foster parents, can create a very unique and distinct foster family constellation. Therefore, based on some of the statistics and known aspects of children in foster care and foster parents, when working with foster families or individuals the helping professional may consider some facts that are a general part of the system. It is imperative to seek an understanding of this particular individual or family and how the blending of these factors has affected functioning and growth.

CONSTRUCTION, DECONSTRUCTION, AND RECONSTRUCTION

As we consider the construction, deconstruction, and reconstruction of foster family constellations, it might help to contemplate the needs that bring the people in a foster family together. As stated in chapter 3 of this text, there are many theories that outline basic human needs. When many of these theories are compared, the most common are physical, cognitive, social, and spiritual. The various dimensions of the family may identify both similar and different specific needs associated with each of these areas. For instance, children are may see their physical needs as safety, clothing, food, and water. Parents may identify these same physical needs for themselves and their children, but may define these needs differently. For instance, the child may think going to the park is safe because he or she has been there many times and it is only half a block away from his or her home. Yet a parent may not see it is as safe for his or her six-year-old due to the environment of the neighborhood and perceived activities that occur in the park. Not only are needs perceived differently by different individuals in a family, but also they do not remain constant but change due to changes in age, maturity, environment, and other variables.

Additionally, different families may define their needs as a collective differently. Some families believe that each child must have his or her own room; other families believe this spoils children and they should be made to share a bedroom even if there are enough rooms in the home for single bedrooms. These may seem like minor differences, but their transactional nature with the other dimensions of need and social institutions in society can contribute to very different meanings of how needs are met among family members and family groups.

When differences in perception and definition are used for understanding foster families, one can see that many different ideas about what is needed converge and transact to affect the being and becoming of the family. Practice wisdom indicates that all humans have a need for love and compassion. Such a view greatly affects the foster family as many foster parents hold this "practice wisdom" as well. Therefore, by providing a safe and clean environment and loving the child, they believe the child's behaviors should change and fit into what they see as acceptable and normal behavior. Many children in foster care will state they are not seeking love from their foster parents. Instead, they share that what they need is for their foster parents to care about them. To care about how they are doing in school, to care about where they are and what they are doing, to care about their safety, to care about their dreams and desires.

The practitioner needs to keep in mind this approach when working with foster families and individuals who are members of foster families. While understanding that each person may approach his or her needs and the needs of the family differently, it is also important to understand how the foster family as a unit constructs, deconstructs, and reconstructs itself. As stressed in chapter 3, people are encouraged to explore constructed boundaries that may limit understandings of family and family dynamics. When a person makes the decision to become a foster parent, she or he does so for various reasons that in turn affect how she or he creates her or his home in a physical and socioemotional sense. The way in which the room where the child will sleep and types of furniture and other belongings might be bought, gathered, and placed all work to construct an environment that the foster parent(s) believes will welcome the child and impress on him or her the norms and expectations of the home. This preparation as well as the training the foster parent(s) participates in, as well as the information provided prior to accepting a child for placement, play a role in the initial construction of a foster family.

Regardless of a child's age at the time of placement, just his or her placement in the foster family begins to deconstruct what was already constructed. This does not mean it is completely dismantled, but aspects that were anticipated by the foster parent may not match the needs and likes of the child now placed in his or her care. As mentioned previously in this chapter, the norms of what to do and how to do them may be very different for the child and for the new family. An infant entering any family affects the unit and the individuals within it in many different ways.

The dynamic nature of how long a child may be placed with a family may make this deconstruction and reconstruction phase different from many other families, especially if the foster family has children or the family is very fixed on how they do things and how they understand the world around them. Each time a new member enters the foster family, the dynamics between members and the understandings that people have of how things need to be may change. This experience is similar to all families whenever a new member joins or a member of the family leaves the home. However, children in foster care often feel that they are a guest in the family even when they have lived with the family for several years. Many times there is still an attachment to their family of origin, regardless of the circumstances. The affect of entering and exiting an existing family constellation not only impacts the child, but also the other foster family members, and is instrumental in the deconstructing and reconstructing of the foster family.

The level of understanding given by foster parents as the foster family is deconstructed and reconstructed with each child's entry and exit will have a profound impact on the identity development of the child as well as on each member of the family. When an environment is provided that embraces the child's norms and feelings of allegiance to his or her biological family while integrating the child into the foster family as a valued member of the family, adjustment and identity development can be enhanced. What is important is for the foster parent(s) to meet the child where he or she is relative to how he or she fits into the foster family or fits with the family of origin, and for the foster parent(s) to provide an environment where questions and feelings can be voiced. As reflected by the content in this section, foster family constellations are in a constant state of being and becoming.

BEING AFFECTED BY AND AFFECTING

In the first section of this chapter, this author stated there were many different lenses through which one might view foster families: the child in foster care; the foster parent; the biological parent; the case worker or other helping professional; the attorney for the child, parent, and county; the court or judge; the county official; the state; and so on. The fourth premise proposed by Guadalupe and Welkley for this multidimensional model for family constellations is further demonstrated when considering these various lenses: one can look at not only the different viewpoints of these entities, but also at the interaction between them that is reciprocal within the foster family as a unit.

The foster family does not only exist as it is described on paper, but also is more complex than the written word could possibly illustrate. The statistics reported nationally or locally do not provide a robust picture of the foster family. Many people believe that foster parents only go into this arena for the money and that more abuse of children occurs within foster homes than outside of them. Other stereotypes of foster families are that they are primarily in poor communities and therefore children in foster care are not cared for as they should be. This author is not going to attempt to demonstrate that these situations do not exist, rather that they are not indicative of all foster families. There has not been the evidence to support the view that abuse or neglect occurs more so within foster homes than outside of them, nor any evidence to demonstrate it is close to the same level. Finding national and state statistics that report demographic statistics on foster parents is not easy to find and current statistics is even more difficult. Something that has been evident is that foster parents come from various socioeconomic status levels, with many being from middle-class families. Regardless of the socioeconomic status, foster parents are required to adhere to specific guidelines set by the state or controlling agency and need to be monitored by the appointed professional to ensure children's needs are being met.

The paradox between cultural influences and cultural choices discussed by Guadalupe and Welkley in chapter 3 is very apparent in the constellation of the foster family. Current cultural influences on foster families entail the adoption of a policy called Family to Family, an initiative of the Annie E. Casey Foundation (Fiester, 2008), that has been adopted by many states throughout the United States. This policy is considered family centered and has many strengths-focused principles. One of the strategies of this initiative is to place children who are removed from their homes in foster homes located in neighborhoods where they originally lived. This can pose many issues for the foster family because many want a certain degree of anonymity with the biological family due to physical and emotional safety for themselves and the child placed in their care. At the same time, such an approach provides the opportunity to broaden the investment of the community and to provide mentors to biological parents within their community. However, with the criticism from the larger society that children are being placed in lower-income homes that are already stretching their resources, this strategy could feed into that stereotype, becoming more of a reality because, although children are removed across socioeconomic levels, a very large percentage of children are removed from homes in low-socioeconomic neighborhoods.

The resiliency of individuals and families is also demonstrated through this dimension of affecting and being affected by other institutions in society. Despite limited resources, so many foster families provide healthy and supportive environments for children in need. Whether this is for one night or ten years, the warmth of caring and steadfastness of provision are carried out in order to promote stability in our communities. This is done at times with the help of caseworkers, attorneys, and biological family members who are invested but cannot provide ongoing care. However, it is also done in spite of these same entities' impositions. Additionally, children in foster care and foster families continually affect these institutions when they stand up for additional resources needed, added support (including social and mental health services), ensuring siblings in care are able to maintain contact, and avenues for pursuing higher education.

As federal and state authorities examine and reexamine policies and initiatives for foster families, an important point to keep in mind is that "no one family has ever been able to satisfy the human need for love, comfort, and security" (Gillis, 1996, p. 240). This is also true for foster families. To propose that all foster families will be able to maximize the growth and development of children in foster care by adhering to one set of principles may do more to oppress and confine than to uplift and support a foster family.

Consideration of Nonstereotypical Skills Promotion of an Eclectic Approach

As Guadalupe and Welkley indicate in chapter 4 of this text, it is important to remember that most eclectic approaches attempt to embrace inclusiveness of diverse aspects affecting and being affected by the family while encouraging practitioners to move beyond stereotypical and dogmatic paradigms. In order to move toward this goal of identifying preconceived ideas one has about foster care and foster families, the practitioner could ask himself or herself these questions:

- Why do I think foster parents choose to become or remain a foster parent?

- What do I think the typical foster home looks like?

- What do I think is the care generally provided to children in foster care?

- Why do I think children in foster care are in care or remain in care?

- If a child in foster care has been in many different placements, why do I think makes that the case?

- What do I assume are the common presenting issues for children in foster care?

This list of questions is by no means exhaustive, but if one takes the time to think about them and related questions prior to providing services to a foster parent, child in care, or a biological parent of a child in care, there might be a better opportunity for exploration with the client.

While considering pieces of the following case study, keep in mind the four premises that are central to the eclectic practice model introduced in chapter 4: multidimensional contextual nonstatic living entity, multiple memberships, being and becoming, and affecting and being affected by—reciprocity of forces. A short discussion of each area will accompany this case study illustration.

Case Study: Summer (age eighteen)

Summer, an eighteen-year-old white child in foster care [In the state of Illinois it is not uncommon for youth placed in foster care prior to the age of eighteen to remain in care beyond that age due to their particular needs and circumstances], is moving in to a new foster home in Elgin, Illinois. She meets the foster parent, Edna, who tells her and her adult friend and mentor, Abigail, which room to put her belongings in. The room is rather small, with a set of bunk beds and one dresser to be shared by both girls. Edna shares with Abigail that she has six foster children in the home, four girls and two boys. She has rules that all the children are expected to abide by, but they will get their needs met as long as they are in her care. She indicates that she takes the phone off the cradle when she leaves the house so that no one can make a call when she is not home. She expects the children to attend school and, if they are over the age of fifteen, to have a part-time job. Edna inquires of Abigail why Summer had to leave her previous foster home to which Abigail replied that it would probably be better for Summer to share that with her. Once Abigail and Summer finish unloading the car of all her belongings, Abigail lets Summer know she can call anytime and maybe they can get together once in awhile even though she lives forty minutes away. Summer has very low affect as they say goodbye and overall is nonexpressive. She gives a half smile as she waves goodbye and Abigail drives away.

Intrapersonal assessment considerations would entail reflection on Summer's cognitive, mental, emotional, and biological needs. It appears on face value that her basic biological needs will be taken care of in this placement. However, it might be important to explore to what extent they have or have not been met over the past eighteen years. The impression given by stating she had "very low affect" may provide some indication of emotional or mental issues, but this cannot be fully assessed without further exploration through dialogue and other assessments with Summer. Exploration of what her beliefs are about self, what messages she has received from others regarding the type of person she is and should be, as well as does she see herself as fitting the images that others seem to think of her as? Also, does she see the image others have of her as not matching how she sees herself? These are all important facets to investigate. These arenas would be a start to understanding Summer's intrapersonal issues.

With the information shared about this case, a practitioner could begin to delve into assessing the interpersonal issues. Discovering the importance that Abigail has in Summer's life might be an important area to explore. How long have they known each other? In what capacity did they come to know each other? How close are they? Does Summer see Abigail as a confidante or just another adult in her life? Each of these questions might provide insight as to how significant Abigail is and to what degree she is significant to Summer. Another important area for assessment in this realm would be to learn if there are other friends in Summer's life and whether they are peers or adults. Determining whether Summer has been or is involved in any community groups or school activities would provide more insight into her interpersonal connections.

Before exploring the next two premises of the eclectic professional competence approach, let's consider more information relative to this case.

Close to a month after Summer moved into her new foster home, Abigail receives a call from her. Summer is at work and says she cannot talk long but she really needs to talk to Abigail. She asks why Abigail has not called her since she left her at Edna's. Abigail replies that she has called three times and left messages. Since she did not hear back from Summer, she assumed she did not want to call her back and was getting adjusted to her new home and school. Summer said she did not receive any messages. Then she stated that she had to go since she was at work, but that she would be home the next day at 4:00 and could Abigail call her then. Abigail agreed.

The next day when Abigail called Summer, Edna answered the phone. When Abigail requested to speak to Summer, Edna inquired who was calling. Once Abigail identified herself Edna indicated she was glad she called and maybe she could talk some sense into Summer and then gave the phone to Summer. Summer would not say much on the phone and Abigail had to ask basic questions to have any dialogue with Summer. Abigail inquired if they had just had an argument or if there are other things going on between her and Edna. Summer replied, "Other things all the time." Then Summer held the phone away so that Abigail could hear Edna shouting at one of the other foster children and cussing at them. When Summer put the receiver back to her ear, she whispered, "This is how it is most of the time. She won't yell at me right now because I am on the phone with you." Abigail did not want the conversation to become one of question and answer, so she asked if Summer could talk at work while she is on break. Summer gave her the work phone number, which she said was a donut shop. She stated she really liked her job because they paid her well and she could eat donuts. Then she asked when Abigail was going to come see her. Abigail replied they could talk about that when they talked next and asked when she would be at work next. Summer said she would be working two days from then, Sunday, from 10:00 a.m. to 7:00 p.m.

Consideration of Summer's social–cultural–political–environmental realm cannot be fully examined with the information provided but a little exploration can be made. She states that she is working and that she enjoys it. This can be identified as a strength for Summer's situation relative to her home environment. Considering the phone conversations and the yelling overheard it might appear that this foster home has some tumultuous energy and does not provide a lot of nurturing and emotional caring for Summer and possibly the other children in the home. The culture of this foster family appears to be dogmatic and from the first part of the case study shared is very structured with many expectations. The dynamics of the home may not be matching Summer's expectations and possibly her past experiences. This would be an area for further exploration to better understand Summer's reaching out after a month in this environment. Edna had indicated that there are six children in foster care in the home, which seems like a large amount of children to have in the home and may make the home environment less homey and more institutional like. Without more information this is mere speculation. Before further supposition, let's take into account some background information on the case.

Ten months prior to Summer's move to the foster home with Edna, she became a resident of a group home where Abigail worked. Upon being assigned to Abigail's primary group (a set of four young women for whom she ensured case plans were written and basic needs attended to) she identified with Abigail quite quickly. Abigail felt a connection with Summer that she did not always feel with all of the girls in the home. The focus of the group home was to serve adolescent girls ages fifteen to nineteen as they developed independent living skills and could move out on their own once they graduated from high school.

Summer was in the group home for about three months. She was quiet initially but began to come out of her shell. She seemed to gravitate toward youth at her school that were known for breaking the rules and receiving detention. She began to dress provocatively and would not always come home at her curfew.

She would have periodic conversations with her biological mother, but unless she felt she could get her mother to buy her something she seemed disinterested in the contact. She has one younger sister (age fifteen) and a younger brother (age seven). Her sister was in the juvenile section of the department of corrections (DOC) and her brother still resided with their mother. Abigail took Summer to visit her sister at the DOC. Summer seemed fascinated with the rules and the toughness exhibited by many of the youth that were there.

On another occasion Abigail took Summer to visit her mother and brother. During this visit Summer took her brother a little gift and appeared quite happy to spend time with him. She would engage with him and smile while playing with him. However, when any attempts were made by her mother to talk with her or sit with her, she became abrasive or unemotional.

While traveling to these visits Summer would share her background with Abigail and indicated she was angry with her mother for not protecting her from one of her mother's boyfriends. She was also upset that her mother still had custody of her brother: she believed he was going to be neglected and not cared for just as she and her sister were. Before being in the group home, she had been in one foster home where she felt close to the foster mother, but the family moved away and could not take her with them because the court stated she would be too far away for visits with her mother.

At the end of March, with Summer turning eighteen, a court hearing was scheduled. She had not been following the rules of the group home and the director was giving notice that Summer would not be able to continue to receive services there. Although she had not yet graduated from high school, Summer's county worker was recommending to the court to discontinue services since she was not responding to services. A recent psychiatric assessment indicated she had a borderline IQ (meaning her score on IQ scales was not low enough be considered mentally deficient nor high enough to be labeled as having normal or average intelligence) and was in need of special education services, behaviorally and emotionally.

As the designated staff person at the group home to advocate for Summer's needs, Abigail investigated the laws and spoke with an attorney who advocates for children in foster care who are in need of special education services. According to federal and state laws, the attorney stated that the court could retain custody of Summer until the age of twenty-one because she was in need of special education services and the state had not been providing those services. She was entitled to continue receiving support from the state. During the court hearing, a guardian ad litem was appointed and it was recommended that a foster home be found for Summer.

A friend of Abigail's contacted Summer's county worker and became a licensed foster parent two weeks later at which time Summer moved in. Abigail would pick her up for church and spend time with Summer from time to time. After four to five months in this placement, Abigail received a call from her friend, Summer's foster mother, stating she had just received a call from the police station that Summer had been arrested for selling and possession of drugs at school. The foster mother stated that she could not keep her if she was going to be dealing with drugs. When Abigail went to the jail to talk with Summer, she stated they were not her drugs but the guy she was dating had asked her to hold them for her. This is a brief overview of circumstances that led to Summer's move to Edna's.

Consideration of this background information relative to Summer's situation provides greater context. At the same time it provides greater opportunity for stereotypes and assumptions. Although not a lot of specificity is given regarding Summer's faith or spirituality, there are points of intersect to explore further with her as the client. It is mentioned that Summer would go to church with Abigail, which may indicate Summer has some type of religious connection. However we do not know why Summer goes. For instance, does she go due to the worship and spiritual nature of the church or does she go due to her faith or religious upbringing? Another possibility is that she may attend because it is a way to do something with Abigail, and that it has less to do with the religious practices themselves. These types of questions provide a framework for beginning to unravel the realms of nonordinary reality; in other words, exploring what is meaningful to Summer in terms of her own spiritual or religious understanding. Another area to look at here is Summer's coping skills when dealing with loss and pain. Learning what she does and to what degree she believes those methods help her resolve these feelings may also provide insight into her nonordinary reality as this may provide a window to her beliefs regarding what exists in the physical realm of society's essence.

The practitioner who embraces this eclectic practice modality will not only employ assessment and interventions associated with each of these realms, but also will keep in mind the four primary premises of multidimensional contextual nonstatic living entity, multiple memberships, being and becoming, and affecting and being affected by—reciprocity of forces and how they intersect with the four realms and each other. For example, when looking at the nonstatic living dynamic of the family and the individual in this case, one should consider the various family constellations Summer was a part of just from the limited information available. One might identify her family of origin, the first foster family she was a part of that moved away, the group home, the second foster home, the foster home where we join her story, as well as Abigail as all being a part of Summer's family. When the human service practitioner is assisting Summer, recognizing the importance and the role that each of these entities have played in Summer's life is vital. However, it is also essential to understand that their levels of importance may be different and change over time for Summer. Additionally, recognition that this will continue to change can assist the practitioner to embrace a family-centered approach and see Summer as the expert regarding the symbolism and associated meanings of these various family forms and their importance to her.

Recognizing that Summer may not see herself as leaving any of these constellations but simultaneously being a member of several of them at any given point in time gives inclusion to the premise of multiple memberships. From some of the information shared one might see that Summer seems to fragment portions of her families relative to how she relates to them separately. Her family cultures appear to be very diverse. It becomes apparent when trying to assist her with her emotional issues that Gillis' (1996) statement that "no one family form has ever been able to satisfy the human need for love, comfort, and security" (p. 240) is applicable.

The family constellations that Summer becomes a part of were both affected by her and affected her (while being and becoming). Without talking with Summer it is difficult to discern any of the specifics but it might be speculated that she was hurt but gained resilience in her family of origin. At the same time, in her family of origin she provided a role of caretaking to her younger siblings and possibly at times to her mother. Her family of origin was affected by her absence as well as affected her possible sense of anomie (a state of normlessness) or disconnection (Durkheim, 1951). She may have a sense of abandonment due to feeling that her mother did not protect her from the abuse that caused her to enter the foster care system. She then becomes attached to another family, which moves away and does not take her with them. It is unclear what level of attachment she built within this family but this constellation influenced her life and worldview. Therefore, she may be dealing with an attachment issue (Ainsworth & Bowlby, 1991). Further exploration could occur regarding the being and becoming effects of the various family forms and attachments, but what is most important is to be aware of this dynamic and possibly assist Summer as the client to understand that just as she was affected, her essence affected each of these constellations as well (affecting and being affected by). There are many other areas that could be considered when reflecting on this case (i.e., her education, special education status, etc.), demonstrating the complexity of Summer's family constellations.

Summary

The many constellations of foster families and the numerous reasons that a child is placed in a foster home may make us take for granted that one will take a multidimensional approach when working with clients who are children in foster care. It is apparent that there are at least two different families that may be included in treatment and services for the child. However, only looking at multidimensions from that point of view may serve as a barrier to engage in multidimensional practice. As when connecting with any individual or family system, it is important that the helper heighten his or her awareness of his or her own stereotypes about children in foster care, foster homes, and foster care as a whole. Recognizing that this family system is nonstatic and affects those around it and is affected by all that is around the family (the environment) is very important when assessing the needs and strengths of children in foster care and of foster families. Such an understanding will provide for better identification of interventions that will be of assistance for the client as she embarks on her journey of life.

Questions to Promote Further Critical Analysis

Here is another case study followed by some questions for critical analysis of this multidimensional approach when applied to foster care families.

Case Study: Brittany (age ten)

As Nina, a county child protective services social worker, reads over the case file for a new client assigned to her case, she becomes horrified with the details of abuse and neglect experienced by this young girl. Brittany is a ten-year-old African American girl living in Jacksonville, Florida. The file indicates that she and two of her siblings, an older sister and younger brother, were taken into care approximately four months ago due to severe neglect and abuse. A call was made to the county regarding suspicion of abuse in her grandmother's house. When the police arrived at the home to investigate, they found Brittany in the garage, where it appeared she had been secluded for at least several weeks. There was the strong smell of urine and fecal matter in several places in the garage. Brittany was found huddled in a corner where it appeared she had been sleeping on a thin blanket. Although this was in Florida, it was late December, when the temperature stays in the fifties or lower. On this particular night, it was in the thirties.

After interviewing adults and children in the home, it was unclear the exact time frame but that Brittany had been locked in the garage for anywhere from one to three weeks (the timeframe was reported different from each person). Brittany had lost her concept of time, having been in the garage for so long. A bag of dog food was found in the garage, which appeared to be all that Brittany had eaten during her time in the garage. Her younger brother reported that his sister had gotten in trouble at school before she was put in the garage and that his grandmother had said, "Maybe that would help get the devil out of her."

As investigations continued into this case, it became known that the children's mother had abandoned them five years before by leaving them with their grandmother. She would come visit from time to time but never for very long. All indications were that the mother was addicted to heroin; she had been arrested several times for prostitution over the course of the past ten years. The children had open cases previously but had not been placed in foster care prior to the occurrence when Brittany was found in the garage. The grandmother was screened and approved as an appropriate kinship placement. However, after finding Brittany in the garage all three children were removed and placed in foster care. Initially, the two sisters were placed together and the younger brother was placed in a nearby home. The siblings were able to visit with one another two times a week. However, their behaviors seemed to escalate into acting out behaviors after having visits with one another. Additionally, the two girls were not able to get along in their foster home, and had to be placed in separate homes. The acting out behaviors included masturbation while in a group setting (i.e., the living room with other people around, at school on the playground), hitting each other and other children, yelling obscenities at their foster parents and teachers, not following directions, stealing other's property, etc.

Nina will begin visiting Brittany this week at her new placement where she was placed one week ago. Brittany's sister and brother are also on her caseload, which will make it easier to arrange and monitor sibling visits. Last week Brittany had her first visit with a therapist and the recommendations noted from that therapist is that Brittany receive therapy twice a week for the next few months and that a psychological evaluation should be conducted. The therapist also noted in her initial evaluation notes, that Brittany reports hearing voices that tell her to do bad things. During the interview with the therapist, the therapist noted Brittany's voice tones change a minimum of three times into distinct voice and attitude representations. When the first therapy session ended Brittany asked when she would be able to see her brother and sister again.

Questions for consideration based on this case study:

- What are the multidimensional contexts of this nonstatic living entity?

- What are the multiple memberships for Brittany?

- How can the concepts of being and becoming be of importance when assisting Brittany's growth and development?

- In what ways is Brittany affecting and being affected by—reciprocity of forces—family, school, the County, foster care, her foster home, and so on?

- When considering each of these facets of a multidimensional approach, how does exploring them through each of the following lenses sharpen your understanding for assessment and intervention with Brittany: intrapersonal (micro capacity), intrapersonal (meso capacity), social–cultural–political–environmental (macro capacity), and nonordinary realm (magna capacity)?

- Based on your understanding of the multidimensional approach to understanding the family, what are additional questions to ask and areas to explore to maximize Brittany's growth and development?

References

Adoption and Foster Care Analysis and Reporting System (AFCARS). (2010). *The AFCARS report*. U.S. Department of Health and Human Services, Administration for Children and Families, Administration on Children, Youth, and Families, Children's Bureau.

Ainsworth, M., Blehar, M., Waters, E., & Wall, S. (1978). *Patterns of attachment*. Hillsdale, NJ: Erlbaum.

Ainsworth, M., & Bowlby, J. (1991). An ethological approach to personality development. *American Psychologist, 46*, 331–341.

American Academy of Child and Adolescent Psychiatry. (2006). *Facts for families: Foster care*. No. 64. American Academy of Child and Adolescent Psychiatry, Washington, DC.

Bowlby, J. (1979). *The making and breaking of affectional bonds*. London: Tavistock.

Bowlby, J. (1988). *A secure base*. New York: Basic Books.

CASAnet Resources. (1997). *Why children are in foster care*. Retrieved March 17, 2008, from www.casanet.org/Library/foster-care/why.htm.

Durkheim, E. (1951). *Suicide: A study in sociology*, New York: The Free Press.

Fiester, L. (2008). *The story of family to family. The early years 1992 2006*. The Annie E. Casey Foundation.

Gillis, J. (1996). *A world of their own making: Myth, ritual, and the quest for family values*. New York: Basic Books.

Sources for Further Study and Understanding

Barber, J. (2004). *Children in foster care*. London: Routledge.

Cain, C. S. (2006). *Attachment disorders: Treatment strategies for traumatized children*. Lanham, MD: Littlefield.

Johnson, J., & Grant, G. (2004). Casebook: *Foster care*. Boston: Allyn & Bacon.

Lipscombe, J., Moyers, S., & Farmer, E. (2004). What changes in "parenting" approaches occur over the course of adolescent foster care placements? *Child and Family Social Work, 9*, 347–357.

Little, M., Kohm, A., & Thompson, R. (2005). The impact of residential placement on child development: Research and policy implications. *International Journal of Social Welfare, 14*, 200–209.

Louise, R. (2003). *Somebody's someone.* New York: Warner Books.

Rhodes, K., Cox, M. E., Orme, J. G., & Coakley, T. (2006, December). Foster parents' reasons for fostering and foster family utilization. *Journal of Sociology and Social Welfare, 33*(4), 105–126.

Rygaard, N. P. (2006). *Severe attachment disorder in childhood.* New York: Springer.

Smith, W. (2001). *Hope meadows.* New York: Berkley Books.

Springer Verlag Schofield, G., & Beek, M. (2005, March). Providing a secure base: Parenting children in long-term foster family care. *Attachment and Human Development, 7*(1), 3–25.

CHAPTER TEN

Blended Family and Multipartner Family Constellations

Errol Bolden
Shirley Newton-Guest

No longer widely considered to be an "alternative"
or "nontraditional" family form, blended families
have emerged as a relatively mainstream,
though complex, entity.

EB and SNG

Any union of a group of people under the umbrella of family experience is both dynamic and complex. The research literature on family forms clearly indicates that the traditional family forms that were more dominant as late as the mid-twentieth century are no longer as dominant. Evidence for this reality is demonstrated by an increased divorce rate over the past four decades (Carter & McGoldrick, 2005). Furthermore, studies report that a large number of those who were divorced are remarrying or are living together (Portrie & Hill, 2005). One report claims that as high as 40 percent of marriages are remarriages for one or both of the couples. This report further states that 61 percent of divorced individuals remarry others who are divorced (Diderich-Balsam, 2005). Adding to the discussion regarding the changing family structure, the following quote captures the current context within which many families operate: "The structure and function of American families have evolved over time. In contrast to earlier eras, today's families are organized very differently. Each arrangement reflects the choices people have made about how they want to live their lives within the cultural and historical context. Today's families are a diverse mix of original two-parent families, single-parent households, remarried families, cohabitating couples, and more. There appears to be no single prototype of the American family" (Seipel & Brown, 2008, p. 174).

No longer widely considered to be an alternative or nontraditional family form, blended families have emerged as a relatively mainstream though complex entity that is represented by various family structures that are not easily defined (Helton & Smith, 2004). Diderich-Balsam (2005) projected that by 2010 a dominant family form in the United States will be what is referenced as the binuclear, or reconstituted family constellation. As we entered 2010, we could see that blended family forms had become a common family structure in the United States. In a study of household economic studies in 2004, it was reported that "of the 51.0 million children who lived with two parents, 87 percent (44.5 million) lived with their biological mother and biological father. Additionally, 10 percent (5.3 million) lived with a biological parent and a stepparent, usually with a biological mother and a stepfather (4.1 million)" (U.S. Census Bureau, 2008, p. 3). It was further reported that 71 percent of these children were living in blended family constellations.

In their review of current research on blended families, Portrie and Hill (2005) stated, "current research on blended families does not speak to the diversity and need for awareness of multi-cultural issues. Research indicates the importance of understanding the diverse needs of blended families; however, no information currently addresses blended families of color, gay and lesbian families, and the joining of culturally different families" (p. 450). Portrie and Hill present a very important observation reflected in the literature. Blended families present practitioners with new challenges. On the one hand, blended families present practitioners with the opportunity to explore the complexity of family constellations when there are multiple unions (i.e., parent and stepparent, child and stepchild, brother and sister, stepbrother and stepsister, as well as half-brother and half-sister). On the other hand, this complexity is amplified when considering the fact that blended families may also reflect multiethnic or multicultural affiliations (i.e., Latino and African American couples, Asian and Caucasian couples).

Emerging research suggests that, although children fare better in households where there are consistent parent practices, children who are raised with both biological parents are more likely to not fare as well as children who live in a blended family household (Gennetian, 2005; Mincy & Oliver, 2003). It is widely reported that as many as half of all marriages end in divorce and rates seem to be growing. As a result, "children are increasingly being reared in single-parent households or other diverse family structures" (Harrison-Hale, 2005, p. 382).

Research on family structure clearly shows an emergence and increased acceptance of various nontraditional family forms or constellations. Consequently, there is a need for a paradigm shift in our work with families that allows us to be more responsive to the diversity of these family units. This chapter discusses these arrangements within the contexts of the experience of blended and multifamily constellations. The dynamics of the interactions and exchanges of these arrangements will be presented; as with previous chapters in this text, our discussion will occur within the context of human diversity within this family arrangement. Finally, questions to promote further critical analysis will be explored.

Inside the Blended Family

The term "blended family" has been used to refer to "two single-parent families or one single-parent family and one childless spouse are joined under this arrangement" (Becvar & Becvar, 1996; Collins, Jordan, & Coleman, 2007). Although this definition is clear and straightforward, various images of the blended family have historically been presented that are sometimes inconsistent and conflictive and may present a welcoming or negative image of stepparents and blended families. For instance, stepparenting is a common theme in fairytales (Collins, et al.). Consider the following messages that have fostered various stereotypes. Do you remember Cinderella and her wicked stepmother? On the flipside, what about the television shows *Step by Step*, *Life with Derek*, or the loveable classic *The Brady Bunch*? In the case of Cinderella the blended family relationship was antagonistic and in the other examples, the relationship was harmonious and supportive. What is clear is that the outcome of blending is not automatic. The expectation of instant readjustment and the recreated nuclear family are just myths (Becvar & Becvar, 1996, 2008).

As the new family is created there is certain to be a period of conflict as family members adjust and readjust to new cultural mores, roles, rules, responsibilities and boundaries. The children are sometimes confronted with the battle over the compliance to, and respect of the role of the new stepparent and their loyalty to their noncustodial parent. This battle may not only pose a problem for the child, but also for the custodial parent who may be desirous of an emotional break (Becvar & Becvar, 1996, 2008). It must be kept in mind that a number of stepfamilies are born of loss: death, divorce or separation. The new family constellation then can be experienced as the antidote for dealing with the damaged emotions so as to fill the void left from the previous family form. Yet this does not mean all blended families are a direct result of the previous family relationship or of the issues that may have been present in the previous family structure.

The blending of families may also involve the various family constellations put forth in this text. Blended families reflect the first and second premises presented in this text. Blended families are multidimensional contextual nonstatic living entities where individuals often experience multiple memberships. For example, these arrangements may include biological parents, parents within polygamous arrangements, or parents that self-identify as gay, lesbian, bisexual, or transgender. The definition of a multipartner family is complex and highly controversial, especially when viewed within a traditional or dominant family value lens. This type of family arrangement is seen as in direct opposition to the widely held paradigms of nuclear or heterosexual family arrangements. Polygamy is one type of multipartner family. The legal response to polygamy and bigamy is clear:

> The law in every state [in the United States] prohibits a man or a woman from being married to more than one living person at a time. The crime of having more than one current spouse is called either bigamy (having two spouses) [or] is a subset of the crime of polygamy (having more than one spouse), and the law makes no practical distinction between the two. Even in states that separately criminalize both polygamy and bigamy, either crime is committed when a married person first enters into an unlawful marriage with a second person. However, additional marriages beyond the second would support prosecution for additional criminal counts and possibly a longer sentence. (Net Industries, 2011)

Unlike the wives or husbands of bigamists, the wives or husbands of polygamists generally live together in the same household.

The fact that the polygamous family lifestyle is not considered legal suggests that such families would be marginalized by both family members who do not endorse such unions as well as the larger society. Benefits that would be automatic for legally recognized unions would be absent for these families. The children and other members of the family may be looked at as different and may be the victims of cruel jokes and other slurs. Some sources report the effects as more stressful than monogamous relationships, while others provide findings that indicate the relationships are more complementary (Daynes, 2001).

As we can see, the social and legal acceptance or nonacceptance of polygamous families complicates the family experience of those in and connected to this family form. Although polygamy is a less-common form of family constellation in our society it does not mean that many individuals do not practice this type of family unit. This form of family constellation may be illegal. However, its practice is often influenced by emotional or social commitment beyond the status quo. It could be argued that both polygamy and bigamy could be perceived as additional reflections of blended families due to the multiple partners that are now a part of the family structure. Generally, when one refers to a blended family, it is thought to be made up of stepparents and children where one or both of the spouses have been previously married.

Another more contemporary family form that has been receiving much attention is unions of gay, lesbian, bisexual, or transgender individuals. This family form adds to the complexity of defining blended families. A report published in 2000 by the Child Welfare Information Gateway suggested as follows: "Defining the family structure of gay and lesbian parents can be a challenging task. The most common type of homosexual household is step or blended families. These are gay and lesbian parents who had their biological children in a former heterosexual relationship, then 'came out,' and created a new family with another partner. Other types of family structures include single gay or lesbian parents and couples having children together. Both of these family types may be created through adoption, but more frequently reproductive technology is being utilized" (Rohrbaugh, 2000, p. 2). One indication of the scope of blended families is captured in a report produced by the National Adoption Information Clearinghouse (2000). This report indicated, "In 1976, there were an estimated 300,000 to 500,000 gay and lesbian biological parents; as of 1990, an estimated 6 to 14 million children have a gay and lesbian parent. And, between 8 to 10 million children are being raised in gay and lesbian households." More recent statistics estimates the total United States lesbian and gay family population to be 601,209, a 314 percent increase from 1990. Even so, it is believed that these census data are underreported (Gay and Lesbian Families, 2004). It is common knowledge that homosexual family forms experience many of the same obstacles other families face. Due to societal views and discriminative social and legal behaviors homosexual family constellations find themselves attempting to create their own traditions and familial roles that support their well-being.

As Guadalupe and Welkley have conceptualized, families are in a constant space of being and becoming. Through the aforementioned discussion on blended family constellations, we can briefly observe that this family form is complex. Currently, we can see that as a society we have some understanding of how blended families are formed and of their experiences. Yet as nonstatic living entities, blended family constellations continue to undergo a process of construction, deconstruction, and reconstruction of identities and experiences. This reflects an opportunity for nonstatic practices that embrace an understanding of how blended families affect and are affected by interpersonal, intrapersonal, environmental, and nonordinary realms of existence, previously explained by Guadalupe and Welkley.

Personal Issues Affecting and Being Affected by the Family

In the first four chapters of this text, Guadalupe and Welkley introduced the reader to the notion that the family is not only a recipient of cognitive, emotional, and social issues, but also simultaneously a participant or contributor to the perpetuation or modification of these issues. The blended family is no exception to this idea. Below we attempt to identify some issues that affect and are affected by the blended family. However, these are not the only family constellations that encounter these issues.

MENTAL HEALTH AND WELLNESS

One major challenge for blended families is coping and living with a member who has a mental illness. The complexity and stress of a reconstituted family of multiple relationships may cause complicated adjustment challenges. Studies have revealed that depression, anxiety disorders, and other emotional issues are common occurrences in divorces and remarriages (H. Cleaver, Nicholson, Tarr, D. Cleaver, 2007; Kirst-Ashman & Hull, 2008; McClennen, 2008; Schewe, 2008). Care for a family member with such challenges can be a tremendous burden on a family and its resources. A blended family may have to deal with the additional challenge of reflecting on how its new family constellation affects its members as well as the multitude of members affected and influencing issues related to mental health challenges.

The goals of intervention for a blended family dealing with mental health challenges are to help the family understand the nature and causes of these challenges, reduce symptoms, and perhaps engage the family in counseling to help improve family interaction and communication (Bentley, 2002; Collins et al., 2007). The blended family must also rely on its resources and strengths while addressing those challenges (i.e., family members' ability to communicate their feelings as well as their capacity to deal with conflicts generated by mental health challenges, extended family support, and community resources). It is well understood that the more members a family constellation has (in this case, blended families), the more factors come into consideration such as diverse and multiple needs, various perspectives on how to address the presented situation, as well as practitioners' abilities to be inclusive in their approaches.

INTIMATE PARTNER VIOLENCE AND DOMESTIC VIOLENCE

Intimate partner violence (IPV) refers to any behavior that purposely inflicts violence on another person in an intimate relationship including spouses, but also cohabitants and nonmarried intimate partners. IPV and domestic violence is universal and can occur in all cultures, all races, ethnicities, religions, sexes, and socioeconomic groups, as well as multiple family constellations. Batterers can be both male and female; however, statistics reveal that males are more likely the perpetrators (Kirst-Ashman & Hull, 2008).

Domestic violence includes, but is not limited to, hitting, kicking, threats with weapons, verbal abuse, sexual abuse, emotional abuse, intimidation, and economic deprivation. Physical assault, sexual abuse, and stalking are criminal acts. Although emotional, psychological, and financial abuse are not criminal behaviors, they are just as demoralizing and can lead to criminal violence that is punishable by law (Kirst-Ashman & Hull, 2008).

Accurate statistics on IPV and domestic violence are difficult to obtain because of widespread underreporting. However, it is estimated that "[a]pproximately 1.5 million women and 834,700 men are raped or physically assaulted by an intimate partner each year. About 588,490 or 85% of victimizations by intimate partners in 2001 were against women. IPV made up 20% of all nonfatal violent crime experienced by women and 3% of the nonfatal violence against men. 1,247 women and 440 men were killed by an intimate partner in 2000" (Office of Minority Health and Health Disparities, 2004). These statistics are startling. It has become common knowledge that family conflict and domestic violence, regardless of family constellation, can profoundly affect the development of children in their attitudes toward school, interpersonal relationships, and even themselves. As discussed before, blended families are complex, due to the multiple memberships individuals may experience. When adding the occurrence of domestic violence to this family form, the complexity is amplified. Imagine children who move between two family constellations if in one household (or both) domestic violence is a constant reality. A challenge for children in this situation can be how to make sense of these different environments and how they may affect their own well-being. The negative effects of exposure to violence on children include emotional distress, somatic illnesses, developmental delays, aggression, anxiety disorders (posttraumatic stress disorder), sleeplessness, and poor academic performance (Cleaver et al., 2007; McClennen, 2008; Schewe, 2008).

The roles of parenting and discipline in blended families must be major considerations for domestic violence. Blended families might want to consider assigning roles and responsibilities, such as who will discipline whose children. What are the rules regarding parental authority? A lack of clarity can create a volatile situation both within the marriage and between the biological parent and stepparent. For instance, thirteen-year-old Bobby reports to his biological father that his new stepfather is constantly disciplining him for "nothing"; the biological father responds with threats of physical violence if maltreatment of his son continues. The newly blended family is in crisis. How can rules be established without what may appear to be outside interference? Will the pressure from the biological father create a conflict between the newly married mother and stepfather? How can tension be reduced and a positive relationship established with the stepchild? How should parenting and discipline be managed? In most blended families, the biological parent assumes the primary role in both parenting and discipline. This can minimize the possibility of emotional turmoil or abuse. However, when there is no clear delineation of roles, or when the biological parent relinquishes his or her power and authority, the likelihood of maltreatment may increase. Maltreatment can have long-lasting negative effects on the child that may persist well into adulthood.

An example of long-lasting effects of family violence occurring within the context of a blended family constellation is reflected in Chloe's case study of a fifty-four-year-old single female whose childhood and adolescence were marked with spousal and child abuse and extreme familial conflict. She describes her experience:

It affects how you operate in your relationships; you operate in fear. The male–female thing is more difficult because my stepfather was the batterer. I was afraid of opening myself up to anyone or putting my feelings and emotions on the line. I was used to having my feelings and emotions stepped on. It is hard to trust because there was no safe place in my home. I was never able to tap into my own emotions to identify my own feelings because I had never been in a situation where feelings were discussed— only physical assault.

My greatest conflict was the resentment I felt toward my mother. It seemed so simple to me—if you leave him then we will be safe. But she chose to stay rather than leave. Our society views mothers as special; therefore I must be an awful person because I resent my mother. I suppressed my feelings and became the protector of my younger siblings. I had to be the parent because my mother was too beaten down to be effective and my stepfather was too abusive to care. My childhood and adolescence were lost.

All of this spills over into your relationships. I am still a nurturer. I have a tendency to seek out the only child or the youngest child in the family as a mate. I have sabotaged many good relationships because I did not know how to be the recipient of anything good. I could not trust and I never felt worthy. After many failed relationships, I had to get off the merry-go-round and take a good look at myself.

Where do I begin? First, I stopped dating and became celibate. Getting past the problem began when I figured out that I was the only common denominator in the failed relationships. I turned to the Lord and the church for support and solace. I also sought help from a therapist. I came to the realization that I had anger issues. One day I was talking to my therapist and crying uncontrollably about problems on my job when I suddenly blurted out, "And he shot me!" I had never dealt with being shot by my stepfather when I tried to stand up to him. I had suppressed my anger rather than confronting the situation. I had all of these feelings inside of me and I did not know how to deal with them. I simply left home; my mother stayed. As hard as it seems, I now know that being shot was my deliverance from violence and continued abuse. I have learned to deal with my anger and resentment toward my mother. I have to love myself, therefore I now can love my mother. I have developed a better understanding of my mother's decision to stay in an abusive relationship.

My mother lost her mother at the age of fourteen. She became a part of multiple blended families (passed around from family member to family member). She never had a stable family of her own. So marriage to my stepfather and acceptance of her child from a prior relationship represented the stability that she longed for as an adolescent. He had accepted her and her child, therefore she gave him full parental power and authority. Her ultimate goal was to keep her husband at all cost. This understanding has freed me of my resentment and I am gaining control of my life for the first time. The cycle of violence must be broken so that it will not be visited upon our children. Perhaps, subconsciously, being single and childless is my insurance policy against violence.

It is unclear as to the reason for Chloe's mother to remarry yet one thing that seems obvious by Chloe's story is that she was exposed to violence by someone who was not her biological father. Multiple lenses could emerge through this observation by posing various questions:

- What role did the biological father play during Chloe's childhood experience?

- Are the siblings mentioned from her biological father, half-siblings, or stepsiblings?

- What role did grandparents (maternal, paternal, and step) play?

- How did the role that Chloe played in the family provide her with strength and resilience to survive this experience, as well as the survival of other family members?

GRIEF AND LOSS

As stated earlier in this chapter, blended families may be born out of loss. A blended family differs from the traditional nuclear family in that it may suffer many significant losses, including relationships (i.e., one person gets "custody of friends"), family home, daily contact with the absent parent, personal belongings, and a sense of security (Kirst-Ashman & Hull, 2008). Several studies indicate that some children have reported that remarriage was more difficult than the parental divorce (Falci, 2006; Ham, 2004; Jeynes, 2006). Children frequently have difficulty accepting the reality that their parents will never get back together again. Remarriages represent an end to their dream of being an intact family again. They may mourn the loss of their previous family and struggle with loyalty issues, especially if animosity between parents exists (Collins et al., 2007; Kirst-Ashman & Hull). Grief is likely a normal emotional reaction to these losses. Grief and loss are a natural part of life; the duration and intensity of grieving varies according to the individual's capacity to accept the reality of the loss or change.

Additionally, a blended family has a greater chance of dealing with a further loss, another divorce. According to Newman and Newman (2006), 66 percent of second marriages end in divorce, especially when children are actively involved. This loss disrupts their family life cycle and grief is revisited.

Research studies reveal that children who experience divorce often suffer from psychological distress and experience lower academic achievement than their peers in intact families. These findings often are also true of children in blended families. This is all the more devastating for children who must endure a second or third divorce (Ahrons, 2006; Wallerstein, 2005).

Adult children of divorced parents have also reported the lingering pain of the loss of their intact family. Many report acute anxieties and insecurities about love, commitment, marriage, and parenting (Ahrons, 2006; Wallerstein, 2005). These findings have major implications for the family life-cycle perspectives, which is especially true when using one of the traditional models described in chapter 3. For example, the primary family developmental task during the adolescent stage in the family life cycle is that of preparing the child for greater freedom and responsibility to interact with the elements within the environment (i.e., peers, employment, etc.). The developmental task also requires preparation for dealing with potential dangers such as drugs, pregnancy, and delinquency (Duvall & Miller, 1985; Zastrow & Kirst-Ashman, 2007). Successful parents of adolescents assist their children in mastering decision-making skills, provide nurturing and support, set high moral standards, and boundary setting in needed areas to ensure growth and autonomy while still being assured that family guidance is readily available (Newman & Newman, 2003; Zastrow & Kirst-Ashman).

When the family reaches the adolescent stage of the family life cycle, socialization of the children in terms of development of moral values is essential. Successful completion of adolescent developmental tasks is linked to the parents' successful completion of their tasks. If parents are not successful in their efforts, the children will have difficulty emerging from the adolescent stage as competent adults (Duvall & Miller, 1985; Zastrow & Kirst-Ashman, 2007). Parental divorce can cause a major disruption in the life cycle; research reveals some negative outcomes of this disruption. Research on adult children of divorce supports this theory (Ahrons, 2006; Wallerstein, 2005; Zastrow & Kirst-Ashman). It is well understood that divorces are not always experienced as negative, and may be an opportunity for new beginnings.

Traditionally, one may observe that the literature tends to concentrate on emotional, social, and economic challenges generated by a loss, whether it is caused by a divorce or a death. However, blended families often present opportunities not previously encountered nor do they all come about from the same set of circumstances. The experience of loss may or may not be present, and may be experienced differently by various blended families. For instance, loss caused by a divorce may have been inevitable in order to sustain family well-being, especially if the divorce was caused by domestic violence. In this case, new or healthy choices and experiences may be encountered in the newly formed blended family where domestic violence is no longer a part of the family dynamics. A loss presents family members with an opportunity to explore individual family strengths to address cognitive, emotional, or social adversity. Part of the family's strengths that may be discovered or strengthened by a loss could be the family's inner ability to communicate experiences as well as an ability to confront the loss while relying on each other's support. Blended families by nature seem to have more individual members that may provide opportunities for more resources. Within the context of being affected and affecting an experience, one may observe a couple going through a divorce or cultivating new relationships with other partners, thus amplifying available assets.

Consideration of Family Potential Strengths and Challenges

Many families prevail over the great challenges of blending two families. What makes these families resilient? What are the common factors that keep these families stable, while others disintegrate? Good communication skills within a family have proved to be a key factor in successful resolution of conflicts. Adequate resources or resourcefulness are also factors that ensure family stability. Financial stability or knowledge of community resources can sustain a blended family during a crisis. Education is a major asset and may increase blended family members' capacity to better understand challenges and creatively problem solve (Hawkins & Langston, 2008). Spirituality, the belief in a higher power is often cited in the literature as a major strength in times of challenges.

Blended families interact with multiple facets of the wider society and communities that serve as a continuum for identity formation. They are dynamic and constantly evolving, and are in the process of being and becoming. Blended family constellations are active participants in this social change and are not simply being acted on. In some cases, this participation may promote family unity, while in others it may create transitional difficulties.

Interestingly, the strengths perspective has gained great merit among practitioners. For example, the strengths perspective encourages practitioners to focus on clients' positive attributes, characteristics, assets, and resources, rather than on weaknesses. In addition, the strengths perspective encourages practitioners to build on clients' strengths and competencies to empower them to use their own resources to understand their current situation and develop creative ways to make positive changes (Bentley, 2002; Glicken, 2003; Miley, O'Melia, & DuBois, 1995; Saleebey, 2009).

As mentioned earlier, the experiences of blended families have the potential for generating multiple resources. Using a strengths perspective, one could suggest that children raised and supported by two or more family units, referred to here as blended family constellations, could have opportunities to be exposed to diverse family lifestyles, cultural experiences, and conflict management skills. It has been said that children are raised by a community. Blended family constellations could be considered a microcosm of the larger society. The more exposure to different experiences, the more the likely it is that individuals will draw on a wider array of resources. Consider the following case study:

Maria and Robert are step-siblings. Maria's mom is Latina and Robert's dad is Caucasian. Maria's mom is bilingual (speaks both Spanish and English) and is proud of her Latina traditions. She encourages the entire family to celebrate holidays that she grew up embracing (i.e., Three

Wise Men Celebration, January 6th, and Dia de los Muertos—Day of the Dead) and attempts to speak Spanish in the house as much as possible. Robert's dad is of Irish descent with a strong Catholic background, something he and his wife share. He sees March 17, St. Patrick's Day, and Super Bowl Sunday as being just as important as national holidays. He expects that the family will be together on these days regardless of other obligations. While being exposed to these two ethnic-cultural experiences Robert and Maria are presented with the opportunity to learn different customs, perhaps languages, traditions, values, and belief systems, thus cultivating or increasing their bicultural capacity to navigate through what could be assumed to be two different worlds.

While developing a bicultural life orientation through the experience of this form of blended family constellation, one could argue that issues such as ethnocentrism (the tendency to judge other people's behaviors and beliefs using one's own cultural yardstick) could be reduced or challenged. Viewing this blended family constellation through a strengths perspective could indicate that the experiences that Maria and Robert are being exposed to can increase their ability to broaden their worldview of themselves, their families, and the world around them.

Although the strengths perspective is quite relevant, understanding challenges is also essential for effective practice. Practitioners must be knowledgeable about challenges that clients face on a daily basis to ensure the best outcome for the client. Consider the following scenario where an adolescent male, who will be referred to as Ricardo Gonzales, is now a member of a blended family of five.

Ricardo's biological father, Enrique Gonzales, is in a same-sex family constellation. His maternal grandparents, with whom he lived for a year, are part of a spiritually based family constellation that adamantly opposes his father's family arrangements. Ricardo loves his father and finds it difficult to listen to his grandparents, whom he also loves dearly, speak negatively about his dad. This was a source of friction among Ricardo and his grandparents. During the year he lived with them, he began spending significant amounts of time with some of his peers who are believed to be members of a local gang. Ricardo sees these so called "gang members" as family; spending time with them was a way for him to escape the tension in the home. He now lives with his mom, Juanita, who is married to a successful businessman, Juan Pedro, who was previously married and has two children of whom he has custody. Ricardo sees him as a good father not only to his own children, but also to him. However, he is very committed to his dad, who his step-dad is not particularly fond of but tolerates. Ricardo gets along well with his new family although he does not understand why they are so concerned about the time he spends with his dad. His stepsisters, Luz and Marta, have said on more than one occasion that it seems like he prefers to spend time with his dad's new family rather than with his mom's. He does not like their questioning his loyalty to the family. Ricardo is concerned that so many folks have isolated themselves from his dad and he wants them to know that he wants his dad to be actively involved in his life. His mother appears less concerned about the time he spends with his father although she does not support his father's family arrangements. Ricardo sometimes finds it challenging to juggle the relationship with his new family, his dad, and both sets of grandparents.

A traditional treatment approach with this family would miss a great opportunity for the development of a culturally sensitive contract with the client. Assuming that the dynamics of working with a blended family would be the same as a nuclear family, or that all blended families are virtually the same, would be shortsighted. Furthermore, failure to recognize or accept the multidimensional contextual family constellations in seeking to work with the family in the case scenario would not be indicative of an approach that values the uniqueness of each client. As Guadalupe and Welkley discuss in chapter 2 of this text, the assessment and intervention would fail to see the constellation of blended families as multisystemic and proactive. Therefore, strengths and challenges must be considered during the application of an eclectic approach when working with blended family constellations.

An Eclectic Professional Approach: Beyond Stereotypes

These authors have attempted to promote some understanding of the complexity and vastness of blended family constellations, while making the observation that blended families are multidimensional contextual nonstatic living entities through which individuals experience multiple memberships. Our discussion has also briefly reflected how blended families are in a constant state of being who they are within context and yet continuously experiencing a process of evolution, reflecting Guadalupe and Welkley's third premise of family constellations of being and becoming. We also have given examples of particular issues affecting and being affected by blended family forms. The authors hope that this discussion has provided the reader with an opportunity to recognize the importance of an eclectic approach when addressing strengths and challenges faced by diverse forms of blended family constellations. Below we provide the reader with examples of possible applications of eclectic approaches to working with blended family structures.

MICRO AND MEZZO CAPACITY: A CASE EXAMPLE

The case of Chloe, a fifty-four-year-old single female previously introduced, will be used as an example at the micro level. Since Chloe is an
adult, the case will be analyzed retrospectively. The goal of this exercise
is to develop effective intervention strategies to help the family, thus
minimizing the negative consequences of domestic violence. Let's
assume that Chloe's mother, Mrs. Parker, gathered her seven children
and left while Mr. Parker was at work. The first intervention used will be
crisis intervention, a brief and time-limited approach where service
providers help individuals cope with or adjust to extreme external
stresses (Kirst-Ashman & Hull, 2008). Other interventions are included
throughout the case. (Stages of the helping process as outlined by Kirst-
Ashman and Hull are indicated with asterisks.)

Step 1: Assessment*   *Mrs. Parker comes to the office at midday with
seven small children in tow. She is severely bruised and frightened. She
looks anxiously around the room. The worker introduces herself and asks
what had brought them into the office. Mrs. Parker recounts years of battery and fear. She is convinced that someday her husband will eventually
kill her, so she had decided to escape.*

*The assessment process gathers information about how Mrs. Parker
views the situation and its impact on her. She says she feels helpless,
worthless, and ashamed. She is isolated from her family and only her
children know of the terrors that exist in the home. She has limited support systems. After more discussion, the worker learns that Chloe, the oldest child, is from a previous relationship, and the other six children are
from her marriage to Mr. Parker. The worker notices that Chloe is very
parental in her interaction with her siblings and mother. There is no mention of Chloe's biological father at this time, so it is unknown to what
degree he is still involved. The worker concentrates on gaining additional
insight into Mrs. Parker's perceptions of the situation and herself. The
worker knows that she will need long-term supportive counseling—that
is, counseling inclusive of diverse approaches in order to assist the family
to regain a sense of power over their family situation. However, the family's immediate need for safety is the priority. The family is placed in a
shelter for battered women where access is limited to clients and workers.
Other immediate needs are clothing, financial resources housing, and
eventually job training for self-sufficiency.*

*The worker carefully questions Mrs. Parker about whether she wants to
file criminal charges against her husband, because battery is a legal matter. She declines to do so, saying that she could not have her husband and
the father of her children incarcerated. The worker also offers information about her right to seek a protection order against her husband*

through the court. She declines again. She denies suicidal and homicidal ideations.

Step 2: Planning* *The worker's evaluation of the crisis situation reveals that the family's home is volatile and clearly dangerous. Mr. Parker is an alcoholic and is probably enraged by their leaving. Mrs. Parker has no means of support for herself and her children and is clearly depressed. The children are anxious and clinging, although Chloe tries to appear strong. She and her mother are the primary targets of her stepfather's rage. She feels like an outsider and believes that her stepfather hates her because she is not his "real" child.*

Although the family situation looks bleak, the worker senses that Mrs. Parker possesses much strength in that she has made a courageous stand to escape the violence and save herself and her children. Mrs. Parker and the worker conclude that returning to her home is not a viable option.

Mrs. Parker and the worker addresses her primary problems first: finances and housing. She is referred to the department of social services to determine eligibility for financial support and housing assistance. This agency could assist with both if the family meets eligibility criteria. The department of social services also could assist with other resources such as food, transportation, and job training.

Another challenge for Mrs. Parker is her fear for the family's safety. Legal intervention may be necessary to resolve this problem, as Mr. Parker could be court ordered to stay away from the family, seek substance abuse treatment, and anger management counseling. Legal intervention could increase the family's chances for safety and stabilization. Another problem facing this family is emotional distress caused by years of abuse. Furthermore, Chloe and her mom need individual therapy to deal with the emotional turmoil of physical and emotional abuse, feelings of isolation, low self-esteem, and for Chloe the recognition that she is a child and not a parent.

Step 3: Implementation* *Mrs. Parker and the worker meet biweekly for one month and are nearing termination. Mrs. Parker has been conscientious in keeping all appointments and has qualified for both financial and housing assistance. She is given permission to remain in the shelter until housing becomes available. The children feel safe and are well nourished and sleep peacefully at night. They are slowly beginning to show signs of childhood joy. Chloe has begun to slowly but progressively assume the role of child, rather than a surrogate parent. Her mother has begun to value her own role as a competent parent. The family for the first time, stated Mrs. Parker, is somewhat stable. It is important to notice that during* the course of intervention, community and other family resources have been identified. Mrs. Parker has attempted to contact Chloe's biological father and grandparents. However, Chloe's biological father is not emotionally available due to drug addiction, and her paternal grandparents are deceased. Instead, her paternal Aunt Beth and her husband have become an emotional and economic asset to Mrs. Parker and the children.

Mrs. Parker also has followed through on the counseling referral. She is involved in assertiveness training at a local mental health center to help her gain control over her emotions and her life. She also is engaged in individual and group counseling. She says she has developed greater insight into her inner self. The worker can see an increase in her self-esteem, self-advocacy, and parenting skills.

The children are engaged in group therapy with other children who also have encountered abusive situations. They are learning that they are not alone. The family is becoming more outgoing and is reaching out to relatives (i.e., Mrs. Parker's siblings) with whom they have lost contact. They go to church regularly and view faith as a great source of strength.

Chloe continues to be involved in individual therapy. She is exploring issues relative to her biological father and how she fits into the blended family created by her mom and stepfather. Beth, Chloe's aunt, has served as a supportive system while Chloe progressively addresses the pain generated from feelings of abandonment related to her relationship with her biological father and rejection related to her stepfather.

Mr. Parker is working on his issues as well. However, Mrs. Parker does not trust him with her well-being or those of her children. She plans to move into her own apartment when it becomes available within the next forty-five days.

Step 4: Anticipatory Planning* Mrs. Parker is making tremendous progress. She is no longer the frightened, dependent woman who appeared in the worker's office four weeks ago. She has worked hard in making her children feel safe. She apologizes to Chloe during a family session for not protecting her, and for relinquishing her parental rights and authority to her brutal stepfather. She has learned new coping skills, insight into her behavior and fears, and ways to be assertive without being aggressive. She is practicing her faith and also seeks greater understanding of spiritual teachings. The children are well on their way to healing. The worker has encouraged Mrs. Parker to continue in therapy to learn additional coping skills to deal with life stressors and Mrs. Parker has agreed to do so. The case has been closed, yet months later in a follow-up with Mrs. Parker the worker learns that the family (Mrs. Parker and all seven children) has moved back in with Mr. Parker.

MACRO CAPACITY: ANOTHER CASE EXAMPLE

In focusing on the social–cultural–political–environmental (macro capacity) contexts, the practitioner needs to take into account its specific meaning for the family. Healthy communities offer healthy environments. As our communities become healthier, so will their inhabitants, leaving professionals the task of working with those who have the most critical need (Glicken, 2003).

As with nonblended families, blended families must adjust to a culture and subculture that influences it through beliefs and ideologies. The community to which families must respond may be spatial or ideological. Johnson's (2001) review of the literature provides an expanded definition of community, to include therapeutic community; formal service providers; the intimate community of family, friends, territorial communities (streets, neighborhoods, nations); and common interest communities (religious, ethnic, sporting, etc.) related to feelings of attachment and a sense of identity. As families interact with each of these communities, it is the nature and strength of their contacts and connectedness among and between persons with whom the family engages that ultimately determine identity construction, deconstruction, or reconstruction.

In working with the blended or multipartner family constellation at the macro level there are various levels around which a working relationship can be developed as the worker seeks to respond to social, political, economic, and environmental forces that affect the family. Following is one suggested approach that has been adapted from the work of Dhooper and Moore (2001) using the Ricardo Gonzales case, previously introduced.

Step 1: Assessment   *We begin with an awareness of the realities of Ricardo's blended family. Ricardo, his mother Juanita, his stepfather Juan Pedro, and his two stepsisters Luz and Marta, come to the agency for help because they are struggling with coming together and functioning as a unit.*

Step 2: Intervention   *The issues that the family brings to the counseling situation may be addressed at the macro capacity using several intervention strategies. The following illustrates possible interventions:*

1. *Support for a community or support group for blended families could be established. Such a group would allow for an organized effort when seeking to influence policies or to whom legislators and other policy bodies could turn to for leadership. Such a group would assist families by providing a forum in which others, who face common concerns, could evaluate their choices and reflect on challenges or gaps. Blended families could address any concerns about what they*

may feel pressured or encouraged to give up or modify as a member of the new expanded family structure. For instance, what does each sibling believe he or she must surrender? What relationship(s) does he or she feel should now be given less weight? In other words, should Ricardo be expected to give up the quality time that he enjoys with his dad (who is involved in a same-sex relationship) in order to be more fully embraced by his new family? This forum would also allow for the mirroring of strengths among group members. This could allow the family to focus less on what they may have lost or be challenged with and more on what they currently have.

2. *Explore the impact of social policy as it relates to the constellation of blended families. To what degree are policies prohibitive for any of these groups? For instance, are same-sex blended families treated the same under the law as are other blended families, or families in general? Meaning, are they afforded the same family benefits that are readily accessible to other family constellations relative to custody, visitation, and so on? Historically, there have been social policies that are "anti" same-sex families. As Dhooper and Moore (2001) suggested, feedback on policy should be obtained prior to policy development and implementation and could be assessed through focus groups, surveys, and town meetings.*

3. *The worker can help educate the family on all relevant policies and involve the agency in identifying mechanisms to ensure that the voices, input, and ideas of blended and multipartner families (including same-sex families) are heard. This is more likely to occur when there is limited or no marginalization among family members within blended family constellations. The helping professional should become an active advocate for such families.*

4. *As previously stated, an array of myths, both negative and positive, exists regarding blended family life. In their role as advocates for greater individual and collective empowerment of families, human services professionals should work to ensure that the media receive accurate information regarding blended family constellations. In so doing they should challenge myths that are being advanced. Such advocacy could help alleviate conflicted dynamics as the one reflected in Ricardo's case. As previously mentioned, due to their religious orientation, Ricardo's grandparents are not supportive of Ricardo's relationship with his biological father. They may embrace unsubstantiated views of homosexuality and the impact of a homosexual parent on his or her child. Dispelling myths about homosexuality and children of same-sex parents might help strengthen the overall blended family dynamic in this case.*

5. *Community organization efforts should be supported, particularly among those who may seem to be further away from the mainstream structure of both traditional and contemporary families. Blended families may at times face isolation, stigmatization, and marginalization. Therefore, the type of community organization model that may be used when working with blended families should depend on the level of resources the community has, the level of sophistication or influence the community has, and the types of exchanges that occur among its community members. Community organizations in this instance are further challenged by the fact that they are not limited to a specific geographical area, but common interests or needs of blended families. This approach could be of value to Ricardo's family in helping members to enjoy healthy exchanges with key systems that directly or indirectly influence the dynamics of this blended family. For instance, Enrique Gonzales' (Ricardo's father) homosexual union should not be seen as an oppressed group but as a group confronting oppression, whose strength could further support stability rather than chaos in Ricardo's life.*

Step 3: Evaluation   *One may look at both process and outcomes in assessing the degree of success of the efforts at the macro level. For instance, the level of Ricardo's family members' involvement in empowering activities and their leadership of key efforts in support of their needs, lobbying and other political activism, and their establishment of formal and informal support systems are all efforts that could be assessed, although the incremental process may be greater for some family members than for others. These authors further contend that the model presented in chapter 1, figure 1.1, may also be used to evaluate the level of success at the macro level. For instance, if there are higher levels of interactions as determined by contact-connectedness among and between the members of Ricardo's community and the exchanges are healthy, a greater sense of community would be fostered that would have an empowering effect for the families involved. Contact and connectedness would not simply be determined by quantity but rather by the meaningfulness of the interactions and exchanges to the blended family functioning. Greater contact-connectedness within and between the blended family of Juanita and Juan Pedro as well as Enrique Gonzales could result in a clearer understanding of the meanings given to the experience of families in this blended family constellation. The degree to which such exchanges could be viewed as healthy would depend on the level of respect shown for the differing perspectives, especially by the blended family structure that is seen as closer to the more traditional or dominant end of the continuum.*

MAGNA CAPACITY (NONORDINARY REALITY): INDIVIDUALIZING PRACTICE ISSUES

In their research on successful families, Krysan, Moore, and Zill (1990) noted that many researchers identified a religious or spiritual orientation as an important component of strong families. In defining religiosity or spirituality, these authors noted that spirituality involves more than just the frequency of one's attendance at a religious service and may include attendance at such events as charitable functions or membership in some form of religious subgroup. Religiosity or spiritualty may also relate to the meaning a person attaches to life or compliance to some values system or moral code.

Expanding the definition of spirituality, Glicken (2003) defined spirituality as "the means by which one finds wholeness, meaning, and purpose in life. It arises from an innate longing for fulfillment through the establishment of loving relationships with self and community. Spirituality suggests harmony with self, others, and the world" (p. 65). He further stated, "It is our way of finding meaning in the social and cultural forces that affect our lives. It is our way of seeing ourselves in relationship to others against a background of shared meaning and purpose" (p. 65).

The nonordinary realm (magna capacity) requires the practitioner to explore the role that faith or spirituality plays in the way the blended family approaches life and filters input and output based on meaningful exchanges that occur with this demanding family form. The magna capacity is probably one of the more difficult levels at which the worker may intervene. Various reasons for this difficulty have been advanced:

1. Support for spirituality as a topic of interest in behavioral health education is a recent occurrence (Evans, Boustead, & Owens, 2008).

2. Training in spirituality is not widely integrated in the human services curriculum (Canda, 1998).

3. The way clinicians treat their clients is influenced by their own values and experience.

4. Religion is equated with rigidity and dogmatism (Kilpatrick & Holland, 1990).

5. Some people perceive that religion always promotes excessive guilt, advances a belief in a God that is punitive, rather than a perspective of healing, which encourages believers to be passive (Joseph, 1988).

6. Religion encourages the believer to focus on "other-worldly" matters rather than on the here-and-now.

The therapeutic environment can be intimidating under certain cir-cumstances. Discussing sensitive issues in a group, even with blended family members, can be uncomfortable. In conducting an assessment regarding spiritual matters, the worker should first create an atmos-phere that makes it comfortable or easy for blended families to discuss spiritual matters. As Cascio (1998) pointed out, in creating such an atmosphere, the worker acknowledges the legitimacy of spiritual mat-ters and the reality that discussing such concerns is acceptable. There-fore, the contract that the worker enters into with the blended family should reflect an openness to discuss how he or she focuses on other-worldly matters that may be influencing the here and now. For instance, some examples of topics or concerns that may surface or at least res-onate with blended families include spiritual beliefs about marriage, divorce, remarriage, cohabitating, child rearing, homosexuality, polygamy, single parenting, and gender-related issues.

As the worker seeks to explore the client assessment of the meaning of life, it is critical for him or her to understand the role of various rituals and the meaning of various symbols. For instance, the role of faith versus science is a matter that could be conflictual, especially if directly related to one's physical or psychological health. A sacred moment as Guadalupe and Welkley note in chapter 4, is one where we have the opportunity to create tools and practical resources while allowing space for a miracle or the unexpected to occur. Reflecting once more on Guadalupe and Welkley's model regarding the dynamics of interactions and exchanges (chapter 1), consider a deeply religious blended family who prays to their god daily. As the blended family prepares to start their day, they interact with their god through prayer. Through prayer, there is a connection with their higher power that results in awareness of their power (as defined by this blended family) in their lives. Prayer is exchanged for blessings in their lives because they have a keen awareness that their god is directing their thoughts and blessing them with a spirit of discernment to know how to act. Any action outside of compliance with what is perceived as the will of their god will be determined as inappropriate.

Step 1: Assessment   Let us revisit the case of Ricardo Gonzales' family.

Ricardo Gonzales, age fourteen, is the only male child with two female stepsisters. His mother Juanita is married to Juan Pedro, who is the custo-dial parent of the two girls, Luz age ten and Marta age twelve. Ricardo's biological dad is in a homosexual union. His mother and stepfather are devout Catholics whose doctrinal teachings state that homosexuality is against the will of God. Yet Ricardo, who also professes Catholicism, loves spending what other family members perceive is a disproportionate amount of time at his dad's home relative to that of his new home. Although his dad does not claim Catholicism, he also sees himself as being deeply religious. The blended family of Juanita and Juan Pedro is struggling to function as a unit, complaining that their teenage son seems passive aggressive in his interaction with his stepfather. The siblings love their stepbrother but claim that they do not know how to engage Ricardo at a meaningful level.

The worker's first task is to create an atmosphere that allows the blended family to share its understanding of the tenets of the Catholic faith and its meaning for their lives. An assessment that focuses on the family's spiritual values and how they affect other relevant blended family constellations such as Ricardo's dad's family and the family of his peers (the gang) should shed some light on how their belief guides their interaction. A clear assessment of what religion in general and the tenets of the Catholic faith means for how each member views life and approaches relationships and interactions with others must be addressed. For instance, how does Ricardo feel about his involvement with a faith that classifies his dad, whom he loves dearly, as deviant, immoral, or abnormal? What convictions or conflicts does that pose for him and how are they resolved?

Step 2: Intervention   Cascio (1998) noted several intervention methods that are worthy of consideration. Again, we encourage the reader to ensure he or she is properly trained in these modalities prior to using them with clients. Blended families seeking strategies to develop better as a reconstituted family may find some of these recommended interventions effective:

1. Gestalt techniques (i.e., psychodrama and the empty chair technique)

2. Journaling

3. Bibliotherapy

4. Metaphor

5. Various forms of prayer such as meditation and ritual

Let's examine two of these techniques for possible application with Ricardo's blended family. We begin with psychodrama, where the practitioner may or may not use the empty chair technique. The key emphasis is to engage the family member in an intense exploration of issues the family is confronting. Issues such as trust, faith, morality, loyalty, entitlement, shame, submission, freedom, love, self-image, fear, self-disclosure, self-sacrifice, and tug-o-war are some of what could be explored through the exploration of impeding or enabling factors. An open and honest expression of one's feeling about these issues could represent a cathartic moment. These issues could be discussed within the context of faith or religion.

Another technique that can be used to explore the issues is biblio-therapy. The poem, "Is It Worth It," has a spiritual foundation where the focus is harmony with self and others. Meaning is explored through interactions and exchanges with others where there is introspection and questioning as the person is taken to that nonordinary realm where the meaning of one's life is explored. A central theme is how the conclusion to the question posed compels the individual to interact with others.

Is It Worth It

Is it worth it?
This is the question I ask myself
As I hide behind a veil
That has been my source of comfort,
Or has it?
As I travel through life with its
Moments of uncertainty, I clutch
Each corner of the veil, fearful that if lifted
The revelation would result in scorn and disgrace.
And so I journey through life threatened by each
Step that might disclose the truth that some might
Find too much to handle and so I suffer in silence,
Convinced that this semblance of martyrdom
Is my lot in life.
The charade continues as I mask
What I should freely share: the fullness of my love,
Not misguided, not inferior, or deviant, but a love
That is as clean as an unmarked snowflake.
But can I freely share without shame if shrouded
In a veil? I find myself pondering whether
The veil cheats others or me of an experience of freedom—
A freedom that is governed by truth and love; that is not
Shackled by unrealistic expectations or unscripted images
Neatly packaged in a case that does not fit: a square peg
In a hole that's round.
At the end of it all
Will I still ask myself
Was it worth it?
Or will I celebrate truth and honesty unmasked,
Satisfied with simply being everything my heart desires.
Is it worth it?
Masked or unmasked?

E. Sebastian Bolden © 2003

In addition to the meaning assigned to specific blended family rituals, the meaning of symbols such as a cross or crucifix, a flag, a tattoo, body piercing, hairstyles, and clothing are all symbols that have spiritual meaning for some. Whether the worker endorses any of these symbols or not is irrelevant, unless it hampers his or her ability to effectively work with the blended family. The significance for the client whether it symbolizes membership affiliation, commitment to a higher being, or that the client is functioning in a specific spiritual realm that directs his or her approach to life is what should be of interest to the worker.

The nonordinary realm presupposes a connection with a being that offers exchanges that will facilitate the incorporation of existing norms and values embraced by a blended family or the development of new guiding philosophies that blended family member(s) deem valuable or necessary. Faith in such a realm is central to one's determination as a family and is seen as both an agent of change and a perpetuator of experiences. Despite the potential challenge of incorporating spirituality when assessing the family's strengths, this dimension cannot be ignored because it is seen as central to how many blended families approach their world or culture (Evans et al., 2008).

Summary

The presence of traditional nuclear families as the norm has been diminishing over the last few decades. In seeking to be more successful in responding to the needs of diverse family forms, new paradigms such as those presented in this text have been advanced. This chapter supports the premise of other authors in this text who purport that families (in this chapter, blended families) are active participants in their own journey to greater well-being. The approaches to working with blended families are constantly evolving in response to changes among family constellations. These authors have proposed an eclectic approach to responding to the total needs of the blended or multipartner families. These proposed approaches are by no means exhaustive.

In instances where case examples were based on real life experiences, key identifying information was modified and permission from parties involved was secured. The case examples are meant to facilitate the student's application of suggested approaches and to stimulate further discussion. The poem, "Is It Worth It?" is an original poem by one of the authors and is meant to promote discussion regarding hidden or sensitive topics.

Questions to Promote Further Critical Analysis

1. How does the growth in number or recognition of nontraditional families affect the quantity and types of services to children in blended and multipartner families?

2. What changes are needed to the curriculum in higher education to better prepare professionals to capture the strengths of blended family forms and respond to their challenges?

3. If cultural context is so dynamic, how reliable would data be from longitudinal studies on blended and multipartner families because they are heavily affected by political, social, and environmental factors that do not transcend time?

4. Beyond a healthy relationship among family members as well as with the human services practitioner, how is success determined in working with blended families?

5. How does one determine the appropriate criteria for ranking competing factors or values when working with blended or multipartner families?

6. How can objectivity be assured by having blended families in highly sensitive or politicized situations as active players in the development of solutions to addressing their problems? How can the practitioner guard against politics driving the solution, or should that be a concern?

References

Ahrons, C. (2006). Family ties after divorce: Long-term implications for children. *Family Process, 46*(1), 53–65.

Becvar, D. S., & Becvar, R. J. (1996). *Family therapy: A systemic integration* (3rd ed.). Boston: Allyn & Bacon.

Becvar, D. S., & Becvar, R. J. (2008). *Family therapy: A systemic integration* (7th ed.). Boston: Allyn & Bacon.

Bentley, K. J. (Ed.). (2002). *Social work practice in mental health: Contemporary roles, tasks, and techniques.* Pacific Grove, CA: Brook/Cole.

Canda, E. R. (1998). *Spirituality in social work: New directions.* Binghampton, NY: Haworth Pastoral Press.

Carter, B., & McGoldrick, M. (Eds.). (2005). *The expanded family life cycle: Individual, family, and social perspectives* (3rd ed.). New York: Pearson.

Cascio, T. (1998, September). Incorporating spirituality into social work practice: A review of what to do. *Families in Society: The Journal of Contemporary Human Services, 79*(5), 523–531.

Cleaver, H., Nicholson, D., Tarr, S., & Cleaver, D. (2007). *Wider effects of violence and substance misuse in the family.* London: Jessica Kingsley.

Collins, D., Jordan, C., & Coleman, H. (2007). *An introduction to family social work.* Belmont, CA: Thomson/Brooks/Cole.

Daynes, K. M. (2001). *More wives than one: Transformation of the Mormon marriage system*. Illinois: University of Illinois Press.

Dhooper, S. S., & Moore, S. E. (2001). *Social work practice with culturally diverse people*. Thousand Oaks, CA: Sage.

Diderich-Balsam, M. C. (2005, August 12–16). *Sibling relationships in nuclear families, divorced families, and remarried families*. Paper presented at the 100th Annual Conference of the American Sociological Association in Philadelphia, PA.

Duvall, E. M., & Miller, B. C. (1985). *Marriage and family development* (6th ed.). New York: Harper & Row.

Evans, C. J., Boustead, R. S., & Owens, C. (2008). Expressions of spirituality in parents with at risk children. *Families in Society: The Journal of Contemporary Social Services, 89*(2), 245–252.

Falci, C. (2006). Family structure, closeness to residential and nonresidential parents, and psychological distress in early and middle adolescence. *The Sociological Quarterly, 47*, 123–147.

Gay and Lesbian Families. (2004). *Family Trends, 1*(3), Institute for Families School of Social Work University of North Carolina–Chapel Hill.

Gennetian, L. A. (2005). One or two parents? Half or step siblings? The effect of family structure on young children's achievement. *Journal of Population Economics, 18*, 415–436.

Glicken, M. D. (2003). *Using the strengths perspective in social work practice: A positive approach for the helping profession*. Boston: Pearson/Allyn & Bacon.

Ham, B. D. (2004). The effects of divorce and remarriage on the academic achievement of high school seniors. *Journal of Divorce and Remarriage, 42*(1/2), 159–177.

Harrison-Hale, A. O. (2005). Fluctuating forces with families: Psychosocial implications for children. *Forum on Public Policy, 1*(4), 375–390. Retrieved June 27, 2011, from http://forumonpublicpolicy.com/vol1.no4.child.psychology/toc.vol1.no4.htm.

Hawkins, C. L., & Langston, L. (2008). Intervening with domestic violence using the family health perspective. In F. K. O Yuen, G. J. Skibinski, & J. T. Pardeck (Eds.), *Family health social work practice: A knowledge and skills casebook* (pp. 65–77). New York: The Haworth Social Work Practice Press.

Helton, L. R., & Smith, M. K. (2004). Children and family relationships. In C. Munson, M. K. Smith, & L. R. Helton (Eds.), *Mental health practice with youth: A strengths and well-being model* (pp. 81–93). New York: Haworth Press.

Jeynes, W. H. (2006). The impact of parental remarriage on children: A meta-analysis. *Marriage and Family Review, 40*(4), 75–95.

Johnson, A. K. (2001). *Tactics and techniques of community intervention* (4th ed.). Itasca, IL: F. E. Peacock.

Joseph, M. V. (1988, September). Religion and social work practice. *Social Casework, 69*(7), 443–452.

Kilpatrick, A. C., & Holland, T. (1990). Spiritual dimensions of practice. *The Clinical Supervisor, 8*(2), 125–140.

Kirst-Ashman, K., & Hull, G. (2008). *Understanding generalist practice* (5th ed.). Belmont, CA: Thomson/Brooks/Cole.

Krysan, M., Moore, K. A., & Zill, N. (1990). *Identifying successful families: An overview of constructs and selected measures.* Washington, DC: Child Trends.

McClennen, J. C. (2008). Intervening with domestic violence using the family health perspective. In F. K. O Yuen, G. J. Skibinski, & J. T. Pardeck (Eds.), *Family health social work practice: A knowledge and skills casebook* (pp. 65–77). New York: The Haworth Social Work Practice Press.

Miley, K. K., O'Melia, & DuBois, B. L. (1995). *Generalist social work practice: An empowering Approach.* Boston: Allyn & Bacon.

Mincy, R. B., & Oliver, H. (2003). Age, race, and children's living arrangements: Implications for TANF reauthorization. *New Federalism: National Survey of America's Families.* Retrieved March 11, 2010, from http://www.urban.org/url.cfm?ID=310670.

National Adoption Information Clearinghouse. (2000). *Adoption and same-sex couples: Basics.* (U.S. Department of Health and Human Services Publication). Retrieved March 11, 2011, from http://www.family.findlaw.com/adoption/.../same-sex-adoption-intro.html.

Net Industries. (2011). Polygamy: The crime. Retrieved June 26, 2011, from law.jrank.org/pages/9272/Polygamy-Crime.html.

Newman, B. M., & Newman, P. R. (2003). *Development through the life cycle: A psychosocial approach* (8th ed.). Belmont, CA: Thomson/Wadsworth.

Newman, B. M., & Newman, P. R. (2006). *Development through the life cycle: A psychosocial approach* (9th ed.). Belmont, CA: Thomson/Wadsworth.

Office of Minority Health and Health Disparities. (2004, October). *Highlights in minority health.* Center for Disease Control and Prevention Publication. Retrieved March 11, 2010, from http://www.cdc.gov/omhd/Highlights/2004/HOct04.htm.

Portrie, T., & Hill, N. R. (2005). Blended families: A critical review of the current research. *The Family Journal: Counseling and Therapy for Couples and Families, 13*(4), 445–451.

Rohrbaugh, J. B. (2000). Lesbian families: Clinical issues and theoretical implications. *Child Welfare Information Gateway.* Retrieved March 11, 2010, from www.childwelfare.gov/pubs/f_gay/index.cfm.

Saleebey, D. (2009). *The strengths perspective in social work practice* (5th ed.). Boston: Pearson Education.

Schewe, P. A. (2008). Direct service recommendations for children and caregivers exposed to community and domestic violence. *Best Practices in Mental Health, 4*(1), 32–47.

Seipel, M. M. O., & Brown, J. (2008). Promoting American families: The role of state legislation. *Families in Society: The Journal of Contemporary Social Services, 89*(2), 174–182.

U.S. Census Bureau. (2008). Living arrangement of children: 2004 Household Economic Studies. Survey of Income and Program Participation, 2004 Panel. Retrieved October 2, 2009, from www.census.gov/population.

Wallerstein, J. (2005). Growing up in the divorced family. *Clinical Social Work Journal, 33*(4), 401–419.

Zastrow, C., & Kirst-Ashman, K. K. (2007). *Understanding human behavior and the social environment* (7th ed.). Belmont, CA: Thomson/Brooks/Cole.

PART III

Final Reflections

In this final part, the authors reintroduce the five premises discussed throughout this text. Furthermore, the authors present the reader with an opportunity to consider other aspects of family dynamics and experiences beyond the scope of the content addressed. A vision as to the potential of family constellation within the context of a society is presented. The reader is encouraged to move beyond the notion of absoluteness while embracing a sense of possibilities.

CHAPTER ELEVEN

The Family

Considering Further Possibilities

Krishna L. Guadalupe
Debra L. Welkley

The human spirit has reminded us that while the mind can be, and often is, limited by its own boundaries, the soul carries us into the infinite.

KLG

As reflected throughout this text, the family is viewed here as a complex biopsychosocial, cultural, nonordinary phenomenon that transcends any single definition. Its absolute identity is infinite, although glimpses of understanding are revealed from one context or time to another. It seems that when we think we understand the family, new occurrences are unfolded, reminding us to be mindful and embrace the wisdom of uncertainty (previously described as an inner knowing or innate intuitive power that reveals understanding of living experiences beyond conscious reasoning). Although total understanding of the family is elusive within the structure of our current human mind, when exploring the family within the context of history several experiences seem to ring true. Families

- are multidimensional contextual nonstatic living entities (first premise),

- provide opportunities for individuals to constantly experience multiple family memberships (second premise),

- are constantly in a process of "being and becoming" (third premise),

- affect and are affected by multiple realms of existence (fourth premise), and

- can be better served through an eclectic approach (fifth premise).

As nonstatic living entities, families are part of a continuum where each experience becomes the leading edge for ongoing evolution. Thus, in order to understand the notion of past, present, and future, an exploration of the family needs to be considered.

Addressing the complexity of family existence and evolution supports the initiative to advocate for ongoing professional assessment and intervention approaches that move beyond dogmatism, stereotypes, or monodimensional lenses. Social or human service practitioners are encouraged to recognize that there are multiple ways of knowing, doing, and being, all of them experienced by the family. Practitioners are encouraged to tune in to the experiences of families that they are working with as if each moment was the first, each moment sacred. While engaging in a continuous exploration of family constellations, both conventional and transcendent wisdom must be considered. One must be careful, however, not to promote the notion of predictability that is often nourished by conventional wisdom. It is important to remember that the mind can be, and has often been, limited by its boundaries, perceptions, logic, and reasoning, whereas the human spirit encompasses nonordinary realms of reality that encourage ongoing curiosity. Thus, acceptance and honoring of the uniqueness of diverse family encounters can assist practitioners to move beyond compartmentalization or fragmentation of family experiences.

No Absolutes—Only Further Food for Thought

Multiple professional lenses exist within the study of the family, each reflecting strengths and restrictions. The lenses introduced throughout this text are no exception. As the reader already knows, no text can ever illustrate an absolute understanding of family constellations or ways to address familial dynamics of communication, being, and doing. This text presents an attempt at inclusiveness through its five premises, as previously reviewed. Another strength of this text is its demonstration of the aforementioned premises within the context of a number of diverse family constellations discussed in various chapters (i.e., multigenerational and blended family units, opposite-sex and same-sex family groups, single parenting, and foster care family constellations). Each of the family constellations discussed in this text could generate enough information for a number of books. Only selected themes were discussed here. Furthermore, the reader is encouraged to be aware that family constellations exist beyond those addressed in this text including, but not limited to

- family constellations without children, either by choice or due to physiological or biological implications;

- multipartner family constellations, different from blended families in that partners may have chosen to willingly engage in and commit to multiple emotionally and sexually intimate relationships where children may or may not form part of the family equation;

- communal family groups, often related by a sense of common purpose, set of obligations, responsibilities, or other ties (i.e., legal, adoptive, genetic, etc.) where a primary objective of communal families is to sustain the well-being of its members and assist with child care and rearing;

- transitional family constellations often cultivated by social and cultural experiences such as halfway houses for people encountering life transitions that include but are not limited to alcohol or drug rehabilitation; and

- spiritually based family constellations reflected within contexts such as ashrams or other spiritual living arrangements. Communal families connected through a spiritual commitment that exists among and between members.

Family constellations do not necessarily exist in isolation from one another. For instance, a communal family group's sense of common purpose could be spiritually based as well as transitional as people move in and out of the specific contexts or agreements. Furthermore, a communal family group may not be defined by a geographical location, but rather by a bond shared by people due to ascriptive ties such as common cultural beliefs, religious heritage, or ethnic backgrounds.

The premises addressed in this text are viewed as proactive, interactive, and interdependent by nature. As mentioned earlier, the primary intention of these premises is to assist the reader to move beyond stereotypical paradigms regarding family constellations while being exposed to some of the complexities observed in family experiences. The chapters written by diverse contributors (in order of appearance, Myles Montgomery, Dale Russell, Ann Moylan, Jan Osborn, J. Errol Bolden, and Shirley Newton) have courageously attempted to explore family complexity beyond stereotypes and within the context of multi-dimensionality. Thus, readers are reminded to take what they need and leave the rest, while remaining true to the intention of a family-centered approach for practice. As stressed in previous chapters, human service practitioners are encouraged to honor and embrace the wisdom of uncertainty, a sense of trust in not knowing that can promote curiosity and a willingness to be open to continued learning. Social or human service practitioners are also reminded of the importance of a practice that incorporates ongoing professional self-evaluation with the intention to gain professional awareness, which is useful when attempting to enhance professional competence while servicing diverse family constellations.

When selecting a professional approach to assess and work with a family constellation it is recommended that human service practitioners consider the following areas:

- *Make sure that the approach is family-centered.* That is, does the approach honor and respect family commonalities and uniqueness through its premises and techniques? Is the approach inclusive of multiple realms of existence (i.e., intrapersonal, interpersonal, environmental, and nonordinary) affecting and being affected by family dynamics? Does the approach perceive the family as a nonstatic living entity in a constant space of being and becoming? Does the approach honor and attempt to embrace the sacredness (i.e., innate essence) of family constellations?

- *Make sure that the approach is not built around stereotypes and dogmatic paradigms.* That is, does the approach encourage the exploration of commonalities and uniqueness among family members as well as between family constellations? Does the approach attempt to explore the family's strengths while addressing its challenges? Does the approach move beyond generalizations or marginalization of family experiences?

- *Make sure that the approach encourages professional or personal self-evaluation and awareness.* That is, does the approach expose practitioners to its principles and guidance while simultaneously encouraging them to tune in to their intuitive wisdom as well as engage in necessary healing (moving beyond the wounded healer—personal wounds held by human service practitioners that might be unattended either consciously or unconsciously [Carl Jung as referred to in Dunne, 2000])? Does the approach encourage practitioners to explore and address their biases?

- *Make sure that the approach is user friendly while you attempt to embrace the complexity of family constellations.* That is, is the approach practical? Can the approach be used and conducted within an appropriate time frame?

These areas can strengthen the foundation of any approach used to assess and work with diverse family constellations. These are guidelines for enhancing our decision-making process when engaging in diverse capacities (i.e., micro, mezzo, and macro) within the field of family practice. Although we have attempted to describe some of the dynamics and complexities of family constellations, we understand that the vastness of family experiences move beyond the ideas examined in this text. As an attempt to briefly expose the reader to other dimensions that could be included when addressing family constellations, we are introducing the notion of transcended consciousness. It goes without saying that human service practitioners should never use techniques and approaches in which they have not properly been trained to apply when working with diverse family constellations. No one book or experience can carry an absolute magical remedy for professional competence. Professional skills and practice wisdom (an ability to consistently apply theoretical and practical knowledge with the intention of producing optimum family wellness) are generated from accumulative conceptual and practical experiences.

Transcending Consciousness

The content in this text supports the notion that the more inclusive an approach is regarding family experiences and dynamics, the higher the possibility for embracing what was referred by Paulo Freire (1971) as "awakening consciousness." In other words, intrapersonal processes reflected within or between family constellations could not be comprehensively understood without considering social, cultural, political, and economic phenomena observed in a society. Within this text another important ingredient has been added to Freire's perspective: the link between nonordinary realms of existence and the role that these are likely to play in intrapersonal, interpersonal, and sociopolitical–economic contexts and occurrences.

Throughout our human chronological sense of time, the human race has been exposed to what could be categorized as nonordinary realms of existence or realities, revealing and instigating synchronistic experiences far beyond the understanding of the human mind. A number of books based on science have addressed the notion that life began with the creation of the universe itself and that conception or birth can be considered an aftereffect. The argument has been made that what we currently consider matter or material substance was initially energy vibrating in its simplest form, hydrogen. According to the field of quantum physics, through its evolutionary process hydrogen atoms started to gravitate together, beginning a more complex movement of elements reflecting higher vibration. According to quantum physics, matter is energy manifested in what appears to be a solid form. The same could be said when we talk about family constellations. That is, although families may appear as individual units that dynamics of interactions could be measured and observed, families are complex and vast entities constantly evolving and changing.

A number of spiritually based books have stressed the notion of spirit as the living force of all creation. Spirit, it is argued, is a manifestation of divine intelligence—infinite source of our essence—the creator itself. As briefly observed, although the initial source of creation may differ depending on the lens, both science- and spirit-based paradigms to some degree embrace the notion that life exists beyond the physical and mental body. In applying this concept to family, we can see that families coexist through what we define as conventional reality (the idea of cause and effect) and transcendent reality (the notion of a higher purpose or power).

The premises addressed in this text support the notion that ultimately one cannot separate the inseparable (i.e., the observed from the observer, the creation from its creator, human beings from nonordinary realms of existence). An attempt at separation can only create fragmentation, partialization, and ultimately marginalization of the whole. Therefore, the study of the family through the lenses addressed in this text encourages the need for transcending consciousness, which promotes the idea of maintaining professional awareness of cognitive and social conditions often reflected in the experiences of family constellations as well as potentiality cultivated and enhanced through the family's nonordinary reality experiences.

Through personal and professional experiences, these authors have witnessed the importance of assisting the human mind to recuperate from its domestication, from time to time promoting the notion that only those experiences that can be touched, heard, smelled, seen, or tasted are real or exist. As mentioned earlier, in many cases science has assisted us to experience a gateway into the once considered unknown. While educational programs move more extensively toward what can be referred to as evidence-based practice (the use of scientific and research studies to identify and determine best ways of approaching family assessment and intervention), we must not negate possibilities not yet claimed by evidence-based practice as right ways. After all, it is well understood that research and science are often constrained by restricted parameters. Through the use of science and research, and without neglecting vastness of possibilities, we can continue to build bridges within and between family members, family constellations, or society as a whole, reminding each other of our interdependence and the need to heal our human wounds created by misunderstandings that often are influenced by exclusiveness.

The development or strengthening of transcending consciousness reminds us that through human experiences we create boundaries based on multiple roles we engage in (i.e., partner, parent, sibling, etc.), statuses that we experience (i.e., group memberships and positions), as well as things that we possess. These boundaries often become possible restrictions or confinements influencing our familiar interactions and exchanges within diverse contexts and settings. Thus, the realization that our human or familial boundaries do not reflect our absolute identity is vital when recognizing our infinite existence. Such recognition can assist us to support one another from a place of nonattachment. We can distinguish being responsible to each others' lives (a sign of unconditional love in action that can be demonstrated among and between family constellations) from attempting to control each others' experiences, reflecting a human condition of a need for power and control over others. This was previously reflected in our discussion of dominant familial paradigms in comparison to the notion of inclusiveness, intended throughout this text.

Multiple conflicts often mirrored within families or society as a whole (i.e., violence, oppressive forces, etc.) are generated by a need for control, manipulation, and power based on an intrapersonal sense of rigid identification with earthly roles and statuses. The emergence of transcending consciousness helps us reunite with our core essence that supports our process of human healing or transformation of intrapersonal and interpersonal human conditions (i.e., greed, selfishness, biases, prejudices, cruelty, oppressive behaviors, and ultimately a sense of separation). The emergence or strengthening of transcendence consciousness can assist us to live within the space where matter and nonordinary vibration coexist. As Eckhart Tolle (2005) stated, "Human is form. Being is formless. Human and Being are not separate but interwoven" (p. 104). Family constellations can consciously serve, and often do serve, as agents of transformation, where we learn to deprogram the conditional mind through a commitment to transcendence consciousness, a tool for embracing our oneness, the universal family constellation.

Einstein once said, "A problem cannot be solved by the same consciousness that created it." Therefore, if we continue to perceive and approach the family and its dynamics from dominant or familiar paradigms that are exclusive, we may not strengthen or assist individuals or families in their evolution and growth. Eckhart Tolle (2005) further illustrates Einstein's notion while demonstrating the importance of being open to a consciousness that transcends the conventional sense of reality, especially if our ultimate objective is to create harmonious familial relationships based on equality or equity. He wrote,

> In the human dimension, you are unquestionably superior to your child. You are bigger, stronger, know more, can do more. If that dimension is all you know, you will feel superior to your child, if only unconsciously. And you will make your child feel inferior, if only unconsciously. There is no equality between you and your child because there is only form in your relationship, and in form, you are of course not equal. You may love your child, but your love will be human only, that is to say, conditional, possessive, intermittent. Only beyond form, in Being, are you equal, and only when you find the formless dimension in yourself can there be true love in that relationship. The Presence that you are, the timeless I Am, recognizes itself in another, and the other, the child in this case, feels loved, that is to say recognized. . . .
>
> To love is to recognize yourself in another. The other's "otherness" then stands revealed as an illusion pertaining to the purely human realm, the realm of form. The longing for love that is in every child is the longing to be recognized, not on the level of form, but on the level of Being. If parents honor only the human dimension of the child but neglect Being, the child will sense that the relationship is unfulfilled, that something absolutely vital is missing, and there will be a buildup of pain in the child and sometimes unconscious resentment toward the parent. 'Why don't you recognize me?' This is what the pain or resentment seems to be saying. (pp. 105–106)

By keeping our attention only within the realm of form, or the notion "if it is not measured it does not exist," we restrict and marginalize our existence. By marginalizing our existence, we limit our experiences. This seems to be part of a domino effect. Such marginalization or limitations are likely to be perpetuated through the experience of cultural influences as well as through our familial relationships. Children practice what they learn. As children grow into adulthood, what they have learned they often teach. Therefore, it is not uncommon to observe perpetuation of cognitive, emotional, behavioral, and spiritual patterns from one generation to another as well as in society as a whole. Thus, as adults within family constellations, attempting to teach children to be honest and authentic in evolving or transcending relationships, we need to model through words and actions. Adults need to sit, listen, and be aware of the voice of inner intelligence (an innate, nonlinear, and nonconfined ability to reflect and act holistically as well as paradoxically). The role that adults play in child development as well as the role that each person plays within each relationship (i.e., partner, practitioner, etc.) needs to be constantly self-assessed in order for necessary changes to be recognized and acted on. Awareness of family members' interactions, exchanges, and effects is an initial step for promoting family well-being, which in turn is likely to affect our society as a whole. It is well understood that awareness alone does not guarantee change. It helps with the clarity of options needed to participate in the process of transformation.

Although using a parent-child example to demonstrate the importance of recognizing our Beingness beyond human forms, Eckhart Tolle's illustration can be equally applied to all our relationships within the context of a society. The choice is ours to be skeptical or to engage in such an active exploration, one step at a time. As the reader you may ask, what tools are available for connecting or embracing transcending consciousness? The tools and approaches are endless and beyond the scope of this chapter. However, some of the common approaches discussed in multiple books that can be used in combination are these:

- Journaling (i.e., free writing—venting out or writing with an intention, etc.)

- Passive or active meditation approaches (i.e., mindfulness practice—sitting in silence focusing on the breaths—inhale . . . exhale—while witnessing thoughts without attachment; use of mantras; chanting; visualization approaches; affirmation techniques—repetitions of statements or declarations that a goal is currently being manifested; reading inspiring books or listening to spiritually stimulating music, etc.)

- Use of prayer (i.e., dialogue or way of connecting with divine oneness or intelligence or source of creation, as one understands it. Such conversation or connectedness method is shaded by the type of relationship and meaning given to the specific divine relationship)

- Use of art methods (i.e., drawing, painting, coloring, collages, etc.)

- Breathing techniques (i.e., Long deep breathing: Fill the abdominal area by inhaling through filling in. Hold the breath for a moment once the lungs are completely filled. Slowly the nostrils, then pressing the air consciously into the lower areas, feel the lungs release the breath. Breath of fire: Start with long deep breathing as previously described. Inhale through the nostrils, once the lungs are filled, immediately forces the air out. Without delays, expand the air back in before all the air is out. Speed the breathing while expanding and contracting the breath. Go as fast as you can, focusing on only the exhale. Develop a rhythm that is comfortable for you. Maintain your spine straight. For more information, search Kundalini yoga and breath of fire.)

- Yoga practices (i.e., Kundalini and Hatha yoga approaches)

- Sharing experiences—developing a sense of communal family

- Spiritual ceremonies and rituals—developing a sense of devotion

- Challenging beliefs, values, and life orientations—dare to change beliefs, values, and life orientation that do not nourish your spirit

As observed in these authors' professional practices, some of the aforementioned approaches can be considered nontraditional, in the sense of often not being considered within conventional literature or traditional educational professional programs designed to educate human service practitioners. However, the use of these approaches seems to be gaining societal support as more individuals and family constellations have become more receptive to what can be perceived as "alternative paradigms to dominant practices." Therefore, human service practitioners are encouraged to continue their development of professional competence through ongoing training and education beyond any one size fits all model of practice.

Visions and Hopes

The family affects and is affected by multiple realms of existence. The family is not helpless even within the context of adversity, but rather is filled with potentiality to awaken and promote the creation of new experiences. The family cannot be confined by a geographical location, a structure, a function, or a life orientation, because its existence is spread throughout time, contexts, and settings, and reflects diverse forms and ways of being. Every place we go, the family is. It is carried on our shoulders—genes, cellular memories, by our thoughts and emotions—and through the umbilical cord that transcends our physical encounters.

The family is an active participant within the multiple environments that it encounters (i.e., social and cultural, physical, etc.). Thus, any attempt at promoting substantial individual or societal transformation cannot exclude the family. To do so is to minimize the power of creation activated by family constellations. In other words, the family does not exclusively experience an environment, but it simultaneously participates, at different levels—for different reasons—in different ways, in the process of its creation.

These authors envision and hope that the content presented throughout this text has raised more questions than answers. Thus, the reader is encouraged to respond to several questions:

- What does family mean to me?

- How does, or can, my orientation affect my professional practice?

- To what degree do I relate or differ from the family lens presented in this text?

- How can I contribute to the ongoing evolution of knowledge and skills geared to strengthen family practice?

These authors envision that as the family continues its process of awakening, new and innovative ways for approaching the family will continue to emerge. That is what these authors consider a true family-centered practice: as the family evolves so does the practice. Professional disciplines such as social work, psychology, and counseling, among others, exist to serve the family, and not the other way around. Within these professional disciplines it is wise to be cautious not to promote approaches that are dogmatic and exclusive of diverse family experiences. To do so is to perpetuate oppressive experiences in the name of good intention.

The human family is confronting multiple challenges (i.e., family violence, substance abuse, mental health crises, delinquency and crime, oppressive forces, and the list goes on and on). The human family has also demonstrated resilience, the endurance and spirit to bounce back into wellness during times of adversity. As practitioners and researchers within the context of family practice, we visualize the emergence of new politics that prioritize people over profit, truth over lies, connectedness over separation, compassion over hatred, peace over war, love over fear,

and politics that embrace and support the family during times of challenges and despair. These authors foresee the family continuing to consciously contribute to the emergence of such politics through its dynamics, power, willingness, and commitment to heal its own wounds.
Individually, family constellations are subsystems of a broader phenomenon, a social order. The power of intention (an ability to set an objective),
courage (bravery to transform beyond human conditions), and the ability
to act on the intention constructed are qualities inherited by every
human being. We must set a clear intention for wellness and not continue
to pass down from one generation to another inherited human madness.
An initial point of reference, for setting and acting on such an intention, is
to recognize our interdependence, connectedness, or oneness.

Often when the terms diversity or human differences are used, the
notion of separation or disconnection is perpetuated. Diversity of family constellations, as presented in this text, is recognized as the point or
interface at which people differ and yet connect. Human diversity is
about the recognition of uniqueness that collectively forms the whole.
Diverse family constellations can be viewed as the human body that has
multiple and unique bones (i.e., skull, vertebral column, ribs, sacrum,
etc.), organs (i.e., heart, lung, liver, stomach, kidneys, large intestine,
etc.) and systems (i.e., nervous systems, respiratory system, cardiovas-
cular system, digestive system, muscular system etc.) that are interwoven and form one whole. Diverse family constellations form the body of
each society, each family playing a significant part in the oneness of
existence. No one family can live or survive in isolation from the whole.
As once stated by Martin Luther King, Jr., we are our brothers and sisters' keepers. Adding to that notion is the recognition that as long as
some people or families experience oppression, no one is absolutely
free. Thus, human and social service practitioners are poised to make an
impact of compassionate action that is both supportive and empowering—that fosters both the honoring of tradition and movement for necessary change. We can reflect on Mahatma Gandhi's words when he
stated that in order to find ourselves we need to lose ourselves in the
service of others. We would like to add that the sense of others are reflections of self. Join the ride!

References

Dunne, C. (2000). *Carl Jung: Wounded healer of the soul.* Sandpoint, ID: Morning
      Light Press.
Freire, P. (1971). *Pedagogy of the oppressed.* New York: Herder & Herder.
Tolle, E. (2005). *A new earth: Awakening to your life's purpose.* New York: Penguin.

Index

Contributors

ERROL S. BOLDEN

Professor Errol Sebastian Bolden is associate professor and field coordinator in the Department of Social Work at Coppin State University in Baltimore, Maryland. He also serves as a part-time senior lecturer at the University of the West Indies, Cave Hill campus, in Barbados and as a visiting faculty member at Addis Ababa University in Ethiopia. Professor Bolden's research agenda focuses on community and organizational capacity building as well as on disengaged dads and males in the academy. His teaching portfolio includes such courses as International Issues in Social Work, Macro Social Work Practice, Community Development, Capacity Building and Planned Change, and Program Planning and Evaluation. He is committed to serving as an educational mentor to bachelor's, master's, and doctoral students. Professor Bolden has more than fifteen years of experience as a macro practitioner and serves on a number of local, national, and international boards. He has lectured or conducted workshops or presentations throughout the United States, the Caribbean, South Korea, and various African countries. Professor Bolden received his BSW from Northwest Nazarene University in Nampa, Idaho, his MSW from Howard University in Washington, DC, and his MPH and PhD degrees from the University of Pittsburgh, in Pennsylvania. He is also a motivational speaker and owner of Universal Inspirations.

JEAN ANN MOYLAN

Ann earned her master's degree in child development and family studies from Purdue, and her doctorate in child and family development from The University of Georgia. She is currently professor of family studies and director of the Center for Family Studies in the Department of Family and Consumer Sciences at California State University, Sacramento. Ann has experience working in several early child development programs, consulting for early childhood education, and overseeing youth and community sexuality education programs. The focus of her work has been on early childhood development, early intervention, and family support services, including support for parenting. Her recent research has focused on the adoption of infants from China to the United States and the ensuing attachment process. Other related areas of interest include infant mental health and hospice youth services.

MYLES MONTGOMERY

Myles Montgomery is a Licensed Clinical Social Worker and graduate of McGeorge School of Law. Myles works primarily with children and families. While in law school, Myles was most interested in the issues of the Constitution and family law.

SHIRLEY NEWTON-GUEST

Professor Shirley Newton-Guest is currently the chair of the Department of Social Work at Coppin State University in Baltimore, Maryland. She serves as the faculty advisor of Phi Alpha Social Work Honor Society, Theta Rho Chapter. Prior to her appointment as chair in fall 2006, Professor Newton-Guest developed and provided leadership and training to private and nonprofit comprehensive community-based mental health facilities in Washington, DC. She was also employed as full-time professor at Virginia Commonwealth University School of Social Work from 1995 to 1999, and is adjunct professor at Howard University School of Social Work. Professor Newton-Guest is a Licensed Independent Clinical Social Worker in Washington, DC, and a Licensed Certified Social Worker (Clinical) in the state of Maryland. She has an extensive background in programmatic oversight, innovative program development, and implementation as well as clinical supervision and training. Professor Newton-Guest has worked in the public and private sector including mental services, maternal and child health services, and substance abuse. She is an experienced presenter at the regional and national levels. Professor Newton-Guest received her bachelor's in social work from Grambling State University, and her master's and doctorate of social work from Howard University School of Social Work.

JANET LEE OSBORN

Jan Osborn received her master's and doctorate in marriage and family therapy from Syracuse University, Syracuse, New York. She has taught in marriage and family therapy programs at Northwestern University, Chicago; and at California State University, Sacramento campus. She is currently teaching at Alliant International University, Sacramento. She has been in private practice for twenty years, and has worked extensively with the lesbian and gay community. She lives in Sacramento with her partner and two sons.

DALE RUSSELL

Dale Russell earned his doctorate in counseling psychology from the University of San Francisco, is a Licensed Clinical Social Worker, and currently is associate professor of social work and undergraduate director at California State University, Sacramento. Dale has spent much of his career as a practitioner working with families where the identified client was a teenager. His academic research interests include best practices associated with the teenage population.

About the Editors

KRISHNA L. GUADALUPE

Krishna L. Guadalupe holds a PhD from the University of South Carolina and an MSW from Rutgers University in New Jersey. He is professor of social work at California State University, Sacramento. He has been certified as an Addiction Counselor through the Alcohol and Drug Certification Board of New Jersey. He has been licensed in Clinical Work through the state of New Jersey and South Carolina as well as in the Island of Puerto Rico. He has been trained in Swedish—Deep Tissue massage (CMT), Reflexology, and Rain Drop Therapy through the Healing Art Institute in Citrus Heights, CA. He has been certified as a Kundalini Yoga Teacher through the Reichian Institute, CA. Other experiences include Breathwork, Shamanic Wellness Work, Acupressure, and Oneness Blessing Giver (Deeksha). Currently, he runs a wellness center in Sacramento with his spouse, Judy, Creative Healing and Arts Center. His most imperative teachings and growth have been influenced by his own commitment to healing and his truth-devoted relationship with his partner Judy, as well as his role as a father to their three magnificent children (Isaiah, Elijah, and Rhia).

DEBRA L. WELKLEY

Debra received her master's of art degree in sociology from Baylor University and has twenty years of teaching experience that span many different college, university, and community college campuses. Currently she teaches sociology courses at California State University, Sacramento, as well as Cosumnes River College, and American River College. In addition to her experience in teaching she has more than twenty years of experience in social services, working as a direct services worker to providing leadership through administrative positions. Her focus has been working with children and families in various venues (i.e., group homes, the welfare system, and in foster care). Her research and primary areas of interest include race and ethnicity, multicultural practice and sensitivity, program development and evaluation, intervention with at-risk children and families (this also includes parenting skills, independent living skills for youth, including foster youth), and the homeless. She provides consultation to area nonprofits and mentors former foster youth as they pursue higher education.